Family Violence: A Canadian Introduction

Ann Duffy and Julianne Momirov

James Lorimer & Company, Publishers
Toronto, 1997

James Lorimer & Company Ltd. acknowledges the support of the Department of Canadian Heritage and the Ontario Arts Council in the development of writing and publishing in Canada. We acknowledge the support of the Canada Council for the Arts for our publishing program.

Cover design: Jeff Domm

Canadian Cataloguing in Publication Data
Duffy, Ann
    Family violence
ISBN 1-55028-583-1 (bound) ISBN 1-55028-582-3 (pbk.)
1. Family violence - Canada. I. Momirov, Julianne. II. Title.
HQ809.3.C3D84 1997   362.82'92'0971   C97-931879-3

James Lorimer & Company Ltd., Publishers
Egerton Ryerson Memorial Building
35 Britain Street
Toronto, Ontario
M5A 1R7

Printed and bound in Canada

Contents

Foreword   vii

Chapter 1
Understanding Family Violence from a Societal Perspective   1
   Family: Haven or Nightmare   1
   Applying a Social Perspective   4
   The Violence of Society   7
   The Study of the Family and Violence   10
   Definitions and Measurement   11
   Conclusions   16

Chapter 2
Violence Against Women in Intimate Relationships   18
   The Experience of Abuse   18
   Naming the Violence   23
   The Name Game Today   26
   Dimensions of the Violence   29
   Patterns Within the Violence   33
      (i) Gender   33
      (ii) Age, Class, Race, Ethnicity   37
      (iii) Alcohol and Drug Use   39
      (iv) Three Other Key Factors   40
   Conclusions   41

Chapter 3
Children Denied Childhood: Child Abuse   45
   The Experience   45
   Naming the Issue: From Spanking and Slaps to
   Torture and Murder   49
   The Changing Historical Construction of Abuse   55
   Mapping the Dimensions of the Problem   61
   Social Patterns of Child Abuse   66
      (i) General   66
      (ii) Gender   68

(iii) Social Class, Race and Ethnicity   72
Conclusions   73

Chapter 4
Sibling, Parent, Adolescent and Elder Abuse   80
  Sibling Abuse   80
    The Experience   81
    Naming the Issue   85
  Adolescent Abuse   86
    Background   86
    The Experience   87
  Parent Abuse   91
  Elder Abuse   95
    Background   95
    The Experience   98
    Naming the Issue   100
    Characterization of the Elderly   101
    Living Arrangements   103
    Detection of Abuse   107
    Conflict Factors/Potential for Abuse   109
    Profiles of Caregivers/Abusers   110
  Conclusions   112

Chapter 5
Looking for Explanations: Exploring Theoretical
Perspectives   114
  The Social Reasons for Violence   114
  Ways of Thinking   117
  The Liberal Democratic Perspective   120
  Patriarchy   123
  The Role of the Media   126
  Psychological, Sociological and Feminist Theories   128
  Why Do Men Batter?   129
    Psychological and Social Psychological Explanations   129
    Sociological Theories   131
    Feminist Theories   135
  Why Do Abused Women Stay?   139
    Psychological and Social Psychological Explanations   139
    Sociological Theories   141
    Feminist Theories   141
  Why Do Parents Abuse Their Children?   144

Mainstream Theories and Models   144
Feminist and Other Approaches   147
Why are Siblings, Adolescents, Parents
and Elders Abused?   151
    Why Do Siblings Abuse One Another?   151
    Why Do Parents Abuse Adolescents?   152
    Why Do Children Abuse Their Parents?   153
    Why Do Elders Become Victims of Abuse?   155

Chapter 6
Looking for Solutions   164
    Woman Abuse   164
       Personal Interventions: Counselling and Related
       Strategies   164
       Institutional Reforms: Criminal Justice Responses   167
       Societal Changes: Feminist Initiatives   176
    Child Abuse   180
       Personal Interventions: Counselling and Therapy   180
       Institutional Solutions: Social Welfare and
       Criminal Justice   182
       Societal Changes: Education and Politics   188
    Elder, Parent, Sibling and Adolescent Abuse   190
       Legislation   197
       Shelter   201
       Education   203
       Community Support and Counselling Services   205
       Research   207

Chapter 7
Some Concluding Thoughts   212

Bibliography   217

Index   233

This book is dedicated to our children,
Alex Nedeljkovic
Mayra Smith
and
Hermana Smith,
and their future.

Foreword

As Duffy and Momirov point out, the media do us a disservice by presenting only the most sensational cases of family violence. By doing so, the media convey the message that family violence is perpetrated exclusively by very pathological — "sick" — individuals, and is not a society-wide problem.

In fact, family violence is a society-wide problem. Almost a million Canadian women are either battered or sexually assaulted each year, and several hundred thousand children are sexually abused. A recent study done by the Centre for Research on Violence Against Women and Children in London, Ontario estimated the annual Canadian cost of violence against women alone to be over four billion dollars. This figure is conservative, as it does not include psychological abuse, the broader categories of violence that apply to disabled and elderly women (e.g., deprivation and neglect), or services to women psychiatric patients and social assistance recipients whose problems were caused by violence other than sexual assault. Nor does the four billion dollar figure include the costs of family violence other than violence against women, or the costs of processing and incarcerating offenders who have family violence in their backgrounds and have committed other crimes. In short, family violence affects almost everyone. Those of us who are not affected directly live, work, or are otherwise closely associated with someone — or, more likely, a number of persons — who are, or have been, family violence victims.

Family violence is primarily a social problem, despite the fact that psychologists remind us — accurately — that social explanations cannot tell us why many persons do not become abusive or violent (e.g., Dutton 1995a). However, the over-individuation of family violence that is routinely accomplished by the mass media justifies the strong countervailing message, delivered by books such as this one, that family violence exists — and remains — largely because our social institutions foster and tolerate it, through their ideological practices of militarism, capitalism, racism, patriarchy, and nuclear familialism, and through the ways in which these same ideological practices account for the appallingly deficient responses most family violence victims receive from their employers, and from our medical, criminal justice, legal, social welfare, and educational systems. As Duffy and Momirov point out, the dismantling of the social safety net, happening in every western country, promises to exacerbate both the incidence of family violence and the inadequacy of our societal response.

The feminist focus of this book is also laudable. Since gender relations are not the only power relations operating in our society, a feminist framework cannot account for every kind of family violence. We feminists who are working against family violence should also include men in our struggles, because we need their help, and because men must not be permitted to dismiss family violence as a "women's problem." Nevertheless, the statistical fact that male violence against women and children accounts for the lion's share of family violence means that socially sanctioned gender power relations must comprise an important part of any meaningful understanding of family violence we develop or share.

If family violence is every person's problem, then every person should make a contribution, however small, toward solving it. I endorse the authors' conclusion that fragmentation and polarization tendencies among contemporary family violence researchers threaten to draw us away from, rather than towards, useful solutions. Yet these tendencies paradoxically demonstrate the success that has been achieved in getting a diversity of people involved. Disagreement and non-communication among the constituencies which carry out research or provide services to survivors reflect the often-frustrating fact that so many persons now consider themselves to be family violence issue stakeholders. But in some places this same fact is facilitating a new era of information-sharing about family violence across disciplines and across the boundaries that once decisively separated practitioners, policy makers, and researchers.

To cite just one example, the five family violence research centres established by Health Canada and the Social Sciences and Humanities Research Council in 1992, were mandated to carry out their action-oriented research and public education specifically by building and sustaining partnerships among academics, policy makers, and family violence workers. During their five years of operation the five centres have experienced excruciating growing pains, because academics and practitioners have found it hard to learn how to march to the same drum. Nevertheless, in just as many instances the collaborations have worked. Indeed, throughout most of the hundred-odd projects so far sponsored by the centres, academic and community personnel have simultaneously done research together and learned to appreciate the complexity of family violence. No academic's or practitioner's effort against family violence has a chance of succeeding without the reinforcing support of persons in other fields. The Canadian family violence research centres have learned the important lesson that eradicating a problem as complex as family violence requires the pooling of the entire range of resources that are represented by academics, policy makers, practitioners, frontline workers, and survivors. A lot therefore rides on the hope that the experiment of these centres will succeed, and that the experience of the centres will provide a useful blueprint for future work. The family violence research centres have helped make Canada a pioneer in the development of collaborative solutions to social problems.

As Duffy and Momirov imply, solving the problem of family violence, at both personal and societal levels, requires strategies that represent the antithesis of asserting control. These strategies include listening, sharing, collaborating, negotiating, and believing that every person around the table has something important to say. It is encouraging that so many people have recently developed an interest in family violence. Even more encouraging is the fact that many more survivors have felt supported enough to come forward to share their experiences. The solution to family violence lies in the social reforms that so many of us desire; it also lies in the everyday processes of talking about and sharing our lives and work. Despite numerous setbacks and backlashes, these everyday processes are gradually moving us to a place where the ugliness inside many homes will lose its private status, violence and abuse will lose their acceptability as ways to conduct family life, and the institutions which serve survivors will find more effective ways to do their jobs. This book represents a significant contribution toward our finding our way to that place.

Deborah Harrison
Director, Muriel McQueen Fergusson Centre
for Family Violence Research
University of New Brunswick

Acknowledgments

To the best of our knowledge, this is the first effort to bring together Canadian material on the general issue of family violence. Over the last five years, we have each taught a course on family conflict and violence at Brock University and, as a result, are keenly aware of the wealth of Canadian research and analysis and the lack of a Canadian book intended to introduce readers to the issue. In preparing the content for the course, we found it necessary to rely on a wide variety of resources scattered throughout a number of different journals and books. Since most of the textbooks written on the topic tend to be American, providing students with comprehensive reading material, particularly relating to the situation in Canada, has meant piecing together information. As a result, when Lorimer editor Diane Young suggested a book in this area, we were decidedly enthusiastic.

Here, we have attempted to provide a unified overview of some of the excellent work being done by Canadian researchers and analysts, such as Linda MacLeod, Holly Johnson, Mariana Valverde, Walter DeKeseredy, Michael Smith, Desmond Ellis, Merlin Brinkerhoff, Eugen Lupri, Donald Dutton, Holly Johnson and Leslie Miller. This does not mean, of course, that all the material presented here is Canadian since many foundational and influential pieces originate elsewhere. Nor do we claim that the book is an exhaustive treatment of the field. It is too large and too diverse to be adequately encompassed in one text. Notably, for example, there is very little here relating to the Francophone experience. Furthermore, because much of the research, especially that regarding the newer aspects of family violence, such as sibling, parent, adolescent and elder abuse, tends to be of a "generic" nature, very little work has been done on family violence amongst ethnic or racial minorities. With these caveats, it is our hope that this book provides a reasonably thorough and provocative introduction to the issue of family violence and that it spurs further interest in this vital area.

We were fortunate to have the support of others in our work on this project. In particular, thanks go to Wendy Weeks, Dusky Smith, Norene Pupo, Walter Watson, Mary Elder, Deborah Harrison, Rebecca Raby, Nada Momirov, Linda Tylee, Elaine Patten, Shawn

Moffat, Doreen Morey, Deborah Lambert, Paul Keen, Barb Chamberlain, the Ontario Arts Council, our families, friends and students for their helpful comments, insights and/or encouragement. Special thanks to Hermana Smith for her research work. Of course, we would also like to thank our editor at James Lorimer and Company, Diane Young, who launched this project and who offered helpful comments and support throughout. However, any errors or omissions with respect to the book's content are entirely our responsibility. The book was jointly authored and we shared equally in its preparation.

Ann Duffy and Julianne Momirov
November 1997

1

Understanding Family Violence from a Societal Perspective

Family: Haven or Nightmare?

Mark[1] loved to watch the sun rise in the morning. It was the only time he felt safe and at peace with the world. Even though he was only eight years old, he had not missed a sunrise for as long as he could remember. He was reluctant to drag himself out of bed because he knew what the day had to offer: a meagre breakfast of toast and peanut butter or maybe just plain toast, getting dressed in his old raggedy clothing and going to school where he would hide in the farthest corner of the schoolyard and try to be as inconspicuous as possible so the other kids would not pick on him. He would watch the other children playing, as he did every day, fervently wishing he could have nice, new, clean clothing like them, craving the kind of life he imagined they had at home with parents who loved and cared about them, mothers who hugged and kissed them, and fathers who played with them. That was all Mark wanted out of life: parents who loved and cared about him. But all he had to go home to were parents who ignored him when they were not abusing him and who otherwise fought, partied and did drugs. Mark had vague memories of his father poking him with a sharp instrument, after which everything would go black. He knew he had been taken away from time to time but he had no recollection of what happened to him during those times; he just knew that it was something he did not want to remember.

As he grew older, Mark learned to be tough so that he could intimidate anyone who might want to harm him. He became known as a "problem" child because his pent-up anger would explode from time to time and he would go wild. His mother eventually kicked him out of the home. He was able to move in with his girlfriend until that relationship ended, devastating him and adding to his anger at the world. Mark attempted suicide a number of times, and he would do crazy, dangerous things, secretly hoping that God would release him from his misery. Having nowhere to live, Mark ended up on the street. He was lucky, though, because he wound up going to a youth centre before he ended up either in custody or in the grave; there he met a counsellor who genuinely cared about him and saw potential in him, despite the tough, wild exterior. He certainly did not trust her at first because he had learned early in his life that others were more likely to try to hurt him than help him. He could not understand why this counsellor thought he had any worth as a human being; after all, he had been told all his life that he was no good. Eventually, however, Mark came to trust her and began to turn his life around, first getting himself a job and then returning to high school to finish his secondary education so that he could go on to university. For the first time in his life, Mark had a future he could look forward to.

Mark's story is a reasonably typical one when it comes to street kids. These are not rebellious teens determined to defy their parents, as many middle-class Canadians believe; they are young people who have known nothing but abuse and deprivation all their lives. Their parents are impoverished individuals who probably suffered the same sort of abuse and misery in their own lives; they are passing on the legacy of their own youth to their children. These are the adolescents that middle-class Canadians often fear — and rightly so. In many cases, without adequate education (often unable to read or write beyond the most elementary level), they have little opportunity to get well-paid jobs. Compounded by their inability to obtain welfare because of government cutbacks or by their homelessness, these adolescents' situations may leave them with no alternative but to turn to a life of crime to survive.

Nevertheless, Mark's story is undeniably sad. It tugs at the heart-strings to think of a small child suffering the way he did. It puts a human face on the social issue of child and adolescent abuse. Meeting Mark makes it all the more tragic because one can see immediately that he is not a "bad seed." He could be anybody's son. He has the same hopes and dreams for his life as any other young man his age. Rather, Mark is a victim — or, more appropriately, a *survivor.* He might not be around today to talk about his life if it were not for caring Canadians responding to the problem of family violence in our society. These are the same Canadians who recognize that while the family may be a warm and loving place for many children, for some it is nothing more than a nightmarish trap from which to flee or, worse yet, from which they are forcibly expelled by parents who simply do not want them. Such Canadians are still in the minority. The majority of Canadians are, as yet, insufficiently informed of the social dimensions of family violence and how these dimensions operate in this society.

Family violence is a subject that a lot of people find unfathomable and repugnant at the same time. Both reactions generally stem from the belief that the family is a "haven in a heartless world" (Lasch 1977) where the members love one another unconditionally and support one another at all times, a place where people retreat to escape the harshness and alienation of the world. If we believe such things about the family, we are then more horrified to discover that in many families individuals are beaten, threatened, humiliated and sexually assaulted. The usual response is to convince ourselves that the people perpetrating such acts of violence must be "sick" and ought to be "locked up." If the victim[2] is an adult, the inevitable question is then "Why doesn't she or he leave?" These responses assume that if social authorities imprison perpetrators or victims leave, the violence will disappear or decrease significantly. They ignore the fact that family violence has a rather long and persistent history.

How can the family be a place of violence? Gelles and Straus (1979), the two "fathers" of the sociology of family violence, list eleven traits of the family that contribute to its violent character. These traits include the amount of time family members spend with one another, the intensity of their interactions due to their emotional ties, the range of activities in which family members engage and the intermingling of different generations and sexes. Ironically, other analysts (Straus and Hotaling 1979) suggest that these same traits can also make the family a loving milieu.

The bittersweet irony of such traits is that intimacy and intensity may lead to love *and* violence. This twofold reality demonstrates how violence can take place within a close, loving environment. While family members may draw comfort from one another and give support, they may also prey on one another. Sharing joy and venting frustration may go hand-in-hand within the family fold.

Yet, other research suggests that abusive family relations differ from non-abusive family relations in ways that do not directly pert to violence. Majonis (1995) argues that family members in abus families tend to be more isolated from one another than in n

abusive families. This means that, rather than engaging in cooperative and interactive activities, the members of abusive families perform tasks and activities that do not involve one another, even though
they take place within the home. Watching television is a prototype
of this behaviour. Family members who are isolated by such activities tend to be more coercive in their relations with one another,
presumably because any bond among them has been weakened by
prolonged isolation and increased distance in their interrelations with
the family. Conflict may ensue and escalate, as may aggression.
There is more social interaction and mutual decision-making among
members of non-abusive families. These observations, which appear
to contradict Gelles and Straus's position, suggest that the amount of
time spent together and the range of activities involved in may not
generate conflict on their own; rather, it is the quality of the interactions among family members that contributes to the production of
violence. If relations are cooperative and respectful, there will likely
be less abuse; if relations are distant and disengaged, abuse is more
likely to occur. Child abuse seems to occur when members of abusive
families who are involved with one another become more distant and
isolated from one another. Thus, members of families who are characterized as "abusive" may spend time together and perform tasks,
such as household chores, and activities, like watching television,
together, as well as alone, but the time spent together places stress
on the members and that stress leads to aggression and then to
isolation.

Applying a Societal Perspective

Yet, blaming the pathology of violence on aspects of family life does
not give an adequate account of why intimacy and intensity should
lead to violence. A leap in logic is required to bind the two concepts
together. Therefore, we must explore other possible reasons for the
occurrence of violence. To do so, we must broaden our focus, take
our eyes off the particular individual, family or, for that matter, social
institution. By keeping our focus narrow, we inadvertently preserve the popular myth of the family: the family-as-haven and the
street-as-threat. This way of thinking allows us to continue to believe
that family violence is a private matter, rather than a social one. Our
focus must shift to the social context in which the family is embedded.

We can accomplish the task of viewing the social context and
its relation to violence within families by using what the

sociologist C. Wright Mills (1959) termed the sociological imagination. In essence, what this means is that we must understand that personal biographies are linked to history. To put it another way, we as individuals live out our lives in a particular time and place, otherwise known as a historical period. What happens, and has happened, in the world around us (that is, historically) influences our personal histories by constraining us or allowing us to accomplish things that at other times and in other places would have been impossible. For example, anyone born after World War II in Canada and coming of age in the 1960s would be more likely to go to university than previous generations because of social and economic changes that made education more accessible. The need for a highly skilled workforce meant that the government and parents encouraged more young people to get a university education. Furthermore, there were greater financial gains for those with advanced qualifications. New universities were built and old ones were expanded (Granatstein et al. 1983: 371). These historical changes profoundly influenced the personal history of that and subsequent generations.

We must take an intellectual step back to view our life histories within their context and to understand how one influences the other. In this way, we are able to recognize that what is happening to us in our personal lives is tied to what is happening in the world around us. Our private troubles are often linked to public issues. When we move between our personal biographies and the social-historical context of our lives, we are exercising our sociological imaginations. This unique perspective helps us understand that family violence is a social phenomenon, not a private matter. Violence is not inherent in individuals and their psyches, nor in particular families, but in the nature of relationships.

In addition, we must address the *gendered* nature of family violence. Prominent social researchers are often silent on the matter of gender, presenting their analyses in neutral terms. Such a presentation implies that both men and women are equally violent. Statistics, however, show that such a portrait of family violence is quite erroneous. There is so much of a gender imbalance when it comes to family violence that some researchers argue that "family violence" should rightfully be renamed "male violence." Not only are males largely responsible for committing violent and abusive acts within the domestic sphere, but females are predominantly their adult victims. Although a number of researchers have conducted studies showing that husbands are abused as much as, if not more than, wives, their studies have several problems (these are explored in more detail in Chapter 2). We argue that to better comprehend the issues involved in family conflict and violence, including the social and power relations that contribute to the phenomenon, it is necessary to address its gendered nature.

In this book, we take a feminist[3] and sociological approach to family violence. We show that the family is rooted in society, that individuals are socialized into particular patterns of behaviour, that these patterns are difficult to change and that social forces external to the family itself have an enormous impact on the processes taking place within the family. We will also endeavour to answer three important questions: (1) What is family violence? (2) What forms does it take? (3) Where does it originate?

Family violence is a social problem that affects all of us and has serious material and philosophical ramifications. The material costs involve the many services required to deal with the aftermath of family violence, such as police officers, social workers, court and prison officials. The philosophical ramification is the breakdown of the social fabric. Relationships among family members are severely damaged by violence; and family members themselves are harmed in numerous ways.

One way individuals are harmed is through humiliation, which results from being violated by someone else. Such violation could be physical, sexual or psychological. It is perhaps particularly humiliating when the person committing the violation is a trusted loved one. The shame will probably be shared by both the one perpetrating the violent act and the one being victimized, although not necessarily at the same time. Humiliation will be experienced by the victim when she or he realizes that she or he has been victimized. The perpetrator, however, will likely not experience humiliation until she or he comes to the awareness of what she or he has done.

Shame, brought on by the belief that one's self is being attacked (Scheff 1990: 80), is a particularly toxic emotion. It may be manifested by people who experience violence in their lives, as perpetrators, victims or witnesses. When the bond between people has been broken or severely threatened, the response is shame. Because shame is recursive, which means "acting back on [itself] in never-ending loops," it distorts the way individuals view not only themselves, but others. In addition, it is "contagious" between perpetrators and victims: shame begets shame (Scheff 1990: 18; see also Bradshaw 1988a, 1988b). A perpetrator who feels shameful may engender shame in the victim. The victim's shame may result in the perpetrator feeling greater shame. Furthermore, the avoidance of shame (or embarrassment) may take on quite an aggressive character (Goffman 1967 as cited by Scheff 1990: 29). Rather than just a matter of defensive gestures, avoidance may become offensive and even belligerent. Violence may eventuate from the desire to avoid shame.

Family violence exceeds the boundaries of the family. It damages perpetrators, victims and witnesses, physically and psychologically. These damaged people, then, go out into the greater Canadian society and have relationships with others. Logic suggests that these relationships, too, will become damaged by the legacy of violence. As the damage spreads throughout our society, it involves more and more people whose relationships are tainted. Societal institutions, such as social service agencies, the police, courts and penal system, become involved in the attempt to stem the flow of this form of toxicity. Yet, family violence does not only originate within families and move into the rest of society; its origins can be found in various aspects of Canadian society.

The Violence of Society

Sociologists have long recognized and accepted the presence of conflict, as well as consensus, in social relations.[4] Lewis Coser, a preeminent American sociologist (1956), argues that conflict can be functional or beneficial for society, in that it can bring about social change. Another sociologist, Thomas Scheff (1990: 7) distinguishes between "good" and "bad" conflict, asserting that if the social bond among members of a society is intact, then conflict may serve a constructive purpose; on the other hand, if the social bond is broken or profoundly threatened, then conflict is likely to be destructive.

Conflict can take many forms, from disagreement to actual aggression, from controlled to chaotic. As a society, we do not like chaotic conflict — riots, angry mobs and high levels of street crime give us cause for fear. We are, however, more willing to tolerate controlled or contained conflict — strikes, the outward expression of conflict between workers and management; peaceful rallies and marches in protest of a social problem; and the types found in movies, on television, in books, sports, video games and other cultural media.

We are also rather more willing to tolerate conflict from particular kinds of individuals or groups because we perceive conflict as part of their accepted societal role. For instance, in our society, aggression is often considered acceptable in males as part of their socially defined masculinity. In addition, when violence is used as a means to an end, to achieve specific goals, it is often considered acceptable. One example is the high tolerance for, and even encouragement of, corporal punishment of children as a means of discipline by some parents and educators. Until quite recently physical aggression of husbands against their wives was tolerated. Many argue that there is still a great deal of tolerance of violence against women, children and other marginalized groups such as the elderly in our society, despite the public commitment of the government to ending such behaviour.

Another instance of a tolerable form of conflict is "peacekeeping." Many Canadians are proud of our country's reputation for providing soldiers for United Nations peacekeeping missions, ignoring the fact that keeping the peace in that form is premised on the threat of violence. Once again, we legitimate violence in this way. We take pride in an activity that threatens to use violence against those who themselves threaten to use violence. The threat, however, is viewed in a positive light because it is "controlled," calculated, sanctioned by officials, not chaotic and random, liable to strike any of us at any moment.

Our eyes and ears are filled with the sights and sounds of conflict and violence on a daily basis. Popular and classical literature abound with conflict, television fare usually deals with conflict, news (in print or on radio and television) is virtually nothing but conflict, even textbooks in sociology and psychology discuss conflict. This pervasiveness tends to legitimize conflict in our society. Since it inhabits most of our waking moments, we tend to see it as a "natural" component of our social life.

Canadian society is especially violent for certain social groups — the poor, women and Native peoples are some examples of these groups. The lives of Natives in this country are often characterized by violence, both on and off the reserve. From domestic violence to racism, Natives suffer victimization as individuals and as a group (see Griffiths and Yerbury 1995). This situation is also true for many women. Not only are they in danger when they venture outside their homes, particularly at night, but they are also in danger in their own homes, where the men they love, and who supposedly love them, may threaten and harm them (DeKeseredy, Burshtyn and Gordon 1995). Sexist attitudes victimize them further when blame is attributed to them by themselves and others if they are attacked by a male in a public setting (Walklate 1989, as cited in DeKeseredy et al. 1995: 71). When the attack takes place inside their own home, these women are even more likely to be subjected to intense scrutiny by others who want to discover whether there is any possibility that they somehow instigated the violence perpetrated against them. Despite what we know about men and violence, we are still programmed to assume that a man would not mistreat his wife or girlfriend without good reason.

Some scholars have argued that the family reflects the violence of society, that it acts as a "mirror" for the social context (Lynn and O'Neill 1995: 272-73). The family "reflects" the inequalities and power relations of the society in which it is grounded. This reflexivity would then account for violent behaviours manifested among family members. Although this characterization is true to some extent, it fails to capture the whole ethos of family violence. Such an assertion makes the family seem excessively passive. Instead, we must be willing to examine power relations and social processes involved in family life and within the violent family specifically. Otherwise, the "mirror" metaphor begs the question Why, then, are not all families in Canada violent?

Much more insidious than these overt signs of societal violence, however, are the deeply entrenched covert aspects. These less obvious features are to be found in our culture and social structure, specifically our economic mode of production (capitalism) and our fundamental beliefs about human beings and conditions pertaining to them (liberal democratic philosophy). Few people are able to identify these elements as having any bearing on family violence. This lack of vision stems from people's inability to connect what happens to individuals in their private context to the social context in which they operate. They fail to see that the conditions of the social context ground their thoughts and behaviours. Patriarchy, which functions as both culture *and* social structure, also contributes substantially, both overtly and covertly, to the violence of Canadian society. The societal aspects of family violence are discussed below.

Conflict and violence are endemic to the Canadian social context. They are not peripheral or alien elements; they are, in fact, part of our everyday lives in some form. Most of us cannot successfully escape them. The implication is that all individuals have internal conflict and violence in some way. Many people believe that without conflict, including family life, is not possible — or desirable. For them, a certain level of conflict is considered to be "healthy."

Despite the knowledge of the existence of family conflict and violence, the discipline of sociology was rather slow to incorporate these issues into its general study of the family. In addition, the popular press has done little to include conflict and violence in its portrayal of the family or to expose their systemic nature.

The Study of the Family and Violence

While the study of the family by social scientists has a reasonably long history, the study of family violence is relatively recent. The second wave of feminism, which arose in the late 1960s and early 1970s, has been credited for putting violence onto the public agenda. Social scientists studying the family began seriously to address conflict and violence in the 1980s.

Killoran (1984) points out that, with the publication of a seminal article regarding conflict within the family in 1969, social scientific literature began to come to terms with the notion that families were not necessarily characterized by harmonious relations. Popular magazines, however, did not reflect this reality to the same extent. Killoran's analysis of *Chatelaine* magazine's content between 1939 to 1980 revealed that of the 245 articles dealing with conflict, only eleven dealt with violence. These articles attributed the violence to the individual perpetrator, citing various psychopathologies rather than social or power relations. By doing so, they perpetuated the long-standing myth of the loving family as well as the myth of abusers as isolated and "sick" individuals.

Maclean's June 1994 cover story, "The Family: Tradition Under Siege," was an eight-page article devoted to the exploration of the current status of the family in Canada. Topics included the battle for same-sex rights to employment benefits and adoption, a lesbian couple raising a child, stepfamilies and how children cope with the divorce of their parents. Other than fleeting references, conflict and violence within the family were not dealt with. Such treatment trivializes the issue and suggests, once again, that conflict and violence within families are uncommon and occur due to individual or particular family pathologies.

Popular literature and the press continue to bury their heads in the sand. Aside from the odd sensationalized case splashed across newspapers or leading off the evening news, the media tend to ignore the pervasive presence of conflict and violence within the family. Killoran's study of *Chatelaine* and the family issue of *Maclean's*, two of the most widely read magazines in Canada, demonstrate that the ideology of the family as supportive and loving still carries the day. Abusers continue to be treated as aberrations who perpetrate such acts due to maladjustment or mental illness, rather than as persons who have, in fact, internalized the various forms of violence in Canadian society, persons who have learned social and power relations in their day-to-day lives and which they enact with members of their families. Increasingly the popular press has become critical of "victim" feminism (that is, feminism that promotes the notion that various groups have been the recipients of oppressive and exploitative behaviours) as an excuse to dismiss violence.

In spite of the failure of the popular literature and press to adequately address the issue, in the past decade or so many scholarly journals have come into being to analyze and promote a systematic study of family conflict and violence. In addition, institutions have been established to study the problem, such as the Vanier Institute of the Family in Ottawa, and various advocacy and therapeutic groups have emerged to deal with the aftermath of family violence.

Undeniably, the social context of family violence is extremely important for an adequate understanding of this phenomenon. However, what may be of even greater salience is how family violence is defined and measured by the public and by people who work in the field in various capacities. We must know exactly what we are talking about — and whether we are talking about the same thing. Therefore, it is imperative to examine the various definitions and means of measuring family violence.

Definitions and Measurement

Definitions and measurements of family violence pose a unique problem because of the nature of family relationships. They take place in private so public officials are not in the position of scrutinizing them. There are few, if any, witnesses. Any witnesses who might be present may be extremely reluctant to admit to what they have seen, even to themselves. So researchers frequently have to rely on self-reports or official statistics.

Official statistics (such as police reports, data from public agencies) often contain what is called a "dark figure" — these are the cases that do not come to the attention of officials but are still occurring. For instance, a woman, reporting on the violence she has suffered from her husband, may tell a researcher that her husband has struck her ten times in the past six months, excluding the numerous incidents in which he threatened to strike her or verbally abused her. The researcher, on the other hand, may consider that the threats and verbal abuse are part of the definition of violence and should be included. In this scenario, according to the researcher's definition, there would be many more incidents of violence but, because of the woman's definition, some of the incidents have been obscured or left "in the dark." We cannot know what that dark figure is. A dark figure will be present in self-reporting because people have varying definitions that are, to a great extent, inaccessible to researchers. Also, research often focuses on one or the other partner, not both. Even when both partners are interviewed, researchers rarely check data to see whether answers do, in fact, match.

Avoiding these problems requires that terminology be as precise as possible in its applicability to empirical phenomena. A precise definition of a social problem means that we should be able to say, beyond the shadow of a doubt, when "normal" or permissible behaviour crosses over into abusive behaviour. Such precision also requires that language be completely lacking in ambiguity and that it be interpreted in a particular fashion. However, both language and behaviour are highly ambiguous and dependent on their context for meaning.

Jones uses "a veil of words" to introduce her argument that the terminology used to discuss the problem of violence within the family often obscures more than it reveals. She argues that using "domestic violence" and "family violence" creates the illusion of gender-neutrality when describing violence within the family. "Male violence disappears in euphemism," she charges. Furthermore, a term like "battered woman" highlights only one facet of a woman's life, reducing the rest of her identity to one variable. It also implies that she is a passive victim of abuse, rather than an active resister or survivor (Jones 1996: 17-18). Using "battered woman" as a blanket term also ignores the fact that a woman may resist being identified as such, even though she may be enduring such behaviour.

Another point that Jones raises is that we generally tend to talk about violence in the passive voice: "women are beaten," "wives are abused," "children are abandoned," and so on. This type of terminology focuses only on the victims, disguising the identity and motivations of the perpetrator. When we are informed about the perpetrator, it is usually an abstract noun: "women are threatened by aggressive behaviour" or "they are battered by the relationship" (Jones 1996: 21). Rarely are we given the explicit details of exactly what was done by whom to whom. The point, of course, is that the use of such euphemistic terms makes the language of family violence imprecise, which, in turn, makes family violence difficult to define and understand.

Definitions of violence against women vary widely in the research literature. Psychological and emotional abuse may be included under the rubric of "family violence," along with financial abuse, verbal abuse and sexual coercion (see Johnson 1996). The same ambiguity exists for violence against other family members, such as children, siblings and elders. Neglect, abandonment, denial of human needs, "rough-housing," "sibling rivalry," spanking, incest, murder — all of these terms arise when researchers begin to discuss violence among family members. Some research instruments include terms like "severe violence" and "very severe violence" with lists of what types of actions belong under each heading.

The wide variation of these definitions and terms raises substantial questions which must be addressed if we, as a society, are going to properly deal with the issue of family violence. How broadly should violence be defined? Is it better to keep definitions narrow and focused on, for example, physical as opposed to emotional abuse? Should we deny the definition of abuse unless at least 25 percent of the body is covered with welts or bruises? Or unless the welts or bruises are no smaller than 2.5 by 2.5 centimetres? Is a smack on the bottom an acceptable form of punishment for a child? Do two smacks constitute child abuse? If an elderly person has to sit home alone all day, with no company but a television, and wait until 7:00 p.m. to have dinner, is that elderly person being abused by her or his caretaker? Are her or his human needs being denied? If one sibling mercilessly teases and humiliates another sibling with stunning constancy, do we classify this as sibling abuse? The answers to these questions will have tremendous impact on how we view family violence, as well as how we respond to it. As a society, Canadians must decide how widely we wish to cast the net of abuse since our societal bond is at stake. Too much or too little will cause that bond to deteriorate decisively. That is, including too many behaviours under the rubric of abuse may result in a breakdown of interactions between people as they label each other's actions "abusive."

However, including too few behaviours under this rubric makes it appear that only certain (usually extreme) actions qualify as abusive; anything else is not labelled in this way. This could result in treatment that drives people apart and makes them suspicious of each other while they are denied redress for their suffering. For example, if just beating someone with fists were considered violent or abusive behaviour, a woman experiencing slaps, shoves, kicks or public humiliation from her husband would not be considered a victim of violence. She might withdraw her love and affection while remaining in the marriage or she might choose to leave the relationship completely because she feels that the relationship is deeply troubled and is suspicious of her husband's actions, even though she may not call herself a battered wife or him an abuser. Furthermore, since his behaviour does not constitute what the public terms "abuse," the wife may not think to go for counselling or examine her experiences. She may find herself being suspicious of other men and leery of entering heterosexual relationships without fully comprehending her own reasons. The point is that, without the proper definitions for her husband's behaviours towards her (because of the narrowness of the behaviour considered "abusive"), the wife in this example is left in a kind of "twilight zone" where she knows that she has suffered wrongful treatment but cannot categorize it in such a way that would benefit her.

Measurement is also a problem, especially when it comes to the instruments used in empirical research. According to Johnson (1996), a number of statistical sources for family violence are problematic. For example, the Uniform Crime Reporting Survey gives an account of criminal acts that have come to the attention of the police in Canada. The problems associated with reliance upon such a survey are the dark figure, which is inherent to all official statistics, and the discretionary power of police officers. Such discretion means that incidents that rightfully constitute family violence may be redefined as another type of criminal act (or as a non-criminal act), thus obscuring actual events.

Family violence is especially prone to underreporting because the family is considered to be a private institution. The myth of the family makes victims too ashamed to report the violence they experience, while dependency on the abuser and sheer terror may keep victims from making their abuse a matter for the public record. Furthermore, a sense of obligation to keep the family intact or a desire not to get too involved in "private" disputes may keep police officers from reporting violent acts between family members as domestic violence.

Another source of statistics is clinical samples (Johnson 1996). These samples are studies that look at behaviours of victims who have sought assistance from agencies such as rape crisis centres and shelters for battered women, or of perpetrators who have been incarcerated. A host of problems accompany such studies. For example, generalization is difficult because of improper sampling methods, which result in samples of subjects that do not represent the population as a whole. Thus the findings may be pertinent only to the subjects of the study, not to all victims of family violence. Self-selection (that is, subjects volunteering for the study) means that the sample of victims may consist of a particular type, or subsample, rather than a wide variety. Perpetrators who have been convicted of offences may be characterized as having had bad luck or having insufficient resources to effectively escape prosecution, rather than as guilty of serious violence. On the other hand, they may be the most vicious of perpetrators. For these and other reasons, clinical samples are highly unreliable.

Population surveys — usually conducted by telephone — are used as another statistical measurement. One of their strengths is that they complement police statistics because the surveys involve incidents that were never reported, in addition to those that were. Another strength is that they are rich in detail. The problem, however, is that the accuracy of the detail is almost impossible to determine. Because of anonymity, interviewees might be tempted to say virtually anything, or the spontaneity of the telephone call could result in the interviewee's inability to recall details on the spur of the moment. In addition, the language of the questions may lead some respondents to eliminate certain data. There may also be some degree of embarrassment about the sensitive nature of the topic or a certain amount of paranoia about the confidentiality of the call, the true identity of the caller and so on (Johnson 1996).

It is evident that family violence is a complex and somewhat elusive phenomenon. Definitions change as power balances in society shift. Measurement of social relations that are so complex and sensitive is a task that requires a refined and prudent instrument. So far, the instruments that are used have drawn criticisms for their tendencies towards inaccuracies. We must, therefore, be cautious when we read reports of family violence, since the findings could have more to do with the instruments used for measurement than with empirical realities.

Conclusions

When we look at the social context of family violence, we see that society has various structures and components which tolerate, contribute to and maintain violent behaviours. Through socialization into our society, to a great extent by our family, we learn to fit into this environment. Some of us may adopt violence as a way of life and internalize it into our identities as a way of getting through life and fitting into society. This internalization demonstrates that family violence is the result of ways of interacting which we learn and which we perpetuate because of our socialization (unless we decide to consciously change our behaviour) and, perhaps even more importantly, because of power relations. If we do not feel powerful in our lives, we may very well seek to exert power over others who are already socially defined as less powerful. So family violence is not difficult to understand and seldom has to do with the pathology of individuals or families. The sociological approach to family violence is that it is a social problem. As such, it affects all of us and is all our responsibility.

Notes

1. Mark is a fictitious character. His experiences are based on a true story conveyed to Julianne Momirov in August 1997.

2. In recent years, there has been a debate over the use of the term "victim," arguing that it is too negative and passive. The term "survivor" has been promoted as being a much more positive and active portrayal of the people who have experienced various forms of family violence.

3. The term "feminist" is applied here to individuals who self-identify as "feminists" in their writings or whose work is included in collections which are described as "feminist" by their editors. It must be understood that the word "feminist" has come to have a diversity of meanings and to cover a complexity of perspectives and conflicts. Feminists certainly do not always agree with one another nor do they necessarily embrace a standard point of view (see for example, Mandell 1995).

4. For other sociological perspectives on conflict, see Dahrendorf 1958, 1959 and Collins 1975.

Violence Against Women in Intimate Relationships

The Experience of Abuse

Perhaps the place to begin and end any discussion of family violence is with the voices of the victims, for it is their experience that we seek to understand. Few of us have not been touched either directly or through the lives of others we care for by some aspect of family violence. Although the quest for understanding the nature and roots of this violence will take us far beyond the personal and individual, it is in our daily lives that we are most likely to first confront the pain of intimate violence. It is the voices and faces of victims, including ourselves, that drive us to seek an understanding of the misery so we can put an end to it.

As with many other areas of family violence, wife abuse may start at a variety of moments. Some women report that their earliest dating relationships were characterized by abuse; others indicate that the violence did not start until they were married and some reveal that physical violence appeared in their relationship only when they became pregnant with their first child. Often, the earliest moments of the abusive relationship are not characterized by physical violence so much as by an overwhelming romantic intensity. In dating relationships, the woman may be flattered by the extreme attention her boyfriend focuses on her; he attends to every aspect of her life including what she wears, who her friends are and where she goes. One survivor remembers:

> I couldn't have any friends at work except those I could talk to between the jobs I had to do during the day. I never could have lunch with a friend or go out for a drink after work. Bob was always there (as quoted in Walker 1979: 116).

Since this intensity fits so closely with ideas about romantic love promoted in the media, it may be deeply seductive. Just as a sexual relationship may seem overwhelmingly intense, the abusive relationship may seem at first to be a deeply satisfying merging of two individuals. However, what may not be clear to the two participants is the predominant role the male assumes in this relationship. Often he wants to possess this woman and lose himself in her but he also fears his dependency upon her and her implicit ability to wreak havoc on his sense of identity and self-worth. Powerful contradictory feelings of attachment and separateness war within him. As a man he is supposed to be manly, unemotional and independent, yet he sees that this woman is becoming dangerously central to his sense of well-being. If he is obsessively insecure, the man may be preoccupied with fears — what if this woman leaves him, what if she spends all her time with the new baby and ignores him, what if she is playing around behind his back with another man, what would any of this say about his manliness, his virility? The media — mainstream as well as pornographic — feed these obsessive preoccupations with images of faithless, oversexed women who make fools of men.

The inner tension generated by these concerns is inexorable and the man looks around his society for solutions. In traditional male and female roles, in mainstream religions, in music videos, in pornography and throughout the cultural order he finds legitimation for one strategic response — dominate this woman. The rational answer seems to be to control as much of her life as humanly possible in order to alleviate his own anxieties. So, he seeks to take charge of what she wears and who she befriends because he feels it is appropriate and safer to control this and other areas of her life.

> Within three months [of marriage at age 17] she was pregnant. It was soon after this, after a party at her sister's, that they arrived home and no sooner had the door closed than Rich suddenly viciously punched her in the face. She reeled back in horror and surprise. He accused her of flirting with her brother-in-law — suggested she had probably been carrying on an affair with him. She denied this and he hit her again (as quoted in MacLeod 1980: 4).

If she rejects his power play — if she overtly challenges his power, discreetly seeks to elude his control or unself-consciously acts in an independent manner — he could use a broad range of strategies to escalate his efforts. He might use emotionally abusive actions, making fun of her and her friends, constantly commenting on her inadequacies and so on. He could socially isolate her by being unpleasant, distant or openly angry when her parents and friends visit the house. He could reduce her economic independence, restricting her access to money, either by limiting her housekeeping money, making it difficult for her to hold a job or insisting she turn her paycheque over to him. He might openly threaten to hurt her in some way, by leaving her and the kids impoverished or killing himself. He could intimidate her — unleashing his violence on property in the home or on family pets or simply by honing the looks and gestures which bring her into line. He could use the children to control her and make her feel that if she goes along with his control the children will be happier and that if she challenges his dominance the children will suffer. Finally, he could mobilize his male privilege and point out that everyone knows he has a right, as a man, to be master of the castle, captain of the ship and that she is attempting to act like a man by challenging this "natural" or "religiously endorsed" pattern of men's and women's lives (Yllo, 1993: 55).

If these strategies prove ineffective, if she demonstrates more independence than he is prepared to countenance or if his inner turmoil demands exorcism, he can always resort to violence. Sometimes this violence is a direct response to the woman's actions. She buys a dress which he considers too seductive (and which triggers his fears of sexual and personal insecurity) and he responds with rage, asking her why she wants to dress like a slut. It doesn't matter how she replies, he is enraged and feels justified in ripping the dress to shreds and screaming obscenities at her. One woman remembers that

> when I just couldn't take it any more he made me burn my favourite dress, because he said it was too tight and made me look even more like a tramp than I already did. Oh, once he also made me cut up all the pictures I had of a good friend because he said she was a bad influence on me (as quoted in MacLeod 1987: 15).

Sometimes this kind of violence ends with an emotional barrage. Screaming obscenities, he storms through the house, slamming doors and smashing objects, or he takes the opportunity to unearth the whole, long litany of her real or imagined offences against him. This might be all that is needed to dominate and control her while soothing his rage.

The danger is that if his rage isn't soothed, he'll turn to physical and sexual violence. He tells her since she wants to dress like a slut, he'll treat her like a slut and he rapes her or in some other way sexually humiliates her. Whether or not she physically resists, he takes the opportunity to exorcise his rage by beating her with his fists or with whatever weapon falls to hand. He may shove her down the stairs or beat her head against the wall.

> Then there was Georgia, a twenty-two-year-old woman whose husband raped her on the second night of their marriage. She reported struggling for close to a half an hour before her husband overpowered her. Even when she vomited on both of them, he still didn't relent. In fact, this made him madder, and he started to punch her (Finkelhor and Yllo 1985: 106).

When the physical and sexual violence ends, he may feel entirely justified in his abuse. It is not clear what he felt in his violent rage, but afterwards he'll shift the blame and responsibility. He probably won't apologize but instead tell his wife it was, after all, her fault. As one husband commented, "You realize that I raped you. You forced me to do it. You didn't want to have sex with me, so I had to force you" (quoted in Finkelhor and Yllo 1985: 43-44). The message is that she should know by now what he expects from her; that she should know the dress (or food or whatever) would "make him crazy." Or, he may minimize the event, saying how great the sex was and how much she turned him on. He might even blame his actions on alcohol or drug use, depending on the well-used explanation that he was too drunk to know what he was doing.

He might, however, be apologetic. He could realize he "lost it," but be unable to explain his own actions even to himself. He'll ask his wife for forgiveness and promise never to be physically abusive again. He probably means it, but won't succeed. The established dynamic in the relationship and the societal context that supports male violence mean that the violence — either physical or emotional — will likely erupt again.

The woman could also respond in a variety of ways. The first instance of serious violence may be enough. She'll pack her bags and go. She knows that nothing — no sexual transgression, real or imagined — justifies the physical or emotional abuse. She values herself too much to jeopardize her life or happiness in an abusive relationship. However, if she is like most women, she probably won't respond this way. Like the overwhelming majority of women, she is (sufficiently well) socialized to have faith in romantic love or to be personally insecure and fearful. Most importantly, she lacks social and economic resources. So she stays. And in the eyes of society, she stays for all the right reasons. She loves and cares for this man and is willing to give him another chance, to work on the relationship and to acknowledge that perhaps she is partially to blame for the abuse.

> You know what hurts me most? We used to be so happy, so much in love. I want those days back. I want to dream again, to make plans, to see a future for us and our kids. I just ache to feel loved again (quoted in MacLeod 1987: 11).

If he has addiction problems, she will hope that solving them is the key to ending his violence. Even a woman who knows the violence is his responsibility might feel ashamed and know that she is likely to be stigmatized and blamed by others if the violence is made public. If they have children, she may decide that having the children's father around and having an economically secure family is more important than ending the abuse. She probably also knows that however violent and enraged he is now, it will be much worse if she challenges him by leaving. She also realizes that it will be hard to hide or difficult to find housing and employment, and fears she will never find another intimate partner who loves her so intensely and exclusively. So much tells her to stay and so little allows or encourages her to leave. A woman whose husband held two doctoral degrees and had a highly visible professional profile said:

> I kept believing he'd change. But I also felt protective of him and his reputation ... Everyone in this small community would have known (quoted in Hoff 1990: 45).

It's very important to know, however, that the abused woman who stays is not necessarily a passive victim. She often works out complex strategies for minimizing and controlling the violence, seeking to anticipate his "bad" mood, keeping the kids quiet, preparing supper the way he likes. These are all strategies for survival. She might also seek to help herself and her children by contacting the local women's shelter for information and support. When indirect efforts fail and he seems open to discussion, she might urge him to seek help for his addictions or suggest family counselling.

If the violence persists or escalates, she might use violence herself or leave or threaten to leave. Even if she leaves and knows she will probably return, she'll send him the message that she has strengths and strategics. Similarly, she may phone the police in the hope of making him realize the severity of his actions and the potentially devastating consequences. In some instances, she might simply want the police to stop the violence, and not want him charged or incarcerated. In other cases, she'll seek police intervention so that she and her children can safely create an independent life. These responses and actions may interplay through the abused woman's life. If the relationship worsens, however, she most likely will become more desperate for change or feel more depressed and impotent. Ironically, when she is strongest, when she lays claim to her rights to a non-violent life by leaving or divorcing her husband, she is at greatest risk.

> The harassment began in the spring of 1993, when Peggy's ex found out she was seeing someone new. He would show up and bang on her door, dump things in front of her apartment. He had assaulted her in the past and as a result, Peggy already had a peace bond stipulating that he not have any contact with her. When she informed police that he was continuing to harass her —following her, sitting in parked cars watching her, slashing and puncturing her boyfriend's tires on at least a half a dozen occasions — they said their hands were tied. [She] said, "What do you want, him on top of me killing me?" (quoted in Turner 1994: C1, C2).

Naming the Violence

Naming the issue of violence against women in the 1960s was such a fundamental turning point in women's history that it is now difficult to understand the times that preceded it. Prior to the mid-nineteenth century, the list of constraints on women's rights and opportunities was almost endless. Denied political, legal, employment, marital and social freedoms, women's adult existence was typically conditioned by marriage, childbirth and childrearing. This pattern reflects the deep patriarchal roots of our society in which women (and children) figured primarily as men's property (Lerner 1986: 212).

Traditionally, daughters' decisions about whom and when they wed were made by fathers and usually in consideration of property arrangements and social benefits. Husbands expected wives to directly provide services and produce children (preferably, male) who would also become productive members of the family. While women were important, even key, to the day-to-day functioning of the household, their well-being depended upon the goodwill of the patriarch. If she failed to fulfil her responsibilities (for example, to produce male children) or if she dared to challenge the patriarchal order, there were few social constraints on his means of discipline.

As property owner, the male had the right to exercise physical force to control and dominate his wife and children. Sir William Blackstone, the influential eighteenth century English jurist, noted, "The common law gave a husband almost unlimited power to control his wife's property; he was, in fact, the titled owner of all her property. He also controlled her person, and had the right to discipline her ... 'the husband ... might give his wife moderate correction' just as he 'is allowed to correct his apprentices or children'" (as cited in Dranoff 1977). Similarly, "Bacon pronounced that 'The husband hath, by law, power and dominion over his wife, and may keep her by force within the bounds of duty, and may beat her, but not in a violent or cruel manner'" (as cited in Strange 1995).

Records of criminal court and divorce proceedings indicate that men made ample use of their right to use violence. Nancy Tomes's examination of the trial accounts reported in the London *Times* from 1841 to 1875 revealed that working-class women were the victims of a "torrent of abuse" (1978). Public complaints emerged only when the violence was so excessive that it led to serious injury or death or created a public commotion. As with whipping and beating children, as long as the husband or father remained within the bounds of socially acceptable violence, his actions were condoned and even encouraged (Pleck, 1987).

The social legitimation of such abuse was only first questioned in the 1800s. The emergence of the temperance movement in North America and Britain led some advocates to link male drunkenness to family violence. The temperance reformers presented excessive wife assaults as further evidence of the ills of alcohol. However, the beaten wife and her drunken husband were assumed to be a working-class and immigrant phenomenon. The solution was, of course, the prohibition of alcohol and punishment (preferably, the whipping post) for wife beaters (Strange 1995; Pleck 1987).

In Britain, these initial steps taken by temperance advocates did lead to a variety of efforts to reform the status of women. In 1857, for example, early women's rights activists founded the Society for the Protection of Women and Children. This society sought to provide women and child victims with legal advice and observers in courtrooms. It also set up the first shelter for victims of assault. Indeed, it was in Britain in 1857 that the term "wife beating" was first used (Pleck 1987: 63, 64).

While these efforts failed to end the social legitimization of wife abuse, they did initiate a few legal reforms. By the early 1900s, special courts had been established in Canada and the United States that attempted to remove family issues from the criminal justice system and provide a "curative rather than punitive approach" (Pleck 1987: 126). The Toronto Women's Court, for example, provided private counselling to couples in conflict and attempted to dispense informal, equitable justice (Strange 1995: 301). These reforms, however, had little effect. Police still continued to routinely minimize "domestics" and sought simply to "patch things up." Courts, preoccupied with preserving the family, offered women and children little in the way of protection or support. For a myriad of reasons, women tended to withdraw their charges. Indeed, their best strategy was often to lay charges to control their husband's violence and then later withdraw the charge. Typically, they and their children were reliant on the abuser's income. Since divorces were extremely difficult to obtain and it was impractical and impossible for most single mothers to acquire sufficient employment income, single motherhood was not a viable alternative. Even if, as rarely happened, the husband was imprisoned, it was typically for six months or less.

This general pattern, which tended to legitimate male violence while trapping women in abusive relationships, persisted well into the 1950s. Violence against women was common, but hidden, in Canadian communities, and societal responses were inadequate and piecemeal. Family violence was still assumed to be the signature of the "lower classes" and, as such, held up to ridicule. Frequently, the woman, and in particular, her housekeeping, were assumed to be the root cause of the couple's conflict. If the wife were "to keep her home and children clean ... [she would] command the respect of her husband." With the popularization of psychology, more sophisticated analysts blamed her for her own victimization by suggesting she must be "masochistic" to stay (Pleck 1987: 139, 193). Or the husband's drunkenness was used to explain away his aberrant behaviour.

It was only with the emergence of modern feminism in the 1960s that these practices and the age-old traditions that supported them were finally challenged in the public arena. English feminist Erin Pizzey, who wrote *Scream Quietly or the Neighbours Will Hear* in 1974, is usually credited with "naming" the violence and establishing the foundation for feminist analyses of woman abuse.[1] Her work was widely read and tremendously influential amongst the many women meeting at women's centres, working in consciousness-raising groups or, simply, reading the new women's literature. In 1980 Linda MacLeod's *Wife Battering in Canada* was published. This Canadian publication was the cornerstone of the battered women's movement. By this point, the shelter movement in Canada had already set down its roots and the lives of all women, including abused women, were being fundamentally altered.

The Name Game Today

Today,[2] now that it is recognized that the violence exists and is unacceptable, wife abuse may seem to be a fairly straightforward issue. Husbands and wives have arguments; sometimes the arguments escalate into physical conflicts and the husbands make use of their greater physical strength to dominate their wives. However, this simple scenario is far from accurate. Violence against women in intimate relations is much more complex, contradictory and multi-dimensional than simple misunderstandings, marital fights or conflicts. It is also much more serious, even deadlier, than arguments that get out of control.

First, the term "wife abuse," since it suggests that the abuse is restricted to women in formal marital relationships, is unacceptable to most activists in the field. Today, with growing numbers of families being headed by common-law couples — about one in ten families in 1991 — such a narrow definition would ignore a large segment of the population (La Novara 1993: 10). Indeed, recent evidence suggests that women in common-law relationships are more likely to be assaulted by their partners than women in formal marriages.[3] Further, women in non-familial intimate relationships, such as those in dating couples, may be subject to very similar patterns of violence. As a result of these kinds of considerations, activists in the battered women's shelter movement tend to opt for the more inclusive term "woman abuse" or "woman battering" in intimate relationships.

Secondly, some social researchers argue that the focus on male perpetrators and female victims is inaccurate. As we discuss below, they cite studies that suggest women in intimate partnerships are also actively violent. Based on this evidence, the term "spousal abuse" or "partner abuse" is recommended since it implies a gender-neutral approach to intimate violence (Wallace 1996: 164-65). While it is important to recognize that many social researchers adopt this "partner" approach, it is not the term we use. While women are clearly capable of violence in intimate relationships, the prevailing pattern in our society is one of male violence against female partners. Females engage in physical violence against their partners but it is often, though not always, reactive violence; that is, they are reacting to physical violence rather than initiating it. Research suggests that male partners are more likely to use "repetitive" and "serious" forms of violence including weapons against their female partners; they are often more capable (owing to a combination of male socialization[4] and biology) of causing serious physical injuries with their violence and it is more often men than women who ultimately kill their intimate partners (Crawford and Gartner 1992; Wilson and Daly 1994; Orwen 1997: A7).[5] Further, in contemporary Canadian society, women are more likely to be economically and socially restrained from leaving the relationship than men (Johnson 1996: 58). Although men sometimes are the primary victims of intimate violence and women sometimes are the primary assailants, research indicates that the typical pattern is one of male violence against female intimates. As a result, we use the term "woman abuse" in this book.

Finally, the term "abuse" is not clear. The assumption that abuse typically takes the form of physical violence (hitting, shoving and so on) and that physical violence is the most serious form of woman abuse is questionable. Not surprisingly much of the research literature has focused on physical violence since resultant injuries are less subjective and more easily identifiable. However, it is important to keep in mind that woman abuse has many manifestations that may or may not be accompanied by acts of physical violence including sexual abuse, economic deprivation, emotional or psychological violence and social battering. Abused women report, for example, being compelled to engage in sexual acts against their will. In the now infamous Bobbitt case, the wife reported her husband repeatedly raped her and forced her to submit to anal intercourse despite causing her physical injury in the process (see, for example, Russell 1982; Finkelhor and Yllo 1985).

Economic abuse is also an important dimension. Women who seek refuge in shelters often report that their husbands provide them with inadequate funds to run the household or feed the family. These same husbands often actively oppose their wives' efforts to obtain paid employment. Economic dependency and insecurity may be a key aspect of the abuse pattern since it effectively locks women into the relationship.

Abuse may also entail psychological or emotional battering. Psychological abuse is often misunderstood as trivial when contrasted to the obvious injuries of physical violence. However, emotional violence may be devastating and pervasive, ranging from constant put downs and furious tantrums to repeated threats to kill the woman, the children, himself or other loved ones (Schmidt 1995: 21). In a relationship marred by violent episodes, tone of voice or slamming doors may create acute fear and anxiety in the abused partner who knows the next violent episode may be in the offing. Lastly, abuse may take the shape of social isolation. Abused women often report that their partners restrict or stop contact with family and friends and lock them into the destructive intimacy of their relationship. Significantly, victims of physical and psychological abuse often indicate that it is the non-physical forms of battering that are harder to bear than the physical pain (Straus and Sweet 1992). Wounds and injuries heal, but the pain of lost dreams and shattered trust lasts a lifetime.

> The thing that's most hurting for me is the way he makes me feel so dirty, so filthy. He treats me like a dog, worse even. He tells me I'm ugly and worthless. He spits on me. It's not enough to hit me and kick me. He spits on me. Sometimes I think the hitting is better than being made to feel so low (quoted in MacLeod 1987: 12).

Based on these considerations, we define woman abuse as a pattern of violence — physical, psychological/emotional, sexual, economic or social — which is intentionally inflicted on a female intimate partner in the course of an ongoing dating, common-law or marital relationship or after one or both partners has ended this relationship. The intent of the abuse is to dominate and control the woman and, in this pursuit, the violence is conditioned by a social context in which men, as a group, tend to have more power and authority than women, as a group.

Dimensions of the Violence

Woman abuse came out of the closet in the late 1960s and early 1970s in Canada. At this time, women were responding to the contemporary women's movement, were being challenged by the new feminist authors and were coming together in consciousness-raising groups and at newly founded women's centres. They quickly identified violence as a key issue in their own and other women's lives. Although women have been raped and wives brutalized throughout history,[6] the social movement energized by modern feminism was able to wage a successful campaign to document the pervasiveness of this violence and its devastating impact on women's lives and to challenge the societal beliefs and values which trivialized and privatized women's suffering. Almost at once feminist analysis translated into social activism and one immediate focus was the creation of shelters (at first called transition houses) for "battered wives." In 1972, the first shelters were established in British Columbia and Alberta. By 1980, there were seventy-one transition houses or hostels across Canada accepting battered women (MacLeod 1980).

No doubt these early efforts would have fizzled if they had not been responsive to many women's and men's experiences. It rapidly became clear that violence against women in their homes was not uncommon or insignificant. In 1978, social researcher Linda MacLeod assembled statistics from forty-seven Canadian transition houses and estimated, based on these results, that about 15,000 women across Canada would stay in a transition house each year. In addition, an estimated 12,000 women requested help from (but did not stay at) transition houses "because they were physically battered by their husbands" (1980: 16-17). These results along with the ongoing demand for shelter services documented that the intimate abuse of women was not simply some private, personal trouble rooted in individual pathology. If one or two Canadian women were the victims of abuse, it made sense to focus on their personal background and idiosyncrasies. When thousands of women were asking for assistance, the problem appeared to be societal and systemic. As early activists argued, this abuse was a public issue that warranted the attention of all Canadians and reflected upon the fundamental beliefs, values and structure of our society. MacLeod went on to update her research in 1985 by collecting statistics and interviewing battered women and transition-house workers at 110 shelters. At this juncture she estimated that yearly 42,000 women were accommodated at the 230 shelters across Canada and almost every shelter was forced to turn "a large number of women" away (1987: 6-7). The publicity surrounding these and earlier figures further motivated social activists, researchers and policy analysts who wanted to determine the actual extent of the problem.

MacLeod's research, while a landmark effort, was exploratory. There was no way of knowing how many abused women were unable or unwilling to contact a shelter or how many were able to use other forms of escape from a violent relationship. What was needed was a much more extensive, and costly, national picture of woman abuse. However, woman abuse by its very nature is extremely difficult to research. In all survey research there is the problem of respondents being unwilling to honestly report their behaviour or attitudes (Northrup 1997). This difficulty is greatly compounded because abusive behaviour and experiences are seen as stigmatizing and shaming. Creating and funding research that would explore this complex and contentious issue on a national basis while protecting the rights and safety of respondents was an enormous challenge.

Throughout the 1980s, considerable academic research addressed the dimensions of woman abuse by employing survey techniques and, in particular, the Conflict Tactics Scale (CTS). The CTS was formulated by one of the pioneer researchers in family violence, American sociologist Murray Straus (1979). The measure consists of eighteen items that are intended to identify a continuum of non-violent and violent strategies that may occur in interpersonal conflict (see Chapter 1). For example, respondents (husbands or wives) are asked to indicate how often, if ever, in the past year they used insults against their partner, slapped, pushed, shoved, threw an object at or kicked their partner.

A number of Canadian researchers have used the CTS to measure woman abuse in Canada (DeKeseredy and Hinch 1991: 21-23). Given the expense of national surveys, it is not surprising that few studies have attempted to measure woman abuse at a national level. However, even city-based surveys suggest that a significant number of Canadian men and women have experienced abuse, even severe abuse. Sociologist Michael Smith (1987), for example, reported that in his Toronto sample of 604 women who were presently or formerly married or in a cohabiting relationship, 14.4 percent had been abused in the past year and 5.1 percent had been severely abused.

However, as a number of researchers have been quick to point out, the popular CTS approach is not without problems. The introduction to the CTS item list identifies the "strategies" as ways that couples seek "to settle their differences." However, many abusive incidents are not precipitated by conflict or disagreement. Some victims report violence erupting without warning. Given the introductory remarks to the CTS it is not clear which incidents respondents would decide to include. Further, the CTS continuum format makes the questionable assumption that physical violence is worse than psychological abuse. Similarly, it assumes that some "minor" forms of violence (slapping) are less physically injurious than "severe violence." Football player James Harris of the Minnesota Vikings allegedly broke his wife's nose and collarbone with a single "smack" (Kaplan 1996: H6).

The CTS format also leaves out other abusive actions such as scratching and burning. Further methodological problems are raised by the fact that the research record indicates men and women do not report and, perhaps, do not perceive the same reality of violence. For example, Brinkerhoff and Lupri (1988) found that women report their abusive acts against their husbands more readily than men report their abusive acts against their wives. Other studies reveal that men's and women's reports on the occurrence and frequency of violence in their relationship are widely discrepant. Clinical studies with violent men also indicate that these men tend to minimize their violent acts and the injuries they cause. In addition, it is not clear from CTS reports whether or not women's violence is a response to male violence or if women's violence is as potentially injurious. Finally, by simply counting the violent acts, the CTS approach ignores the larger context of violence. For example, in a society where men tend to be the principal wage earner for the family and where men are still often assumed to be the "head" of the household, one violent act by the man may have a much more definitive impact on the household than several violent acts by a rebellious wife (DeKeseredy and Hinch 1991: 23-25; Johnson 1996: 56-60). Researchers are aware of these limitations and are making various efforts to refine the CTS instrument as well as to develop new approaches (Smith 1994).

Significant advances in understanding the dimensions of woman abuse were achieved in the early 1990s, when the national Canadian

Violence Against Women Survey (CVAWS), funded by the federal Department of Health, was conducted through the auspices of Statistics Canada. This survey, which involved telephone interviews with a randomly selected representative national sample of 12,300 women using a modified CTS approach, provided Canadians with invaluable understanding of the nature and extent of male violence. This pioneering effort not only provided an informed base for national policies but also stands as a model which is now being replicated by other countries wishing to address the costs and consequences of violence against women (Johnson 1995).

The CVAWS produced powerful evidence that intimate violence is a pervasive and significant issue in women's lives. The researchers found that one-quarter of the women surveyed (aged eighteen or older) experienced violence at the hands of a past or present marital partner since age sixteen. This means that one in four Canadian women will in all likelihood be pushed, grabbed, shoved, threatened, slapped, kicked, bitten, hit, beaten up or sexually assaulted at some point in their marital lives. While "severe" violence such as "choking" or "using a gun or knife" was relatively uncommon in the reports (7 percent and 5 percent of respondents respectively reporting these types of violence), more than one in ten of the women who reported violence in a current marriage indicated they had at some point felt their lives were in danger. This severity is perhaps not surprising since 39 percent of these women reported more than one violent episode in their current marriage and 10 percent reported more than ten episodes (Statistics Canada 1993).

Other recent investigations corroborate that woman abuse in intimate relationships is a relatively common social phenomenon. In 1994, Lupri, Grandin and Brinkerhoff interviewed a small representative national sample of women and asked them detailed questions about physical, psychological and sexual violence. Their findings, which corroborated MacLeod's 1979 study, estimated that on an annual basis one in ten Canadian women were the victims of "wife battering" (59).

Even with the quality of these research efforts, concerns persist that the research methodologies are flawed. The CVAWS, although it generated considerable media attention, was criticized. Some critics feared that it overestimated violence against women because it failed to distinguish between the seriousness of assaults and failed to look for violence against men. While these criticisms have been effectively responded to by the survey's authors and others, they are important symptoms of the ongoing public debate surrounding women's issues and feminism (Johnson 1995; Doob 1995). They also underscore the importance of knowing the underlying strengths and weaknesses of research findings that are being used to create social policy and social change.

While acknowledging these persistent debates about research methodology, it seems fair to say that today a vastly improved research base confirms that violence against women in intimate relationships is a pervasive and persistent social problem. Even a relatively narrow conception of violence generates data that suggest that each year 3 percent of currently married or cohabiting women, in other words about 201,000 Canadian women, are subject to abuse (Johnson 1996:136).[7]

No longer is it necessary to rely on estimates or impressions. Newspaper items that call attention to the "epidemic of violence against women" or refer to the "pervasive abuse of women" now have added credibility. Further, research has given us a much more solid understanding of the parameters of abuse, who the typical victims and abusers are, what the nature of the violence is, where it occurs and so on.

Patterns Within the Violence

Since MacLeod's landmark research in the late 1970s, researchers have been interested in documenting not only the extent of the violence but also its distinguishing characteristics. Clearly, analysts hope that by understanding who is victimized and when the victimization occurs, they will gain insight into why the violence occurs and how to end it.

The growing research literature is now able to provide a clearer picture of abuse patterns.

(i) Gender

There does appear to be a gender pattern in the documented violence. Although research suggests men are more likely to be the instigators of serious, repetitive violence, women are also capable of serious violent acts. In some of these cases, the woman was reported to be responding to years of violence and abuse. For example, in 1994 a forty-eight year old Ontario woman was acquitted of all criminal charges after drugging her unfaithful husband and cutting off his penis. Her lawyer argued that she was suffering from "battered wife syndrome and was acting in self defence ... because she feared [her husband] might kill her that night" (Crook 1992: A4).

It is now widely accepted that some instances of woman-initiated violence are the result of the *battered woman syndrome*. This term, popularized by Leonore Walker, one of the pioneer activists in the movement against woman battering, refers to the theory that women victimized by intimate physical, sexual or psychological violence may eventually feel so helpless and hopeless that they cannot extricate themselves from the abusive relationship. When they feel their own or their children's lives are in imminent danger, they may respond by attacking and killing their abuser. This psychological state, an aspect of post-traumatic stress disorder,[8] has now been successfully used in Canada and the United States to defend women who have killed their abusive male partners (Walker 1993). As a result of a landmark Supreme Court of Canada ruling in 1990, which recognized battered women's syndrome as a legal defence, a 1997 report to the federal government recommended that seven women currently incarcerated for murder be freed from prison, be pardoned or have their sentences reviewed since they were defending themselves against abusive partners.

Regardless of this phenomenon, many commentators insist that women are just as violent and dangerous as their male counterparts. As mentioned above, research that simply tallies up the number of violent acts in a relationship is often presented to support this perspective. For example, a 1992 federally funded survey in Winnipeg reported that 39 percent of women and only 26 percent of men polled indicated they had threatened or physically abused their spouses. According to media coverage of the survey, "most women said self-defence was not the motive" (*Toronto Star*, October 23, 1992: A18). This finding is not as exceptional as suggested by the media coverage. Canadian and American researchers have frequently documented women's violence in relationships. Indeed, Straus points out that there are "30 or more studies showing that women assault partners at about the same rate as men" (1993: 82). The dimensions and implications of women's violence remain one of the key "controversies" in family violence research (Kurz 1993).

Recent research into lesbian battering has also been presented as evidence that women are potentially as violent as men. Certainly, some aspects of violent lesbian relationships are highly reminiscent of heterosexual patterns of abuse. Claire Renzetti's nationwide American survey of violence in lesbian couples found, for example,

that "power imbalance" was an issue in 50 percent of the relationships. As with heterosexuals, lesbian abusers and victims appear to
become locked in a struggle over dominance.

> [There was violence over] any way that I was different from
> her, yes ... I had different friends, and I had to drop them all
> ... there was no room for me to assert my autonomy. I could
> never feel like myself (as quoted in Renzetti 1992: 37).

However, the fact that lesbians can be violent and preoccupied
with dominating their partners does not mean that women in heterosexual relationships are likely to act in a similar fashion. Lesbian
violence is conditioned by the relationship between the couple and
the larger social context. As women, the lesbian couple are likely to
be treated by the larger society as equivalents; as lesbians, they are
both socially defined as members of a generally stigmatized group.
These factors tend to support equality between the partners rather
than reinforcing and legitimating patterns of inequality. Further, the
lesbian community — in established dissonance with mainstream
society — is likely to provide a context which is both more prominent in the relationship and more supportive of healing the couple
than the typical suburban community (Card 1995). The violence
takes shape and has meaning within this societal context. For example, when a woman beats her female lover, she does so within the
context of a homophobic society that represents lesbianism as "deviant." She knows (as does the abused lover) that the police, judicial
system and social welfare agencies will respond to her lover as a
"lesbian" victim and that this will likely translate into dismissive or
overtly hostile reactions.

Similarly, heterosexual women's violence is structured by its social context: a context in which women are more likely to be poor,
less well paid, less well educated and so on. Heterosexual men and
women do not typically confront one another as equals in this society.
Regardless of their personal qualities and abilities, they live in a
society with the inevitable knowledge that this society is frequently,
although with some notable exceptions, led by men, financed by men
and designed by men. When a woman hits her husband or male lover,
she does so with the knowledge of these gender inequalities. She
knows, for example, that if the marriage ends, she will probably take
custody of the children and will, in all likelihood, struggle financially. She knows that at forty-five or fifty years of age she, but not

he, has greater chances of being considered a marital longshot. She may not like these social conditions, but she will be aware of them and they will be part of the meaning of her actions.

In short, when examining the implications of lesbian battering for woman abuse, we must keep in mind that acts of violence are socially constructed. It is the social meaning of the violent act that is important. For example, if someone unintentionally drops a rock on your foot, you may be injured and angered but your reaction is tempered by the social meaning: the other person did not intend to hurt you. If however, the act was intentional or part of a pattern or historical tradition in which other people like you were injured or violated, it acquires dramatically different implications. While lesbian battering does confirm that women are capable of severe violence, even murder, it cannot stand as a parallel to the violence in heterosexual relationships.

Currently, most social researchers and analysts in Canada, even those documenting female violence, seem to subscribe to the view that, while female violence should not be ignored, male violence is key to understanding intimate abuse.[9] Men are the ones most likely to inflict the serious physical and social injuries while women's violence is frequently committed in self-defence (Johnson 1996: xix-xx; Lupri, Grandin and Brinkerhoff 1994: 53n; DeKeseredy and Hinch 1991: 11-12; Gelles and Cornell 1990; Gelles 1993; MacLeod 1987). Dobash et al. also point out that the specific explanations for the violence that are given by victims of wife battering — male sexual jealousy and proprietariness, expectations of obedience and domestic service and women's attempts to leave marital relationships — suggest a reality that is deeply rooted in our society's notions of masculine and feminine roles (1992: 83).

Criminal justice statistics corroborate this pattern of female victimization. It is women who lay the overwhelming majority of complaints of domestic violence with police.[10] It is women who are most likely to appear in hospital emergency rooms with injuries from domestic violence. And, it is women who are much more likely than men to be killed by their marriage partner. Each year from 1974 to 1992 women were three times more likely to be killed by their husbands than men were by their wives, and women were nine times more likely to be killed by their spouses than by a stranger (Wilson and Daly 1994; see also Crawford and Gartner 1992). Further, crime statistics consistently document that extreme violence, such as homicide, is a strongly male phenomenon. Not only are men more likely to be victims of homicide (67 percent of all homicide victims are male), men are much more likely to be accused of homicide (87 percent) (Johnson 1996: 179). The most dramatic and violent expressions of family violence, familicides, where the wife and children (sometimes along with other family members) are killed in one incident, are a distinctly male phenomenon, with men committing 94 percent of familicides (Wilson and Daly 1994: 4).

While, based on this evidence, we reject notions that men's and women's participation in marital violence is equal, we do not want to imply that violent women be invisible in studies or be seen as appropriate role models for children. Rather, we prefer to focus on male violence in intimate relations, since this violence is currently exacting the heaviest personal and societal costs in terms of the number of women and children in shelters, police intervention in domestic disputes and spousal homicides.

(ii) Age, Class, Race, Ethnicity

In the late 1970s the picture of the batterer was extremely unclear. Since that time, as a result of both enormous strides in survey research such as the CVAWS and in clinical research,[11] we have gained a much better understanding of who the typical batterer is, where he comes from and what seems to motivate him.

The CVAWS results suggest that the typical abuser is most likely to be a young man, under the age of twenty-five. More than one in ten men eighteen to twenty-four years old were reported to be violent towards their partners, while only one in one hundred men forty-five years old and over engaged in woman assault in their intimate relations (Johnson 1996:149; see also, Gelles 1993; Kennedy and Dutton 1989; and MacLeod 1987). Since youth is understood to be a difficult period in modern life and the young often lack the resources or experience to make appropriate decisions, this pattern is understandable. It is also reflected, for example, in high rates of violent crime amongst young men (Cote and Allahar 1994: 62).

However, as with every other "typical" characteristic of the batterer or victim, it must be emphasized that there are numerous exceptions. Abusers are generally but not always young. For example, in 1996 Harry Morgan, then eighty-one years old and the former actor of *M*A*S*H**, was charged with beating his seventy-year-old wife (*Toronto Star*, July 11, 1996: C7). Woman abuse is not the exclusive domain of angry young men.

Given the relative youth of many abusers, it is to be expected that many will be in common-law relations, will have low levels of family income and education and will often be unemployed (Edelson et al. 1985; Smith 1990b). The CVAWS reported, for example, that "men living in families where the joint income is less than $15,000 and unemployed men had rates of violence twice as high as those in more affluent families and employed men." Not surprisingly, youth and low socioeconomic status (and common-law marital status) were correlated; that is, very likely to occur together. It seems likely that these features interact in a complex fashion with one another — for example, youthful immaturity, economic insecurity and low level of relationship commitment — to result in increased rates of intimate violence against women.

While it is important to be aware of this pattern, it is also crucial to keep in mind that both survey and clinical research reveal that men from all classes and occupations batter their wives.[12] For example, a recent examination of the lives of military wives in Canada found that abusive violence emerged as an important issue in these women's lives regardless of their husbands' rank (Harrison and Laliberte 1994; see also, *Toronto Star*, August 5, 1997: A9). Two recent high profile cases bring this point home. In 1995, Dorothy Joudrie shot her husband six times. Earl Joudrie was a "corporate giant" and the former chair of the board of Canadian Tire and Gulf Canada Resources Limited. In the subsequent trial, it was revealed that their thirty year marriage had been marred by his acts of physical and emotional abuse (Ford 1996: E4; Woloschuk 1996). In 1994, the wealthy heiress to the Scripps newspaper fortune was beaten to death by her husband. The police issued an arrest warrant for him when he disappeared (*Toronto Star*, January 8, 1994: A10). The well-to-do are not immune to woman abuse (although they may be better able to avoid public and police scrutiny) and violence against women is not endemic to the working class.

A similar point should be made about racial and ethnic differences. The CVAWS did not ask respondents to identify their ethnic or cultural background and very little other research appears to have focused on this issue (see DeKeseredy and Hinch 1991: 28).[13] However, public opinion does appear to subscribe to the view that certain racial and ethnic groups are more likely to experience woman abuse. Research has indicated that Aboriginal women may be particularly subject to woman abuse. MacLeod found in 1985 that 15 percent of the women in Canadian shelters were Aboriginal (1987: 24). The

Ontario Native Women's Association reported in 1989 that eight in ten Aboriginal women were abused. Similarly, Dumont-Smith and Labelle found that 75 to 90 percent of women in some northern Aboriginal communities were battered (as cited in Gurr et al. 1996: 34). Activists and academic researchers support the conclusion that intimate violence against women is particularly acute in Aboriginal communities (LaRocque 1994; Baxter et al. 1995)[14]. A similar relationship between race and woman abuse has been documented in the United States. Research there indicates that "wife abuse" is significantly more common amongst the unemployed and poor and amongst Blacks and Hispanics (Gelles 1993: 33-34).

This relationship between racial/ethnic minorities and abuse does not, however, imply causality. In two recent events, there were suggestions that cultural values and practices (such as arranged marriages) produce woman abuse. In two recent incidents, a prominent Filipino-Canadian woman was killed in a domestic dispute, and nine members of a British Columbia Sikh family were killed by a jealous ex-husband. Analysts dismissed any causal link and pointed out that woman abuse, sexism and misogyny know no racial or ethnic boundaries (Cardozo 1996: A21). These violent incidents more likely reflect the stresses of economic and social marginalization rather than subcultural values that permit or endorse wife abuse. Since economic marginalization and minority group status tend to interact, it is to be expected that woman abuse would be more evident in minority communities. Further, poor and minority groups may be more subject to police and judicial scrutiny and, as a result, the violence is more likely to become part of the public record.

(iii) Alcohol and Drug Use

Throughout the literature on woman abuse, alcohol figures prominently as an aspect of the violence. Many abused women explain their husbands' actions in terms of drinking and, of course, many perpetrators use drunkeness to attempt to excuse their violence. Predictably, the CVAWS reported that "perpetrators had been drinking in more than 40% of violent incidents" against women and that drinking was most likely in cases of violence involving intimates (boyfriends, dates and spouses) (Statistics Canada 1993: 5). Most analysts agree that, despite the hopes and beliefs of both victims and victimizers, alcohol does not cause the violence and the violence will not necessarily stop if the drinking stops. Alcohol and drug use may provide the men with a "socially accepted time out" and it may reduce inhibitions and escalate the severity of the violence, but many men who are abstainers or moderate drinkers assault their wives and many "heavy drinkers" were not "under the influence" when they beat their wives (Johnson 1996: 155-58).[15]

(iv) Three Other Key Factors

The research over the last twenty years reveals that there are three other factors that increase the likelihood of violence. The first is pregnancy. One in five (21 percent) of the women interviewed in the CVAWS report said that they experienced violence by a previous or current partner during their pregnancies (Statistics Canada 1993: 4; see also MacLeod 1980). This has been explained both in terms of women's increased dependency and hence vulnerability during this time period and in terms of the batterer's fear of increased family responsibility or increased competition for his wife's attention.

The second factor that increases the threat of violence and, in particular, life-threatening violence, occurs when the wife expresses a desire to leave or when she actually separates from or divorces her abusive partner. The CVAWS found, for example, that one-fifth (19 percent) of women who experienced violence at the hands of a former partner reported that the violence occurred after or during separation, and one in three of these cases reported that the violence increased in severity when they separated (Statistics Canada 1993: 4; see also Johnson 1996: 169-70; Smith 1990b; Kennedy and Dutton 1989).

As Smith points out, this pattern of abuse against women who have threatened to leave or who have actually left is important when thinking about explanations of women's actions (1990b: 55). Notions that abused women suffer from learned helplessness[16] or are masochistic or depressed are contradicted by the evidence that many abused women take dramatic steps to end the violence by leaving the abuser. The CVAWS found that 43 percent of women who reported wife assault had indeed experienced increased violence when they left their partners either for a short time or permanently (Johnson 1996: 188).[17]

The third factor suggests that perpetrators of violence and their victims are more likely to have been exposed to violence in their family of origin. MacLeod reported that 61 percent of the husbands of women staying in shelters in 1985 had been abused as children, and 39 percent of the women themselves had been physically abused as children (1987: 39). The CVAWS found that women with violent fathers-in-law were three times more likely than women with non-violent fathers-in-law to be abused by their marital partners (Statistics Canada 1993: 5). By the mid-1980s, the research literature revealed "exposure to parental violence to be the only consistent risk marker in women's victimization" (Hotaling and Sugarman 1986).

Conclusions

Several general conclusions can be drawn from the discussion in this chapter. First, since the inception of the modern women's movement, violence against women has been socially targetted as an important social issue. Secondly, researchers have responded to this concern by developing an increasingly detailed picture of both the parameters and features of violence against women in intimate relationships. This research remains at the centre of an intense political debate about feminism and gender equality. Despite the persistent criticisms of the research record, a growing body of findings appears to provide unequivocal evidence that intimate violence against women is a prominent feature in the lives of a significant number of Canadian women. Thirdly, we have an increasingly clear picture of the dynamics of this violence. With this growing knowledge base, analysts are able to evolve a more fine-tuned understanding of the personal and societal roots of violence against women.

Notes

1. Although the term "woman abuse" is more inclusive, the terms "wife abuse" and "woman abuse/battering" will be used interchangeably throughout this text. In part, this reflects the usage employed in the various texts cited; in part, it reflects popular usage. It should be noted that the term "wife abuse" is employed here with no necessary implications for the marital status of the women involved.

2. For a much more in-depth examination of the ways in which various segments of Canadian society struggle to control prevailing definitions of violence against women and, therefore, solutions to this violence see Gillian Walker's *Family Violence and the Women's Movement: The Conceptual Politics of Struggle* (1990).

3. A recent survey of Canadian women found that while only 2 percent of married women reported at least one violent incident

from their partners in the year preceding the survey, this was true of 9 percent of cohabiting (common-law) women. This does not suggest that marital status per se alters the rates of violence. Rather, it seems likely that factors that may be associated with cohabitation, such as youthfulness, weaker expectations of commitment and sexual fidelity, fewer family and community supports and so on may be linked to higher rates of violence (Johnson, 1996: 150-153).

4. Male socialization refers to the social process by which the family, friends, media and educational institutions combine to create a certain socially approved pattern of male behaviour in a particular society.

5. For example, a recent report by Maria Crawford, Myrna Dawson and criminologist Rosemary Gartner indicates that between 1991 and 1994, 70 percent of murdered Ontario women were killed by their male partner. Disturbingly, the number of women killed by their intimate partners is increasing while other crimes involving lethal violence are decreasing (Orwen 1997: A7).

6. The first organized response opposed to wife abuse was launched by the temperance movement in the mid-1800s. Temperance advocates identified violence against wives as yet another outcome of alcohol consumption and further evidence to support the banning of all alcohol. However, in much of their literature wife abuse was portrayed as a feature of working-class lives. There was no appreciation for the fact that women of all classes were subject to violence or that gender inequality was at the root of such violence (Strange 1995). Other historical research based on police reports indicates that violence against wives was common-place in working-class communities (Tomes 1978). However, social activists of the time identified the problem as a "class" rather than a "gender" issue.

7. Dutton (1995: 25) also concludes from a review of the research literature that severe assaults will occur in between 8.7 percent and 12.1 percent of marriages.

8. Post-traumatic stress disorder (PTSD) is a category found in the *Diagnostic and Statistical Manual of Mental Disorders*, which catalogues psychological disorders and their symptoms. It first appeared as a diagnostic category in 1980 and has received

considerable attention as an outcome of exposure to military combat, notably the Vietnam War, or other violently traumatic events. Individuals afflicted with PTSD may experience difficulty concentrating, confused thinking and poor judgment. For a detailed discussion of the criteria for diagnosis of PTSD see Walker 1993: 138-44.

9. The debate is far from over. Witness a recent column in the *Toronto Star* that cited the Winnipeg study and argued there are "shameful double-standards [being applied] to domestic violence issues" (Laframboise 1995: A17).

10. Violent incidents may not be disputes or conflicts at all. Not infrequently victims of wife abuse report that nothing set the stage for the violence; it was completely unexpected. For example, in a recent case in Toronto where a woman and live-in partner were set afire and almost killed by her ex-husband, she reported that their separation and divorce had seemed amicable and that her ex-husband's subsequent anger and violence were completely unexpected.

11. Clinical research focuses on clinical populations, for example, men who participate in programs for male abusers. This kind of research — usually employing an interview format — is more helpful in building a detailed picture than survey research, which relies on questionnaires.

12. While the CVAWS provides high quality data, it does not solve all of the problems entailed in this type of research. As noted, being abused is a stigmatized and socially shamed behaviour which the women respondents are being asked to admit to. It is to be expected that regardless of the use of only female interviewers, non-judgmental and supportive interviewing techniques, etc., some women will balk at admitting to victimization. If the woman being interviewed is married to or living with a man with high social status, she may have additional reasons (involving finances and social standing) for staying in the relationship. She may be understandably loathe to admit that she is staying in an abusive relationship out of financial self-interest. As a result of these kinds of dynamics, surveys such as the CVAWS may still misrepresent the class characteristics of abusers.

13. American research reveals that "wife abuse" is more common in Black households than white ones. However, since race clearly intersects in a complex fashion with income, employment and social status, the role, if any, of racial subcultures and racially distinct value systems is not clear.

14. It should be noted that not all reserves are equally subject to the problems of family violence. Some, such as Alkali Lake, have been able to make dramatic turn-arounds in terms of community and spiritual revival, which result in dramatic reductions in family violence and addiction problems. Indeed, as discussed in the final section of this chapter, Aboriginal communities have been amongst the most innovative in addressing family violence issues (Gurr et al. 1996: 28).

15. As Kantor and Straus point out, alcohol may not be the link to violence. Rather, alcohol and violence may be both linked to a pivotal third factor. For example, both violence towards women and "heavy" drinking may be related to popular conceptions of manly behaviour (as cited in Johnson 1996: 12).

16. "Learned helplessness" is a psychological term that refers to the psychological state created when organisms "learn that they cannot predict whether what they do will result in a particular outcome." Lenore Walker applied this term to battered women to describe the sense of confusion and narrowing choices which often accompanies an abusive relationship (1993: 135).

17. Other evidence also suggests women are far from passive, helpless victims. The CVAWS found that in one-third of all cases of violence, the women were able to successfully end their husbands' use of violence after one episode by leaving (or threatening to do so), by calling the police or by some other method (Johnson, 1996: 140).

Children Denied Childhood: Child Abuse

The Experience

Perhaps even more than in woman abuse, it is impossible to capture the complexity, diversity and devastation of family violence experienced by children. The violence takes such a variety of forms and the perpetrators occupy such an array of relationships with the victims that any simple description can only overlook as much as it encompasses. Further, the lines between abuse and "normal" behaviour, between discipline and violence, are so murky in our society that victims themselves may have difficulty naming and assessing the violence used on them. The following overview attempts to identify some of the dimensions of the abuse while acknowledging the larger complexities and variations.[1]

Although adults may differ in their resources and abilities to mobilize power in their own defence, rarely are the inequalities as great and as glaring as between an adult and a child. Imagine, as family violence commentator John Bradshaw suggests, being yelled at, threatened, terrorized, hit or raped by a giant two or three times as tall as you, weighing twice to three times as much as you. Even the terror we as adults might experience if trapped with such an assailant cannot capture the hopelessness, immobilizing fear and horror felt by many abused childen. For the abused child, there is often no escape, nor any hope of escape.

The parent abuser is frequently the source of everything that sustains life — food, shelter, clothing — and every aspect of life may be dictated by his or her will. Where the child lives, whether she or he goes to school, whether the child has a pet or plays with local children all hinge on the will or whim of the parent. All social institutions — religion, media, schools — tend to reinforce and legitimate the incalculable power of the adult. Parents are to be loved, honoured and obeyed; parents are the centre of the psychological universe and parents are forever. Although children grow out of their physical dependency, many adults go to their graves locked in an interminable emotional struggle with their long-dead parents — still seeking the love, attention, respect or decency that they were denied decades ago.

Child abuse must be understood for its inclination to permeate our social systems and to inject poison into every facet of social existence. Not only do abuse victims become adults who abuse their wives, husbands and children, they become political leaders and generals who fight genocidal wars, authors who promote internecine hatred, religious leaders who sanction intolerance, managers who take pleasure in exploiting their workforce.

It is likely that all abused children struggle with some legacy of pain, shame and anger. The impact of the experience is conditioned by their socially defined status as children. However, there are enormous variations in the violence inflicted on children. Some children are hit, threatened or injured only once in their young lives and as the result of a peculiar and short-term constellation of family factors. In other instances, abuse may last until the child is able to fight back. For example, many children, especially boys, report being beaten until the age at which they were able to physically challenge their abuser and then the physical violence ended completely. For others, the violence may linger well into adulthood. Some victims of incest disclose that they were abused by a parent into their twenties; although they were physically and socially adult, they were unable to end or escape the abuse. Other child victims of psychological abuse go on being scapegoated, belittled and manipulated by their parents even when they are married and have children of their own.

The frequency and duration of the abuse clearly affect the victim's experience. Similarly, the intensity of the violence alters the experience. Many children are the victims of "neglect": the parent(s) does not actively violate the children's rights but rather fails to provide the food, shelter, clothing and care children need to thrive.

> I clearly remember my mother telling me very matter-of-factly that her earliest childhood memories were of being alone, tied into her bed and having her toys on the bedcover in front of her. An elderly neighbour occasionally checked in on her and brought her something to eat. Her mother was at work and since it was during the depression, they would

> not eat if she didn't work. My mother as a toddler sat in bed
> waiting for her mother to return. (Personal reminiscence).

There is a complex overlap between this kind of parental neglect and the neglect perpetrated by the surrounding society that provides inadequate social support services. In many countries around the world children are not only neglected but also prostituted and crippled in response to an economic order that offers no or little support to impoverished parents.

The complexities of domestic violence against children are also apparent in emotional or psychological patterns of abuse. Traditionally abuse has been narrowly defined in terms of physical violence and obvious injuries. Only in recent years has attention increasingly turned to the psychological well-being of children. Although social welfare agencies are still less likely to intervene where children are being psychologically (but not physically or sexually) abused, there is greater public awareness of the issue and more parents are aware that good parenting involves more than providing food, shelter and clothing. The 1997 children's movie *Matilda* provides an interesting example of our increasing public appreciation for inadequate or inappropriate emotional responses to children. Matilda's parents spend most of the time alternately ignoring her existence, yelling at or threatening her or demanding that she meet their needs. A happy ending is constructed, rather bizarrely, when Matilda's loving teacher, Miss Honey, agrees to adopt the academically brilliant child. Needless to say, the real life aftermath of psychological abuse is rarely so promising.

Emotional abuse should not be dismissed as a minor form of child abuse. For some children, it may take on nightmarish proportions. In punishment for any perceived infraction of parental will, they (or other loved ones) may be threatened with death, their possessions taken away or destroyed or they are forced to witness the killing of a beloved pet. They might be forced, directly or indirectly, to witness physical violence between their parents. Victims report living in terror of the next violent rampage, lying in their beds listening to the screams and blows and wondering who will survive. Some are forced to witness their mother being raped or abused. Despite the absence of physical scars, this kind of violence exacts an enormous price from its victims.

> We have talked with two young women each of whom told
> us that when her father was angry with her he killed her
> favorite pet. One girl told how her father put her dog out in
> twenty-below-zero-degree weather, and the dog froze to
> death. The other told of how her father killed a pet rabbit
> and then gutted the rabbit at the kitchen table while the
> young child watched silently (Gelles and Straus 1988: 68).

Emotional and psychological violence also happens when children
are sexually abused. The victimization includes not only the physical
pain and suffering but also the violation of children's trust, their
sense of safety in the world and their sense of self-worth. Some
family members who sexually abuse children are overtly violent and
abusive. They threaten their young victims with retaliatory violence
if the child tells anyone. Part of the perpetrators' personal motivation
appears to be an enjoyment of the pain and suffering they are inflicting on the child. Other perpetrators may be less physically coercive
and more manipulative. They rationalize their behaviour as providing
the child with a sexual education, as a result of their "sexually frigid"
wife or as a "natural" response to the child's seductiveness.

> Pretend you are daddy's woman. A hand squeezes my shoul-
> der at the base of my throat. Before he makes the world go
> dark again he says: say you like it. I turn my head away from
> him. He is on top of me. There is no place to go (Danica
> 1988: 42-43).

In all cases of sexual abuse, the children's emotional well-being
is ravaged; frequently they are encouraged to blame themselves or
to consider themselves as dirty or flawed (Russell 1986). This type
of abuse is sometimes termed "soul murder"; the devastation of the
child's sense of self is so enormous and complete that many cannot
survive in adult life in any meaningful way. They develop, as did
Sybil,[2] fragmented or multiple personalities; they are incapable of
establishing a trusting adult relationship, become completely alienated from affectionate sexuality, withdraw from all social contacts
and in many other ways are denied a happy and fulfilling life because
of the horror of their childhood. The damage is incalculable and,
sometimes, irreparable. Some of the most devastating assaults on
children are precisely this combination of physical, sexual and emotional abuse.

It is apparent that the experience of child abuse is a multifaceted and complex phenomenon. As notable family violence analysts John Bradshaw and Alice Miller point out, we live in a society where very few children grow up in completely "functional" families with mature, loving and supportive parents. Most children experience some level of family dysfunction, where parents are immature, distant or demanding. In addition, many children are directly or indirectly the victims of their parents' economic struggles. Economically pressed or insecure parents may take their frustrations and anger out on their children by physically hurting them, or may neglect their children — leaving them, for example, "home alone." As a result, abuse of children, in general terms, is structured into normal, everyday life in Canadian society. Most children are subject, at least occasionally, to some degree of abuse, particularly psychological and emotional abuse. Indeed, most truthful parents would admit that they have on occasion failed their children by being neglectful, manipulative or coercive.

Within this larger societal reality, there is a subset of numerous children who are subject to severe victimization and damage. These are the children who experience persistent or significantly injurious physical, sexual and emotional violence and, often, these are the children identified by social agencies and the courts. Since the early 1960s social researchers have developed an increasingly clear picture of this "severe" violence against children. However, in the process, it has also become evident that the lines between "acceptable" child-rearing practices and abuse have become murkier while the interconnections between serious violence and normal families have come into sharper focus. The plethora of TV talk shows, paperback books and programs consumed by adults seeking to "heal the wounds of childhood" reflect this growing realization that dysfunctional families and abused or neglected children may be more "normal" than not. As a result, it is increasingly obvious that the experience of child abuse cannot be isolated from the ways our society constructs the experience of being a child.

Naming the Issue: From Spanking and Slaps to Torture and Murder

Although we all assume that we have some basic understanding of the term "child abuse," arriving at a workable, satisfactory definition is, in fact, not an easy task. Indeed, an important key to much of the literature on child abuse is the question of definition. On a common-sense level, the term immediately evokes images of children who are beaten and bruised, neglected and abandoned. We may wonder how parents could perpetrate such violence on defenseless children, why they do not respond to the pain and suffering of "their own flesh and blood," but we rarely puzzle over what we mean by the term child abuse. As with every facet of family violence, closer examination, particularly from a feminist and sociological perspective, reveals a much more complex and contradictory reality — one which often has less to do with monstrous, unnatural parents and more to do with a hierarchical, power-oriented social system.

A tremendous amount of time and energy has been and is being directed to arriving at a satisfactory definition of child abuse. The definitional issues are far from resolved. However, these definitional issues are fundamental since they underlie theoretical explanations, empirical research and policy initiatives. For example, if child abuse is conceptualized in broad and inclusive terms, research is more likely to uncover high rates of abuse and such research is likely to generate a heightened public demand for public or private solutions. Similarly, if legal definitions are narrowly framed — for example, relying on physical injury as the defining characteristic of abuse — legal interventions will be restricted to a narrow range of behaviours.

Currently, most analysts focus on four main elements of child abuse: physical abuse, emotional/psychological abuse, sexual abuse and neglect.[3] Some analysts also focus on family violence (that is, the violence between parents) and ritual abuse. Each of these components is subject to definitional debates. Physical abuse is commonly defined as an intentional act by a child's caregiver that results in physical injury to the child (Wallace 1996: 29; Tower 1996: 64). A more recently recognized form of abuse — emotional and psychological abuse or maltreatment — may be defined as a "pattern" of emotionally destructive behaviour intentionally directed at the child by the caregiver.[4] Included here would be behaviour that is rejecting, isolating, terrorizing, stifling or corrupting (Tower 1996: 121).[5]

Sexual abuse, which previously was assumed to be so uncommon it barely warranted comment, is now the leading research issue. It is defined as incest and sexual exploitation. Incest occurs when the child is forced or manipulated into participating into a sexual act with a member of their family for the sexual gratification of that family member. Sexual exploitation occurs when the child is forced to observe sexual acts or pornography. Sexual abuse encompasses a wide array of relationships between the child and the perpetrator(s), different levels of force and a range of sexual behaviours (Tower 1996: 132-33; Wallace 1996: 58; McGuire and Grant 1991: 2-3).

Neglect is also an extremely complex and multifaceted form of abuse. Children are considered to be neglected if their caregivers fail to provide (intentionally or unintentionally) basic physical, educational and emotional support. This would include failure to provide physical or mental health care, inadequate supervision, child abandonment, inadequate food, shelter and clothing (Tower 1996: 92-93). In the past and at present, the majority of child abuse cases in the social welfare system involve neglect and so, over the last 150 years, there has been considerable effort to provide clear, concise definitions of the term. However, "contradictory views" persist and still the lines between neglectful and adequate parents are often unclear and contested (Swift 1995).

Today, a child's exposure to family violence and a child's experience of ritual abuse are often acknowledged as elements of child abuse. Since the early 1980s, a considerable amount of literature has documented the impact on children of exposure to their parents' violence, especially wife abuse where the mother is beaten. Whether or not the children themselves are the victims of other forms of child abuse (and, of course, many are), growing up in a violent family has long-term negative consequences for children and, in this sense, is abusive (Rossman 1994; Jaffe, Wolfe and Wilson 1990). "Ritualistic child abuse" refers to physical, sexual and psychological abuse of children in the context of rituals. Most publicized cases involve satanic beliefs, practices and cults (Wallace 1996: 116; Rose 1993).[6] However, the inclusion of ritual abuse is hotly debated and one of the leading American texts on child abuse pointedly leaves out any mention of this subject (Tower 1996).

In addition to these key elements, some advocates urge the inclusion of pre-natal abuse in the definitions of child abuse. They argue that women who abuse alcohol or drugs or intentionally expose their fetus to environmental hazards[7] should be considered abusive (Knudsen 1992: 175-78). Finally, a child can be subject to "multiple abuse" such as physical and sexual abuse. Indeed, most forms of maltreatment also involve some form of emotional abuse (Trocme 1994: 42).

To make the picture even more complex, within these elements, there are variations. For example, American sociologists, Gelles and Straus's ground-breaking work on physical violence routinely distinguishes between "minor," "severe" and "very severe" violent acts

(1986: 469). The latter degree of abuse would include, for example, children who are tied to a chair and locked in a closet all day, or children who are beaten so severely that they end up mentally or physically disabled. Very severe violent acts against children are, as child advocate Paul Mones points out, probably misnamed as abuse since they would be more accurately characterized as "child torture" (1991: 32). Other analysts point out that there may be significant variations in the frequency and longevity of the abuse. Although typically abuse occurs over an extended period of time, it is possible for abuse to be a single incident. These variations are important when gauging their impact on children's lives.

While we may believe we have a kind of common-sense understanding of what is meant by child abuse, it is important to recognize considerable controversy still swirls around legal, scientific and popular definitions (see, for example, Watchel 1994; Lenton 1990). In particular, what is missing from the discussion is the role that institutions and society play as the children's caregivers and protectors. If we simply target individual families and attempt to hold them up to some unclear standard of adequate parenting, we ignore innumerable other areas where children are subject to abuse. This would include daycare centres, schools, courts, childcare agencies, welfare departments and correction centres. Further, on a societal level, we would not capture the many ways in which social policies result in vast numbers of children being inadequately fed, clothed, housed and educated (Gil 1980). Accepting a definition that eliminates, for example, societal responsibilities, means ignoring numerous abused and neglected children. While as a society we may agree that parents who intentionally injure or kill their children are abusive, researchers, policy advocates and ordinary citizens do not yet agree on many other aspects of child abuse (Gelles and Straus 1988: 52-59).

Nowhere does this struggle over "naming the issue" become more apparent than in the current controversy over whether or not spanking is a form of child abuse. Repeatedly, opinion polls and other research reveal that Canadians, Britons and Americans both endorse and employ spanking as a means of disciplining children. A 1996 phone-in poll in Toronto reported that three-quarters of callers answered no to the question "Should spanking of children be outlawed?" (Stefaniuk 1996: A7). Most Canadians agree with section 43 of the Criminal Code that allows parents (and other caregivers) to use force against children by way of correction if the force does not exceed what is reasonable under the circumstances (Landsberg 1996a: A2). Similarly, in the United States a 1986 national opinion poll found that a clear majority of persons eighteen and over agreed that "it is sometimes necessary to give a child a good hard spanking." Other research indicates that the overwhelming majority of parents actually use some form of corporal punishment in their childrearing (Straus 1994: 197).[8] Nor is this pattern peculiar to North America. British government research in 1995 provides ample evidence that most children are, on occasion, hit by their parents and many are subject to routine physical discipline,[9] even at a very young age.

While worldwide many parents find spanking, slapping and other forms of hitting suitable and effective, many childcare and family violence experts vigorously oppose the use of any form of violence against children. First, they cite research that suggests that "spanking" results in long-term harm to the child, increasing risks of aggression, delinquency, drinking problems, depression and suicide.[10] Using violence teaches children that violence is an acceptable means to deal with relationship problems and also serves to link violence and love. Secondly, they argue that alternative, non-violent methods of disciplining and controlling a child are as effective and less potentially harmful than corporal punishment (Straus 1994; Brown 1994: B1). Based on this line of thinking, Ontario, British Columbia, New Brunswick and the Yukon have banned "strapping" in the schools, and Newfoundland and Saskatchewan are moving in this direction. Further, there is considerable public pressure to repeal section 43 of the Criminal Code so that adults are no longer able to punish children with force (Cordon 1997: B6; Landsberg 1995: G1; Landsberg 1996b: A1). In 1997 a Toronto advocacy group, the Canadian Foundation for Childen, Youth and the Law, launched a Charter of Rights challenge that would make it illegal for parents to hit their children (Papp 1997: A1). One repeal advocate who has done "extensive research" into the court records pertaining to section 43 argues that the law as presently interpreted considers "slapping, grabbing, pulling, shaking, kicking, hitting with straps, belts, sticks, extension cords and rulers, causing bruises, bleeding, nose bleeds, chipped teeth and welts" as within the parameters of "reasonable force" (Scotton 1994: J4).

Several recent high profile cases have highlighted the division between pro- and anti-spanking advocates. In 1994 an American tourist visiting London, Ontario, was charged with assault after he put his five-year-old daughter on the trunk of his car and spanked her bare bottom at least eight times. He explained his action as punishment for the girl's pushing her two-year-old brother out of the car and then slamming his fingers in the door as he attempted to climb back in. After the pro- and anti-corporal punishment views were aired in court, the judge found the father not guilty (Massecar 1995: A1). A similar popular case emerged in Britain in 1996 when a twelve-year-old boy took his stepfather to the European Court of Human Rights saying he had been beaten. As in Canada, the case generated an outpouring of pro and con views.

In Canada, Britain, the United States and elsewhere there is an ongoing struggle over whether parents will retain the legal right to physically punish their children. If Canada follows the lead of Sweden and Austria, which banned physical violence against children in 1979 and 1989 respectively,[11] the lines between "normal" parenting and abusive childrearing may shift significantly (*Toronto Star*, September 22, 1996: A4). Since such actions would cut to the core of many parents' sense of their rights and their sense of righteousness, any shifts towards non-violent childrearing are likely to be hotly contended.

Not surprisingly, much of this struggle around the use of physical discipline has shifted into a definitional debate regarding the meaning of "spanking" or "gently slapping" or "last resort." Indeed, some advocates of spanking seek to "define" the acceptable form as one or two slaps on the bottom with an open hand for children between ages two and six and only in conjunction with other positive parenting techniques (Larzelere 1994: 204). The shifting terrain of definitional arguments will in all likelihood fail to resolve the public divisions on this issue, but they do underscore how central the issue of definitions is not only to understanding but also to resolving child abuse. Enlarged definitions of child abuse necessarily expand the net of potential abusers and more and more parents are forced to confront the uncomfortable question whether abuse is external and foreign or part of their personal reality. Here, child abuse is defined as acts of commission or omission, usually by those entrusted with the care and nurturing of the child, which function to deny the child the reasonable opportunity to develop her or his potential as a human being. Such a broad definition, of course, allows for consideration of whether or not socially accepted standards of parenting are abusive and whether social agencies, entrusted with both the child's well-being and parental education, such as the education and social welfare system, are acting in the child's interests.

The Changing Historical Construction of Abuse

One of the most important reasons these definitional conflicts persist is a long historical tradition (of many cultures, including Canada's) that endorses the use of violence, including sexual violence, against children. Under traditional patriarchy, children, like their mothers, belonged to the patriarch. It was his responsibility to control and provide for these dependents and in pursuit of these responsibilities it was his right to employ violence, even deadly violence. At the moment of birth, the father in ancient times had the right to either acknowledge the infant or dispose of it. In many cultures, infanticide, through exposure or denial of food, was often practised both to limit demands on family resources and to eliminate children deemed defective. Needless to say, female children were particularly at risk of infanticide since they often required a dowry in order to be married and, as a result, were a drain on family resources. Also, as is still the practice in a number of countries today, children could be sold into slavery or prostitution if the family was in need. For centuries, children were seen as simply another form of property, much like a dog or a goat, and treated with a similar lack of sentimentality (Radbill 1980).

These paternal prerogatives over children's well-being and survival were typically buttressed by religious beliefs and values.[12] In the Judeo-Christian tradition, the need for children's obedience to their fathers is a persistent theme. The belief is, of course, embedded in the Ten Commandments and in the story of Abraham and Isaac. In testing Abraham's obedience, God instructs him to kill his only son, and Abraham proves himself by intending to carry out God's will. Throughout the Old Testament, parents (presumably fathers) are exhorted to physically discipline their children. "He that spareth his rod hateth his son: but he that loveth him chasteneth him betimes" (Proverbs 13:24 as cited in Greven 1990: 48). In Deuteronomy, Moses instructs parents that it is appropriate to stone to death "a stubborn and rebellious son" (Greven 1990: 49).

Not surprisingly, this patriarchal religious ideology played an important part in the evolution of what renowned family violence analyst Alice Miller terms the "poisonous pedagogy." From the 1700s to the present, parents have been advised by childrearing authorities that it is their religious responsibility to break the child's willfulness, to drive out obstinacy and disobedience and to crush rebelliousness (Greven 1990: 60-72; Miller 1983: 63-96). In the mid-1800s parents were advised that this mandate applied even to infants. If a baby cried for no apparent reason, parents were urged to use threatening gestures, rapping on the bed and mild corporal admonitions to "become master of the child *forever*" (as cited in Miller 1983: 5, emphasis in original). Such views did not disappear in the twentieth century. For example, a childrearing authority from the 1970s urges parents to spank a disobedient child until his will is broken; as long as "he is stiff, grits his teeth, holds on to his own will, the spanking should continue" (as cited in Greven 1990: 68). Often the religious rationale behind this advice is explicitly stated: spanking children keeps them from going to hell (Greven 1990: 62). Using physical violence to dominate an unruly child is presented as both a parental right and responsibility.

Traditional paternal rights over children extended beyond physical dominance and included sexual prerogatives. In ancient times, as recorded in the Talmud and Old Testament, female children were considered to be the father's property. In ancient times, girls were betrothed while still toddlers and married off before they reached their teens. If a man raped an unbetrothed virgin, he could take the girl as his wife by making a payment to her father. The father might also force his daughter into prostitution by accepting the payment but not insisting on marriage and thereby making his daughter available to other men for a fee. The rise of Christianity did not eradicate the sexual abuse of children. Although Canon law forbade child marriage, customary practice meant that many young girls were married off before their teens and even very young children were betrothed. While many of these practices were eliminated by the nineteenth century, child sexual abuse in terms of child prostitution remained very evident. In England, the Victorian era was marked by the "cult of the little girl," a period when immature, preferably virginal, females were considered the most desirable prostitutes. In part, this practice reflects the growing fear of syphilis and the popular belief that having sexual relations with a virgin provided a cure for venereal disease. In England, Germany, France, Scandinavia and Eastern Europe procurers targetted girls aged eleven to fifteen, especially those from the poorer classes, to work in brothels (Rush 1980). These various activities suggest a social context in which the sexual abuse of children was to some degree accepted and rationalized.

The redefinition of physical and sexual violence as abusive and unacceptable has a long and tortuous history. In part, the changes emanated from a gradual reframing of childhood. With the rise of education and modern individualism, a more sentimental conception of children slowly emerged. Through changes associated with indus- trialization and urbanization, such as improved health care and birth control, there were fewer children in the family and they were more likely to survive into adulthood (Synnott 1983). The work of Jean- Jacques Rousseau helped popularize the notion that children embod- ied the best in human innocence and naturalness. Buoyed by these developments, social critics and social reformers began to insist upon more humane treatment for children. In the nineteenth century, for example, child labour laws were introduced in many western coun- tries to ensure that very young children were not employed and that children over age fourteen were not subject to beatings or unsafe working conditions. Middle- and upper-class "child savers" sought to help the numerous poor, abandoned and orphaned children on the streets of the new industrial centres (Knudsen 1992: 7). Steps were also taken to safeguard children in the family as Societies for the Prevention of Cruelty to Children (SPCC) — first founded in New York City in 1875 and modelled ironically on similar societies for the prevention of cruelty to animals — were created throughout the western world in the late 1800s to protect children from abuse and forced prostitution (Radbill 1980).

While the United States and Britain played a leading role in responding to child labour and in the establishment of SPCCs, Can- ada and other western countries quickly followed suit. In 1891 the first Children's Aid Society in Canada was founded in Toronto. By 1901 there were thirty children's aid societies in Ontario alone. In 1893 the Ontario legislature passed the *Prevention of Cruelty and Better Protection of Children Act*. Under the Act, local children's aid societies were authorized to ensure that neglected children were cared for and that cruelty to children was punished. Other provinces soon followed with similar legislation. Quebec, which had adopted legislation protecting the rights of children and youth in 1869, relied on church-sponsored institutions and did not introduce child welfare legislation until well into the twentieth century (Swift 1995).

Needless to say, despite the advances achieved earlier, many of the more dramatic changes in social attitudes towards child abuse occurred in the later half of the twentieth century. The landmark work of Dr. C. H. Kempe in the United States is usually cited as a crucial turning point (Kempe et al. 1980). By examining the patterns of bruises and fractures that often came to the attention of physicians attending abused children, Kempe was able to identify in 1962 what

he termed the "battered child syndrome," which doctors could diag-
nose based on x-rays, bruises, etc. That same year, he chaired a
conference on child battery and out of these efforts emerged a model
child abuse law which, within five years, was adopted by every
American state (Radbill 1980: 16). By 1972 the U.S. National Center
for the Prevention of Child Abuse and Neglect had been established,
and in 1974 a *Child Abuse Prevention and Treatment Act*, which
defined maltreatment and provided federal funds to act on children's
behalf, was passed by the United States government (Tower 1996:
13).

While the United States took the lead in several of these developments, other countries, including Canada, very quickly followed. So
much work on child abuse has been accomplished in Canada since
the 1960s that it is only possible to point out some of the landmark
events. Certainly one of the critical milestones was the publication
in 1972 (revised in 1978) of Mary Van Stolk's *The Battered Child
in Canada*. This book both raised the public profile of child abuse
and brought together a variety of Canadian research and policy. It
was followed in 1980 by the Senate Report *Child at Risk*, which
provided the earliest estimates of national rates of child abuse in
Canada. Scientific documentation of some of the dimensions of child
abuse was achieved in 1984 with the publication of Robin Badgley's
1,314-page *Sexual Offences Against Children*. This internationally
acclaimed report included a survey of a nationally representative
sample of Canadian adults. Based on the recall of these adults, the
report determined that an astonishing one in two girls (53.5 percent)
and one in three boys (30.6 percent) under age of twenty-one had
been subject to a sexual offence (ranging from being "flashed" to
unwanted touching to actual or attempted sexual assault) (180-82).
Almost half of the female and male victims sixteen years of age or
younger were subject to attempted or actual sexual assault, including
attempted or actual forced intercourse or sodomy using either a penis
or an object or forced sexual stimulation (179-83). Predictably, this
comprehensive and academically rigorous examination of the sexual
abuse of Canadian children shattered many illusions and triggered
widespread public demand for a societal response; in particular, an
improved criminal justice response to intrafamilial child sexual
abuse.

Throughout the 1970s and 1980s most provinces initiated extensive reforms to their child welfare and criminal legislation, establishing, for example, child abuse registers and mandatory reporting.

Under the latter legislation, professionals who come into contact with abused children, such as physicians and social workers, and in some cases, average citizens, are required to report any suspected cases of child abuse. In recent years, laws tend to be less preoccupied with "neglect" and more concerned with children "in need of protection." Some provincial laws (for example, Alberta's) now include emotional harm, although it has been difficult to prove emotional abuse in court and very few children are removed from parents or guardians on these grounds alone. Finally, much legislation is premised on "the least intrusive principle" and "the best interests of the child"; that is, agencies seek to respond to abuse with the least "interference with the family's affairs to the extent compatible with the best interests of children and the responsibilities of society" (Swift 1995: 44).

Also during the 1980s and 1990s, many private and public organizations emerged to combat child abuse. In 1983, the Ontario Ministry of Community and Social Services, in cooperation with the Canadian Children's Foundation, established the Ontario Centre for the Prevention of Child Abuse. In 1987, the Centre evolved into a private, non-profit charitable organization with a national agenda — The Institute for the Prevention of Child Abuse (IPC). The IPC focuses on research, training, public education and consultation. Many other efforts were mobilized on the community level as grassroots feminist organizations such as local rape crisis and sexual assault centres set up support groups for adult female survivors of sexual abuse, and shelters for battered women developed programs to meet the needs of children who were either directly abused in violent homes or subject to indirect violence by exposure to a battering situation. In addition, shelters and sexual assault centres undertook public education campaigns in the schools and in the community to challenge the beliefs and values that support patterns of family and interpersonal violence. Other groups, such as the International Order of Foresters (IOF), supported the distribution of public education pamphlets and films on family violence and child abuse.

Some sense of the intensity of the public response to child abuse (and to family violence in general) is apparent in the financial support for research, program development and public education authorized by the federal government. In 1982, Health Canada established the National Clearinghouse on Family Violence to provide a national information and consultation service for professionals as well as a base for developing important sources of public education (for example, the Family Violence Film Collection). The Clearinghouse's fact sheets on child abuse and neglect and child sexual abuse have been widely disseminated and, as a result, have played an important role in providing public education. Also in the mid-1980s, the Canadian Council on Social Development, with funding from Health Canada, created *Vis-a-Vis*, a national newsletter on family violence which provided quarterly updates on the latest developments across the country in research and policy.[13] In 1992, Health Canada, in collaboration with the Social Sciences and Humanities Research Council of Canada as well as local organizations, foundations and universities, established five new research centres on family violence and violence against women[14] across Canada. Other centres for research were established prior to 1992, such as the LaMarsh Research Centre on Violence and Conflict Resolution at York University (1980).[15]

Needless to say these initiatives and projects have been costly and have demanded a significant allocation of public funds. For example, in 1986, the federal government launched a $25.1-million initiative on child sexual abuse (Health Canada 1994c). This was followed in 1988 by the $40-million Family Violence Initiative, and in 1992 by the $136-million four-year Federal Initiative on Family Violence. This latest commitment was directed, among other things, to helping frontline workers do a better job, "improving national information on family violence" and improving treatment and support for victims (Government of Canada 1992). This is, of course, only part of the picture, since provincial and municipal governments and organizations have also funded research and program development (see, for example, Marshall 1994 and Crowder 1993).

This explosion of governmental, academic and public concern about child abuse has fundamentally altered our awareness and understanding of the issue. However, as evidenced by the ongoing debate about spanking, all this well-deserved attention has not resolved the definitional disputes. As we enter the twenty-first century, child abuse (along with other dimensions of family violence) remains contested terrain. Numerous modern childcare "experts" continue to advocate a traditional position on childrearing. Some promote a punitive approach to caring for children: "Babies under six months old should never be played with, and the less of it at any time the better ... Never give a child what it cries for; let the child cry out and break the habit" (as cited in Synnott 1983: 87). Social movements have emerged that urge a stern response to disobedient and rebellious adolescents. Many fundamentalist and conservative spokespersons still endorse the use of physical punishment. Fundamentalist LeRoy Pennell is on record as saying, "I believe the Bible is our instruction book for living ... I believe there is a place for physical discipline — not as the only form of discipline but a useful and necessary discipline" (quoted in Scotton 1994: J4). Moved, as we apparently are as a society, by the plight of the defenseless child, many of us are not yet prepared to accord children the inalienable right to be free of violence.

Mapping the Dimensions of the Problem

The absence of any consensus about the parameters of child abuse makes undertaking research and setting policy extremely difficult. Perhaps nowhere is this more apparent than in the absence of national statistics on child abuse cases in Canada. Since the first modern steps to address child abuse were taken, analysts in Canada have been plagued by the absence of reliable national or provincial statistics. Few provinces collected and maintained statistics on child abuse cases until the 1970s (Van Stolk 1978: 3-4). Ironically, almost two decades later, the statistical record in Canada remains flawed. Only in 1997 was a decision finally made to collect Canadian national statistics on child abuse through Health Canada's three-year project that will seek to provide a national standard definition of child abuse and to collect national statistics on reported instances of neglect and abuse (Van Rijn 1997: A4).

Until these data are assembled, all discussion of national statistics on child abuse must be couched as estimates or based on inadequate data sets. Even tallying the number of child abuse cases known to children's aid societies and family and children services across Canada is not possible. Because child welfare is a provincial responsibility and because provinces define child abuse and neglect variously and maintain case statistics in different ways, it is not possible to simply add up the yearly number of new cases (Federal-Provincial Working Group 1994: 5-6). For example, there are considerable differences among provinces in defining the age of a child — these range from fifteen years and younger to eighteen years and younger. Even at a local level, there may be differences in how Children's Aid Societies implement child welfare policies. As a result of this absence of a provincial and national picture, there is an enormous gap in our understanding of the dimensions, regional variations and historical shifts[16] in child abuse.

Other sources of data provide some useful insights. Crime statistics, for example, tend to confirm that the family is one of the most dangerous institutions for children in our society. Forty-one percent of violent crimes against children reported to police departments are perpetrated by family members and almost half (48 percent) of criminal sexual assaults are committed by a family member (La Novara 1993: 54). However, considerable numbers of violent crimes against children never come to the attention of police departments and these statistics are more suggestive than definitive.

Very recently there has been significant progress towards developing a better statistical profile of child abuse in Canada. Once again the Canadian Violence Against Women Survey (CVAWS) has been useful. Its nationally representative sample reveals that significant numbers of children witness parental violence in their home. In 39 percent of violent relationships, the women respondents indicated that their children had witnessed the violence. Extrapolating from these figures, it is suggested that at least one million Canadian children have been exposed to "the trauma of watching their mothers abused" (Johnson, 1996: 173-4). American research suggests that many children who witness abuse will also be victimized themselves. For example, it is estimated that 40 to 70 percent of child observers in violent families also experience sexual or physical abuse or neglect (Rossman 1994: 29).

Another recent breakthrough is the Ontario Incidence Study of Reported Child Abuse and Neglect (OIS), which is providing analysts with the first province-wide report on the annual incidence of child maltreatment cases (Trocme et al. 1994). If, as proposed, the OIS survey is replicated in other provinces, it will finally be possible to accurately estimate the number of reported cases of child abuse and to reasonably gauge any historical shifts in child abuse cases. At present, the Ontario data reveal that in 1993 there were 46,683 child maltreatment investigations. This meant that 2 percent of all Ontario children were involved in reported cases of child abuse in the course of one year. The largest number of substantiated cases of maltreatment involved neglect (36 percent), followed by physical abuse (34 percent), sexual abuse (28 percent), emotional maltreatment (8 percent) and other maltreatment (2 percent) (Trocme et al. 1994: 41). Data reported by other provinces tend to reflect this general picture, with the neglect category (where it is included as one of the dimensions of child abuse) typically containing the largest number of cases (Federal-Provincial Working Group 1994; Swift 1995: 4, 67).

These patterns are consistent with American research. The U.S. government has been compiling national data on child abuse and neglect since the mid-1980s. Most recently, the U.S. National Committee to Prevent Child Abuse reported that there were nearly 3 million reports of child abuse in 1993 and 1 million confirmed[17] victims.[18] In 1993, an estimated 1,299 children died of child abuse; almost all child murder victims (90 percent) were under 5 years of age and almost half died in families previously reported to child protection agencies. In contrast to the Canadian data, almost half the confirmed cases (47 percent) involved neglect, one-quarter (25 percent) concerned physical abuse and one in seven (15 percent) concerned sexual abuse (Edmonds 1994: 8A).

Of course, official statistics are of limited use in understanding the societal dimensions of child abuse since they capture only those instances that have come to the attention of a reporting agency. As with many other aspects of family violence, it is reasonable to assume that many cases would be hidden because of fear of family response, shame and self-blame. Failure to report would be particularly true of cases of child sexual abuse where even adult survivors have difficulty publicly confronting their abusers. In other instances, child abuse — physical abuse, neglect, emotional abuse — might be invisible to the victims and the perpetrators since they define the behaviour as normal and socially acceptable. In other words, creating an accurate research picture entails numerous difficulties. One solution, following Badgley's example in *Sexual Offences Against Children*, would be retrospective research with a nationally representative sample of adult Canadians. However, retrospective research is always problematic since it relies on the accurate recall of events that occurred years previously and that, because they are painful, may be more likely to be forgotten or minimized. Research with adults that explores their parental relationship with their children in the past year avoids these memory issues but may still result in underreporting as parents underestimate their physical or, especially, sexual violence. Certainly the best and most accurate information is likely to come from research that tracks a nationally representative sample of children (interviewing them at periodic intervals) through their childhood. Although such research involves considerable ethical concerns, it is the most promising avenue and it is this approach — a National Longitudinal Survey of Children — that was recently proposed under the "Brighter Futures" program in Canada (Watchel 1994: 11).

Until comprehensive national research is completed, we must rely on a variety of other sources. For example, the 1980 Senate Report, *Child at Risk*, estimated that between 5,000 and 9,000 Canadian children suffer damaging or fatal abuse. A subsequent study suggested that 8,000 cases of physical abuse occur each year in Canada and that there are approximately 250 to 350 cases per million population (as cited in Marshall 1995: 12).

Amongst the most influential and important American studies examining rates of unreported child abuse are Murray Straus and Richard Gelles's 1975 and 1985 national surveys. Using the Conflict Tactics Scale (see Chapter 2) and a national probability sample, they surveyed 6,002 households in 1985. Almost two-thirds (63 percent) of parents in the sample reported hitting their child. In all, 19 out of 1,000 children were, according to their parents' reports, subject to very severe acts of violence; that is, they were kicked, bitten, hit with a fist, beaten up, threatened with a gun or knife or had gun or knife used against them (1986: 469). Although these rates indicated a 47 percent decline since 1975, they continue to indicate "extremely high" rates of abuse (1986: 474).

The most significant and recent Canadian study, undertaken by researchers (notably, Harriet MacMillan) at McMaster University and the Clarke Institute of Psychiatry, provides valuable insight into abuse patterns in the general population. The research was a survey based on a random sample of almost 10,000 Ontario residents over age fifteen. Based on the adult recall of the respondents, the study found that one in three boys and one in five girls suffered physical abuse during childhood. The respondents defined physical abuse as excluding slapping and spanking and including "pushing, grabbing, shoving and throwing objects" when these occurred "often" or "sometimes," and "kicking, biting, punching, hitting with an object, choking, burning, scalding or physically attacking" when these occurred "rarely" (Gadd 1997: A1, A6).

Other research results also confirm that child abuse is a significant social problem. For example, a 1991 Gallup poll reported that one in six Canadians (17 percent) say "they have personal awareness of a serious instance of physical abuse of a child by a parent" (as cited in Conway 1993: 79). A similar finding was reported in the United States where 13 percent of those polled indicated they "personally know children they suspect have been physically or sexually abused" (Edmonds 1994: 8A). Similarly, research on child deaths also suggests the extent of child abuse. Spurred on by a *Toronto Star* inquiry, a task force was set up in 1996 to examine children's deaths in Ontario. Between 1991 and 1995, 238 children died in Ontario. Of these cases, forty-nine were "known" to Children's Aid Societies prior to death, typically because of abuse or neglect. In total, 128 of the 238 deaths were homicides; 39 percent of the victims were under age of two, and in 55 percent of the cases parents were the confirmed perpetrators (Donovan and Welsh 1996: A1, A34).

Gauging the number of cases of abuse is especially difficult when the focus is on specific types of violence. Sexual abuse (particularly, male child sexual abuse) and emotional abuse are, for example, notoriously underreported in official complaints. Victims often do not come forward, even as adults. As a result, official case statistics will often grossly underestimate the size of the problem. Various research studies (such as Badgley's) have provided insight into the actual parameters of these forms of maltreatment (Tower 1996: 137). Reviewing a variety of studies undertaken in the United States, Canada and Britain from 1979 to 1988, researchers concluded that serious sexual abuse (unwanted or coerced sexual contact up to age sixteen or seventeen) occurs against *at least* 15 percent of females and 5 percent of males (Bagley and King 1990: 56-77). A similar review by Tower on American research from 1978 to 1989 concerning male child sexual abuse reported prevalence rates ranging from 2.5 to 17.3 percent (1996: 141; see also, Wallace 1996: 56; Manion and Wilson 1995: 8). The 1997 survey by researchers from McMaster University and the Clarke Institute of Psychiatry reported that one in eight girls and one in twenty-three boys is the victim of sexual abuse. Sexual abuse was defined quite narrowly for this study as "adults exposing themselves to a child more than once; threatening to have sex with a child; touching a child on the sexual parts of his or her body and trying to have sex with a child or having sex with a child" (Gadd 1997: A1, A6).

As evident from all of this research, one of the consistent features of the data has been the greater prevalence of female sexual abuse. However, some analysts are now suggesting that male child sexual abuse remains vastly underreported, even in research (such as the McMaster/Clarke Institute study) based on self-report among an adult population. The causes cited for this distortion are prevailing conceptions of masculinity and sexuality. Some researchers believe that in the future, as attitudes about victimization shift, research will reveal equivalent rates of sexual victimization of boys and girls (Tower 1996: 140).

What is clear from the statistical profile is that child abuse is an enormous social issue. In North America, literally millions of children are growing up without childhood. The media images of the Cosby children and the children in other popular television shows are just cruel reminders for many children who do not live in a loving, supportive and kind family. Violence, abuse, manipulation and exploitation are the norm of their upbringing, and the emotional fallout from living through childhood years filled with fear, anxiety, self-loathing and anger is likely to plague them for much, if not all, of their adult lives.

Social Patterns of Child Abuse

(i) General

As with abuse against women, child abuse is not randomly scattered through the population. There are discernible (if disputed) patterns, and these patterns are the key to understanding the roots of violence against children and, perhaps as importantly, the key to understanding the politics of child abuse. Not surprisingly, child abuse tends to occur more frequently in families which rate high in conflict and in which there is "marital violence." Straus and Gelles report from their national U.S. survey that families where the husband had hit the wife in the course of the preceding year were 150 percent more likely to disclose instances of child abuse than other families (1992: 254). Not surprisingly, parents who came from a violent home, particularly one in which they were physically punished, are more likely to engage in severe violence with their own children. Similarly, parents who simply witnessed violence in their family of origin are more likely to abuse their own children (1992: 255-56). Given the popular endorsement of both violence as an interpersonal tactic and discipline as a parental responsibility, it is not surprising that official child abuse statistics are as high as they are. Further, families affected by substance abuse are seen to be more likely to abuse their children, particularly in terms of neglect and abandonment (Tower 1996: 114). Finally, families which are socially isolated (for example, lacking neighbourhood ties or involvement in organizations such as clubs, lodges, unions, church groups, etc.) are more likely to be abusive (1992: 256-57). Given the breakdown of community in most modern industrial countries, this relationship between abuse and isolation is particularly important.

Research also suggests that certain types of children are more vulnerable to abuse. Children who are conceived or born out of wedlock and children who are born prematurely as well as sickly babies and those born with physical or mental disabilities are more likely to be abused. For example, in the provocatively entitled book *When Children Invite Child Abuse*, the author details connections between child abuse and learning disabilities, childhood depression and nutritional problems (Gold 1986). In other words, any circumstances that add to the already considerable stress of becoming a parent appear to increase the likelihood of some form of maltreatment (Tower 1996: 75).

The age profile of victims of abuse is far from clear. Statistics drawn from reported cases of child abuse suggest that children who are placed "in care" as a result of child abuse concerns are spread rather evenly throughout the age range. Newfoundland reports the majority of its children in care are aged twelve to fifteen (30 percent), while Manitoba indicates that reports of alleged abuse are most numerous for children aged four to ten (47.8 percent of reports) (Federal-Provincial Working Group 1994: 24, 107). Needless to say, it is likely that abuse starts long before it comes to the attention of a reporting agency. Indeed, most analysts point out that in many cases child abuse starts before birth as the child is often battered in utero in the course of violence against the mother or as the mother abuses drugs or alcohol. Not surprisingly, neglect and abandonment are most likely to occur in the period from birth to one year of age and are less likely to occur as the child matures. Deadly child abuse, that is, child abuse that results in the child's death, is most likely to occur before age four. Sexual abuse can occur at any age and has been reported against infants. However, research suggests that the average age for sexually abused boys is four to six and for girls eleven to fourteen (Tower 1996: 101, 140; Bagley and King 1990: 70-72; Thomlison et al. 1991: 67).

The age patterns of abuse, in particular the young age at which so much abuse begins, are perhaps key to understanding why children — even when they are legally adult — remain with their abusive families and why adult children have such difficulty addressing their victimization. As evident from some of the above statistics, abuse may be all the child has ever known. Indeed, despite images from the media and experiences in the families of friends, abuse may seem "normal." More importantly, the child is profoundly connected with the abuser through their shared life history. However angry or enraged the child victim may feel, it may be enormously difficult to challenge her or his abusive parent or to place that parent in jeopardy by reporting the abuse to someone outside the family. Efforts to obtain outside help may simply confirm that children are not believed. Sometimes the abuse is muddied by "good times" with the abuser; sometimes the child victim has been taught to blame herself or himself for the violence or exploitation. Not surprisingly, a childhood of abuse may leave the child with few escape options: run away, lose oneself in drugs or alcohol, report the abuse, commit suicide or commit homicide against the parents (Mones 1991).

More generally, our social conceptions of age are, of course, crucial to any analysis of child abuse. We live in a society where children, simply by token of their age, are denied a wide variety of social, legal and economic rights. We assume, unlike other cultures and other historical periods, that children should be treated as dependants, denied adult rights and prerogatives regardless of their abilities or family circumstances and, in general, segregated from the mainstream of social life. While many would argue that these restraints are in the best interests of children since they ensure that they are not exploited in child labour and are given an opportunity to achieve an education, such social arrangements hinge on the presence of loving, supportive parents. The societal assumptions that children, by token of their age, should be powerless and dependent are precisely the assumptions that help set the stage for prolonged abuse and violence against children.

(ii) Gender

Given that the rights and roles of women form one of the central issues of this century, it is not surprising that gender issues emerge in the discussion of child abuse. Since, as discussed in Chapter 2, family violence amongst adult members of the family is strongly structured by gender differences, it is reasonable to examine whether gender plays a significant role in child abuse (see, for example, Margolin 1992; Muller 1995). In particular, since men engage in considerable violence against women in our families and our society, are they more likely than women to use violence against children and are girls more likely to be victimized? Some researchers suggest using a feminist "power and control" analysis, which would lead to the position that child abusers are predominantly male, and victims are predominantly female and very young males. This analysis is based on the premise that child abuse primarily involves the exercise of power and maintenance of control over others. Rather than needing, for example, sexual gratification, or lacking the ability to control his anger, the abuser is seen as often using and enjoying age-old prerogatives embedded in prevailing notions of masculinity. He has the right, he believes, to use his power to maintain control of the women and children in his life. This patriarchal male, socialized to exercise power and control and freely exercising his will to dominate wife and child, presents a possible scenario for child abuse (Conway 1993). Similarly, given that men are socialized to be the sexual actors in our culture, male sexual abuse against girls may seem more likely than female assaults.

The existing statistical profile provides some useful information. Although the question whether men are more violent and abusive to their children than women is far from fully answered, it does appear that gender is relevant to understanding violence against children, but not along the lines usually anticipated. The precise role played by gender depends on the type of abuse considered and whether official or self-reported data are examined. The Ontario Incidence Study reports that mothers constituted almost half (49 percent) of all those (including father, stepfather, other male, other female and unknown) investigated in substantiated child maltreatment cases. While this may seem damning evidence of female brutality, it must be recalled that the largest percentage of child maltreatment cases involve neglect (failure to supervise and so on). In these instances of neglect, women were considered responsible in 85 percent of substantiated cases. Since 49 percent of these families were single-parent, mother-headed families, the mother was the only parent present who could be held responsible (Trocme 1994: 67). Further, since women in our society are still assumed to be the primary caregivers, it is not surprising that case workers consider them the responsible parent even if a father is present (Swift 1995). Finally, since most of these women are living in poverty, often as single mothers, it's not clear, as many social welfare analysts point out, whether the woman is guilty of bad parenting or, simply, of being poor. As the Ontario Incidence Study notes: "physical neglect [the overwhelming majority of neglect cases] is in many ways the most ambiguous form of neglect ... it is difficult, if not impossible, to determine the extent to which this deprivation is due to neglectful parenting rather than poverty" (Trocme et al. 1994: 51-52).

Leaving aside the issue of neglect, evidence does suggest that women may be physically violent and abusive to their children, but at a lesser rate than men, particularly, if the amount of time spent taking care of children is taken into consideration. For example, Trocme found that mothers were the perpetrators in 39 percent of substantiated cases of physical abuse and in 1 percent of sexual abuse cases (1994: 66-68). This appears to contradict U.S. national surveys that suggest that women are "at least as violent as men against their own children" (Gelles and Sweet 1992: 247). Since these researchers also reported that women were as likely to assault their spouses as vice versa (see Chapter 2), these results must be scrutinized.

Considerable research indicates that women undertake the lion's share of parenting in this society. While there have been some shifts in the division of domestic labour, the bulk of childrearing remains the mother's reponsibility. This is, of course, dramatically evident in custody arrangements, which almost always result in mothers assuming responsibility for the day-to-day childcare. Consequently, given the relative amounts of time that women and men spend with their children, it would seem that women as a group are, indeed, less violent (Cole 1988). This is, of course, consistent with traditional gender socialization in which men are brought up to be both aggressive and dominant and the family disciplinarian.

The role of gender as a factor in sexual offences against children seems more straightforward. Repeatedly, researchers conclude that the overwhelming majority of sexual abuses against children are perpetrated by males. Trocme reports, for example, that fathers were the alleged perpetrators in 16 percent of substantiated sexual abuse cases in Ontario in 1993 (1994: 67). While women are certainly capable of sexually abusing their children, this victimization appears to be very uncommon. In general, about 94 to 100 percent of child sexual abuse against females is perpetrated by males and 85 percent of child sexual abuse against males is by males (Bagley and King 1990: 75; see also, Thomlison et al. 1991). Research suggests that men who are stepfathers in the family are particularly likely to sexually abuse children. Trocme found, for example, that while only 18 percent of all families investigated for child abuse contained a stepparent, stepfathers[19] were responsible for 14 percent of substantiated cases of sexual abuse (1994: 67, 87; see also, Bagley and King 1990: 73).

Finally, the gender pattern amongst victims of abuse is complex. Official statistics tend to suggest that boys and girls are almost equally likely to be investigated as possible victims of abuse and to be taken into care by social welfare agencies (Trocme 1994; Federal-

Provincial Working Group 1994: 24, 106). It seems likely that boys and girls are equally subject to abuse simply by token of their status as children. Age, however, may mitigate some of the effect of childhood. While some evidence suggests that older boys may be more subject to frequent, severe parental violence (Knudsen 1992: 58), other research suggests that boys are more likely to be victimized when they are younger and gradually outgrow this victimization pattern. Girls, in contrast, do not outgrow their powerlessness and are more likely to be abused as they mature into adolescence (Trocme 1994: 82). This pattern is, of course, consistent with a social context in which men, as a group, wield more power than women, as a group.

For many years, research into sexual abuse has suggested that girls are the probable victims. Badgley, for example, reported that one in two females and slightly less than one in three males were victims of unwanted sexual acts before age twenty-one (1984: 180). Again, age intersects with gender. The indications are that girls do not outgrow this victimization. Girls are much more likely than their male counterparts to be sexually abused, and girls' sexual abuse occurs later in their childhood (eleven to fourteen years) than boys' (four to six years) (Tower 1996: 140; see also, Bagley and King 1990: 70-72). However, in recent years, as male sexual abuse has attracted more public attention and understanding, reported rates of male abuse have increased (Lew 1990; Genuis et al. 1991). Some analysts predict that gender differences in child sexual abuse will eventually disappear. While both boys and girls may be equally likely to be victimized, it is possible that age will continue to play a role, with girls' victimization persisting as they mature.

Certainly, even if boys and girls are equally likely to be sexually abused, it remains probable that patterns of female and male upbringing play a part in their victimization. Interviews conducted by the Women's Research Centre in Vancouver with seventeen adult female survivors of child sexual abuse certainly suggest gender is relevant. In some instances offending fathers played the stereotypic, patriarchal role of domineering authoritarian and used male privilege and violence to control and exploit their families. In other cases, even though survivors saw their mothers as dominant in the family, it appears that their fathers were the ultimate authority and key consideration in family matters (1989: 39-40). Finally, offending fathers who presented themselves as "wimps" who were dominated and abused by their wives often used this ruse to secure the allegiance of "Daddy's little girl," turning the daughters against their mothers while obscuring the fathers' own responsibility (1989: 41). There are many relevant gender roles that need not assume uniform or stereo-typic shapes to be important in abuse situations. Sexual offenders may run the gamut from macho men to shy, sensitive types, but their masculinity and its prerogatives remain pertinent. Conversely, whether victims are tomboys, wimps or little ladies, learned concepts of masculinity and femininity may be an important aspect of their victimization. The Women's Research Centre study found, for example, that most of their survivors were brought up to be "proper young ladies" with all the trappings of traditional femininity — passive, conforming, dependent, entertaining and accommodating (1989: 47). Such gender socialization may produce potential victims.

(iii) Social Class, Race and Ethnicity

It has become commonplace to point out that all children — regardless of race, gender and social class — are vulnerable to child abuse (Wallace 1996: 33; Van Stolk 1978: 34; Segal 1995). Daily reading of any city newspaper will certainly confirm that this is true. However, it is also important to make two key points. First, research repeatedly indicates that economic deprivation increases the possibility of child abuse. In a complex interplay with other factors such as violence in the father's or mother's family of origin, ongoing marital violence, social isolation and so on, the family's economic plight has a role to play. Secondly, the economic location of the family — its social class — does determine whether or not family problems are scrutinized and labelled by social agencies. Middle- and upper-class families can afford privacy and private solutions; their respectability and social power make it less likely they will be defined as neglectful or abusive. Poorer families will often seem to fit the stereotype of neglectful or abusive parents and will more likely be in contact with social welfare agencies.

Certainly, the research record, despite the obligatory acknow-ledgement that families of all races and social classes engage in child abuse, indicates that poorer families are much more likely to be labelled abusive. Trocme's study of reported child abuse in Ontario found that more than one-third of investigated families (36 percent) were living on social assistance and almost one-fifth (17 percent) were living in public housing (1994: 96, 97). Rhonda Lenton's survey of child discipline techniques amongst Toronto parents found that mothers and fathers struggling with low family income or un-employment were more likely to use violence in disciplining

(1990).[20] American research follows the same pattern. Gelles and Sweet, for example, report from their national survey that "families earning less than twenty thousand dollars a year have the highest rates of child abuse" and families where the husband is unemployed have child abuse rates 62 percent higher than other families (1992: 249, 251). Recent research continues to confirm that poverty (living in poor neighbourhoods) is clearly associated with increased rates of neglect as well as physical and sexual abuse (Drake and Pandey 1996).

Almost by definition poor families are most likely to be neglectful. However, as many analysts point out, the governmental solution is rarely, if ever, to eradicate poverty but rather to push and pull these individual parents (mothers) into fulfilling their parental obligations.

Since poverty tends to follow certain racial and ethnic lines in Canada and the United States and since poverty is strongly associated with family abuse, it is not surprising to find that there are some clear racial and ethnic patterns of abuse.[21] In Canada, for example, child abuse charges have been rampant in many Aboriginal communities. In the 1960s and 1970s tremendous numbers of Native children were taken into care by provincial authorities. According to some estimates, Native children comprised 35 to 40 percent of children apprehended by child welfare authorities during this period. The result of the "sixties scoop" was the removal of almost an entire generation of children into white foster homes in Canada and elsewhere. For example, in the 400-member Spallumcheen Indian Band in British Columbia an astonishing 80 children were removed and placed in foster or other care in the 1970s (MacDonald 1995).

Conclusions

Child abuse is not an inevitable, natural human constant. Its appearance in any society corresponds to historical and societal circumstances.[22] In the past, social beliefs and values were highly conducive to various expressions of what today is termed abuse, including infanticide, child prostitution and child labour. Even today, the legacy of these social patterns persists in the deeply felt belief of many parents that their children are their property and that they have the right to do with them whatever they wish. In this sense, child abuse is a social construction based on both historical traditions and current beliefs and values.

Child abuse and neglect are also products of economic conditions. As we've seen, poor parents are by definition at greater risk of being unable to provide adequate food, shelter, clothing and so on. By prevailing North American standards of abuse, many Third World parents are guilty of neglect. Further, it seems likely that economic pressures exacerbate the frustrations and anxieties of parenting and increase the likelihood that forms of child abuse other than neglect will occur. As one study noted, "Poverty reduces a family's capacity to respond to stress and contributes to the dislocation and distinte-gration of families" (Aitken and Mitchell 1995: 29).

Given the extensive research documentation of the relationships between lower-income families and child abuse, changes in the econ-omy must be considered significant indicators of future trends. In this regard, current high rates of unemployment, increasing rates of child poverty and reductions in social welfare support for the poor are all ominous signs of what is to come. In particular, dramatic increases in poverty among the young and mother-headed families, along with the highest rates of child poverty recorded in decades, all suggest the likely future expansion of child abuse rates in Canada (Aitken and Mitchell 1995).

Any discussion of child abuse must also acknowledge the global dimensions of the issue. The plight of abused and battered children is far from a local or national problem, and success in solving vio-lence against children must ultimately be judged in international terms. Unfortunately, growing public awareness of child abuse in North America and around the world has only meant, at best, halting progress, and future indications are decidedly grim.

Despite the fact that the U.N. Convention on the Rights of the Child is the "world's most widely ratified human rights treaty," the day-to-day realities of children around the world are far from com-mendable. A British human rights group, Index on Censorship, re-ports that 40 million children worldwide are living on the streets: 12 million die yearly, mostly from preventable diseases: 250 million children are engaged in child labour (usually at long hours, for little pay and often as virtual slaves working to pay off family debts); and in the last ten years, wars have killed 2 million children, injured 6 million and turned 30 million into refugees (*Toronto Star*, March 27, 1997: A19).

In sum, no matter whether you look around locally, nationally or internationally, there is much to be done and enough work for eve-ryone who is willing to fight for the right of children to have a childhood. In this context, it is important to recall Alice Miller's plea for friendly and supportive "witnesses" for children, "witnesses who could be of help to the suffering children. By witnesses I mean people who are not afraid to stand up for children assertively and protect them from adults' abuse of power" (1981: xiii). Every day, in Canada and around the world, children are dying for want of such witnesses.

Notes

1. As discussed in Chapter 5, psychologists have argued that abusive and neglectful parents can be categorized in terms of certain personality problems. For example, neglectful mothers may be described as "apathetic-futile," "impulse ridden," suffering from "reactive depression" and being "borderline" or "psychotic." Fathers who sexually abuse their children are described in terms of having "poor impulse control," "low frustration tolerance," "social and emotional immaturity," etc. (Tower 1996: 108, 145). While it should be noted that a considerable portion of the child abuse literature is devoted to analyzing the personality types of abusers, the emphasis in this book is on understanding child abuse as a social issue. Evidence indicates that the maltreatment of children is socially and historically constructed; that is, the society's beliefs, values and rules contribute to the acceptance of abusive behaviours. While personal pathologies may play a part (particularly in extreme cases of abuse), it is the larger societal context that must be understood as the backdrop to child abuse.

2. Sybil is a book and movie that portray the real-life struggles of a young woman who, as a very young child, was the victim of horrendous sexual and physical abuse. As a result of the abuse she fragmented into a number of separate personalities. The separate personalities apparently allowed her to compartmentalize the abuse memories and survive. With therapy as an adult, she was able to reintegrate and lead a productive life.

3. For example, the Ontario Incidence Study (OIS) focused on five forms of child maltreatment: 1. physical abuse, 2. neglect, 3. sexual abuse, 4. emotional maltreatment, 5. other maltreatment.

   Within this framework, neglect was defined along eight dimensions: 1. educational neglect, 2. abandonment/refuse custody, 3. permitting criminal activity, 4. psychological treatment neglect, 5. medical neglect, 6. physical neglect, 7. failure to supervise leading to sexual harm, 8. failure to supervise leading to physical harm.

Sexual abuse was defined in terms of the following categories: 1. exposure, 2. intercourse, 3. fondling, 4. other.

Emotional abuse was defined in terms of three dimensions: 1. emotional neglect, 2. non-organic failure to thrive, 3. emotional abuse.

In total, there are seventeen dimensions to OIS definitions, each with its corresponding operational definition (Trocme et al. 1994).

It should also be noted that some analysts distinguish between abuse that is intentional on the part of the parents (for example, physical and sexual violence against children) and maltreatment that is unintentional (for example, neglect and exposure to family violence) (Lenton 1990).

4. Within this category are a variety of newly recognized forms of abuse. For example, the Munchausen Syndrome by Proxy (MSBP) has been increasingly recognized in the journals as a noteworthy, life-threatening type of abuse. MSBP typically involves a caretaker (generally, the mother) who fabricates or induces physical ailments in her children and subjects them to extensive medical tests and interventions. While the psychological basis for this behaviour is complex, it seems the mother enjoys and benefits from the medical attention that is directed to her children and to herself, as caregiver (Yorker 1994: 34).

5. O'Hagan distinguishes between emotional and psychological abuse, proposing that emotional abuse is "repetitive, sustained, inappropriate emotional responses" to the child's emotional responses while psychological abuse is any behaviour which undermines the developmental potential of the child (1993: 34-35).

6. A highly publicized Hamilton child-custody/child-abuse case raised the issue of cult/ritual child abuse in Canada (Kendrick 1988).

7. For example, if a woman knowingly exposes her child to secondhand smoke or works long hours on a VDT, is she engaging in a form of child abuse? As evidenced in recent legal disputes in Canada, it is not clear how the courts can effectively protect fetal rights while not infringing on the rights of the mother.

8. Consider Rhonda Lenton's survey of Toronto parents whose attitudes towards and use of child discipline techniques suggests that Toronto parents are "at least as likely as American parents to use violent disciplinary practices" (1990: 169).

9. A 1995 British survey indicates that 91 percent of children have been hit at some time and 77 percent were hit in the year preceding the survey. Three-quarters of children one or younger were hit in the preceding year and 38 percent of four year olds and 27 percent of seven year olds were hit more than once a week. Fifteen percent of mothers indicated they used "severe" punishment (*Toronto Star*, September 22, 1996: A4). This approach to childrearing received some official endorsement when the Archbishop of Canterbury came forward to allow that "gentle slapping" was a way to instill moral values in children (*Toronto Star*, October 28, 1996: E2).

10. For example, noted American sociologist Murray Straus reports in the 1997 *Archives of Pediatrics and Adolescent Medicine* that spanking children only works in the short run. In the long run, the child becomes more of a problem and more likely to engage in antisocial behaviour such as cheating, lying, bullying, deliberately breaking things, disobedience at school and lack of remorse. His results are based on research with 807 mothers who each had a child aged six to nine years old. The mothers were interviewed two years and, then, four years after the initial investigation. The findings suggest that spanked children become more, rather than less, difficult to manage. This study is particularly important since, unlike preceding research, it controls for the influence of socioeconomic status, sex of the child, parenting style and ethnic background (Papp 1997: A1, A32).

11. In Sweden, parents who are reported to be using physical force against their children are not charged with child abuse. Rather, the use of force is seen as evidence that the family is in need of help in managing their parenting role and such help is provided (Straus 1994: 202).

12. Recently, various religious organizations have sought to examine the ways in which religious ideologies have traditionally supported domestic violence and abuse (McAteer 1995: K16).

13. Indicative of shifting priorities and increasing governmental cut-backs, *Vis-a-Vis* was folded in July 1996 (Denham and Gillespie 1996: 3).

14. The Centres are located at the University of New Brunswick, the University of Western Ontario, the University of British Columbia, the University of Manitoba and the University of Montreal. They were each allocated $500,000 which is to be dispensed over five years.

15. Developments occurring in the United States during the 1980s and 1990s provided further support for these Canadian efforts. In 1984 a major centre for research — the Family Violence and Sexual Assault Institute — was established in Tyler, Texas. Numerous new American journals — *The Journal of Child Abuse and Neglect, The Journal of Child Sexual Abuse, The Journal of Child Maltreatment* — were also launched in response to dramatic increases in both popular and academic interest in the topic, and much Canadian research appears in these sources.

16. As with violence against women, there is some evidence that more cases of child abuse are now being investigated than in the late 1980s. For example, Trocme et al. report that from 1985 to 1989 there was a 57 percent increase in the number of documented child abuse allegations (1994: 10). However, it is impossible to know whether this change reflects greater public and agency awareness of the issue and, therefore, more cases being reported or a real increase in the number of actual cases.

17. "Confirmed" cases are those which have been investigated by child welfare agents and found to be substantiated.

18. Ironically, in the late 1970s American experts were estimating that "if there were full reporting" there would be one million cases of child abuse annually. Needless to say these predictions are currently being exceeded (Van Stolk 1978: 3).

19. The McMaster University and Clarke Institute of Psychiatry survey found that adults who were unrelated by blood or marriage were most often identified as abusers. While these adults were "not strangers," they were not family members in the traditional sense (Gadd 1997: A6).

20. This relationship between poverty and abuse is interrelated with the parent's own socialization and gender.

21. Gelles and Straus report that Black children are significantly more likely to be abused than their white counterparts (1986: 252).

22. In this regard, it is interesting to note that the McMaster University and Clarke Institute of Psychiatry survey found increased reporting of child abuse amongst younger generations of respondents. For example, in the over sixty-five group, 7.8 percent of women report childhood sexual abuse. However, in the twenty-five to forty-four year olds, 15.3 percent revealed such abuse. As the report's authors are quick to point out, it is not clear whether this pattern reflects increased rates of abuse, more willingness to disclose it or greater ability to remember it (Gadd 1997: A6).

Sibling, Parent, Adolescent and Elder Abuse

In the past two decades, wife and child abuse have become noteworthy social issues. Elder abuse has recently acquired a great deal of public notoriety and has become a significant area of concern to researchers, social service professionals and workers, and advocates. Less prominent are sibling, adolescent and parent abuse. Very little research into these forms of abuse has been carried out in Canada to date. The same does not hold true for elder abuse, however, an area of family violence into which a good deal of research has been done, although there is still a certain lack of coherence in the research agenda.

Sibling Abuse

The phenomenon of sibling abuse is a fascinating one since, in one way, it is the most commonly acknowledged form of violence ("sibling rivalry"), yet, in another, it is the most ignored. Parents freely admit that their children do not get along with one another and often engage in various forms of aggression, but these behaviours are not labelled as "violence" or included under the umbrella term "family violence." In fact, social norms encourage aggression among siblings to the point where parents believe that it is an inevitable part of growing up. Furthermore, some even view such conflict as "a good training ground for successful management of aggressive behaviour in the real world" (Gelles and Cornell 1990: 85). Therefore, parents are far less likely to attempt to curtail it.

Furthermore, not only do parents have a difficult time seeing that "sibling rivalry" may be in actuality sibling abuse, but they also may not believe their children's accounts of suffering at the hands of siblings, or, worse yet, blame the children themselves for whatever these siblings do to them. This tendency to blame the victims implies that these children "deserve" such treatment, something which can be extremely damaging to the child's self-esteem and detrimental to family relations as a whole, especially when the abuse is of a sexual nature (Wiehe 1990).

The behaviours entailed by sibling abuse are seen to be far more innocent than similar behaviours directed at, for example, small children by parents, or by husbands at wives. In other words, the same actions performed by husbands, parents or caregivers against wives, children or elders would not be tolerated. Yet, because these actions are carried out by siblings, or "equals," they are more likely to be accepted, albeit with some reservation. This acceptance may relate to the notions of "equality" prevalent in our society that are seen to somehow mitigate unpleasant conditions. That is, as long as people are of comparable status, this "equality" somehow makes their actions more tolerable.

Until recently, social scientists have also failed to devote serious attention to sibling violence, largely due to parents' widespread acceptance of it and their belief that such behaviour is necessary for children to learn how to handle themselves. Researchers have even contributed to this position by outlining five "positive" elements of sibling aggression which include "benefits" such as sibling reassurance when parents are unavailable, acquisition of conflict management skills and the promotion of feelings of loyalty (Goodwin and Roscoe 1990).

The Experience

In a 1977 study of sibling abuse, the most difficult aspect encountered by researchers was that of getting parents to record anything but the most extreme cases of violence. This implies that the findings do not necessarily reveal the true frequency of sibling abuse (Steinmetz 1977: 44). Nor do they allow researchers to state with any confidence whether sibling violence is increasing, decreasing or remaining at the same level (Gelles and Cornell 1990: 87). Another interesting finding of the 1977 study was that parents were often used as a resource by the sibling in the weaker position but that parents themselves believed that conflicts were better resolved among the siblings than through their intervention (Steinmetz 1977: 44). This may also reflect the belief that, because such conflict occurs among "equals" or peers, it is not to be taken seriously. Because siblings are members of a loving, supportive family unit, conflict among them is not likely to be truly hurtful or abusive. But the reality is that sibling conflict can be hurtful and that conflict erupts among a certain age group.

It has been found that the number of conflicts and their causes among siblings differs according to age group or stage of life cycle. Conflict is much more frequent in families with young children (eight years and younger) as opposed to those with teenagers (fourteen years or older), perhaps because, as children age, they spend less time with one another and more time outside the home. Young children tend to fight over possessions such as "toys, games or the attention of adults." Adolescents (categorized as aged eight to fourteen years) engage in conflict over personal space while teenagers fight about "responsibilities, obligations and social grace" (Steinmetz 1977: 51, 56). Furthermore, use of physical force as a resolution for conflict decreases as the ages of the children increase because older children are better able to articulate their complaints and, thus, can resolve conflict through discussion.

Goodwin and Roscoe (1990: 454) cite research that reveals that sibling violence may be a better predictor of violence in adulthood than violence between parents. Sibling violence provides the children with practical opportunities to carry out abusive behaviour rather than simply witnessing violence between their parents. One study surveyed American junior high school students (mean age 12.3 years) about their experiences as victims and perpetrators of aggression towards siblings. The findings revealed that 88 percent of males and 94 percent of females identified themselves as victims, while 85 percent of males and 96 percent of females stated that they had been perpetrators. The violent behaviour they experienced included shoving and kicking. These findings indicate levels of violence among siblings much higher than those reported by adults and parents, possibly indicating the lack of serious attention to the problem given by adults and parents. The findings also suggest that females are more violent than males — statistics that contradict findings that show girls are less violent than boys (Straus, Gelles and Steinmetz 1980: 88-89). However, we can assume that other factors play a role when children self-report. For example, boys may be less likely to view certain behaviours as violent or aggressive while girls may be more inclined to describe some of their behaviour as aggressive. Therefore, gender socialization could account for the higher figure of girls reporting being the perpetrators of sibling abuse.

In a similar study, American high school students (mean age 16.9 years) were surveyed concerning violence involving their closest-aged siblings over the previous twelve months (Goodwin and Roscoe 1990). The researchers found that the major source of sibling conflict was over possessions and verbal exchanges. Females were more likely to cite jealousy and preferential treatment by parents as sources of conflict. More males threatened to harm their siblings while more females were teased. In terms of actual physical violence, 65 percent of females as opposed to 64 percent of males reported being perpetrators, while 64 percent of females and 66 percent of males stated that they had been victims. A higher number of males reported using a mild form of physical force as a way of resolving conflicts with siblings than females, who tended to use verbal methods, although such methods included shouting.

The findings of this report support the argument that, as children age, they learn to use language as a way to resolve conflict rather than resorting to physical aggression. However, the level of physical violence at this age, when adolescents are big enough to inflict serious damage on one another, indicates that sibling aggression is still a significant problem. The fact that males used physical force more often than females may indicate social norms that encourage aggression in males as part of their masculine socialization

In Vernon Wiehe's (1990) study of 150 self-identified victims of sibling abuse, most stated that the perpetrator of the physical abuse was male. Since 89 percent of the respondents were female, it would appear from these reports that it is mostly brothers who abuse. Wiehe's analysis is that power in America is gender-related, with males believing that they should have power and that females should be placed into powerless positions. If a brother feels powerless, he may abuse his sister to make himself feel powerful in relation to her. The feeling of power that he gets from abusing his sister is a reinforcement for perpetrating such acts in the future. Wiehe also notes that, when it comes to sexual abuse in particular, it is not only families of low socioeconomic status in which siblings victimize one another. In other words, contrary to certain myths, siblings of middle- and upper-class families are as likely to sexually abuse one another as those from lower-class families.

In Wiehe's study, the respondents described their experiences of physical abuse as screaming and crying for help, separating themselves from their abuser and hiding, abusing a younger sibling in order to reject the role of victim and identify with the aggressor, and telling on the perpetrator to parents (which often resulted in the victim being blamed). Similar responses were experienced in cases of emotional abuse where fighting back was a typical form of resistance. However, very few victims of sexual abuse fought back. These victims pretended to be sleeping or simply submitted. This passivity may be because victims were generally younger and smaller than their abusers. Also, they may not have been aware of what the abuser was doing. Often secrecy and threats were involved, effectively silencing the victim.

Parents may not be made aware of sexual abuse because the victim may not be able to articulate what she or he is experiencing or may not perceive it as abuse. Fear of retaliation from the abuser is another reason victims often do not report sexual abuse to parents. Or they may blame themselves for the abuse, thinking that, if they did not stop it themselves, they were somehow granting "permission" to the abuser. The atmosphere in the home may not allow for reporting such abuse; such subjects may be taboo (Wiehe 1990).

There has been virtually no major research done on sibling abuse in Canada to date with the exception of one study conducted by DeKeseredy and Ellis (1994 as cited in Baker 1996). Their survey relied on a non-random sample of 215 undergraduate students and 34 interviews with children from six to eleven years old who have learning disabilities. Representativeness is problematic due to both their method of sampling and the fact that self-reporting was involved, yet the study should be considered a pioneering effort by Canadian researchers to shed light on the issue. They asked their respondents to report on conflict between themselves and siblings and whether they had experienced harm or had inflicted it upon siblings. Their findings show that 47.8 percent of the undergraduates and 100 percent of the children with learning disabilities had been victims of sibling abuse.

The Canadian study should not be compared with the American findings by Steinmetz (1977) and Straus, Gelles and Steinmetz (1980), according to Ellis and DeKeseredy, because different measures and samples were used, and the definitions of sibling violence were dissimilar. Because enough of the most basic components diverged, the findings were incompatible. This divergence in research in the two countries demonstrates a prevailing problem in family violence research as a whole: without standardized procedures and definitions, establishing a comprehensive portrait of the dimensions of family violence as a whole is very difficult.

Naming the Issue

The sibling bond is perhaps one of the most important in any individual's life. It is also one of the longest relationships anyone has in a lifetime (Tindale et al. 1994). The way that sibling interaction unfolds in a family may have an enormous effect on how individuals interact with others throughout the remainder of their lives. Therefore, the matter of sibling abuse is a salient one. Unfortunately, it has not enjoyed a great deal of legitimacy in the consciousness of the public at large or even among academics, judging from the small numbers of studies that have been done. This is particularly true for Canada.

"Sibling abuse is any form of physical, mental, or sexual abuse inflicted by one child in a family unit on another." Such a definition is useful because it encompasses children who may not be related by blood, but are related through their parents' marriages and may or may not reside in the home on a full-time basis. It also involves children rather than those siblings who are over the age of eighteen (Wallace 1996: 101-2).

Like other forms of abuse within the family, sibling abuse can be categorized into three types: physical, emotional and sexual (Wallace 1996: 102). It should be noted that these various types of abuse often occur together. Seventy-one percent of the respondents in Wiehe's (1990) study stated that they had suffered all three. Physical abuse involves striking, kicking, punching and using objects such as sticks. Emotional abuse consists of name-calling, ridicule, degradation, exacerbating a fear, destroying personal possessions and the torture or destruction of a pet. Emotional abuse is very difficult to identify due to the lack of physical evidence and because legal standards may not be clear enough to establish distinct boundaries regarding what constitutes emotional abuse (Wiehe 1990). The characteristics of sexual abuse distinguish between childhood curiosity and abuse. Some of the divergences involve differences in age and types of activities. Power and control are usually the hallmarks of abusive sexual behaviour between siblings, both of which are absent in cases of childhood exploration. One researcher has argued that sibling sexual abuse is a more serious form of adolescent sexual abuse because of the accessibility of the victim and the privacy of the family, which shrouds the activities of family members in secrecy (Wallace 1996: 102-3). Also, sexual abuse tends to be compounded by shame on the part of both the victim and the perpetrator (Wiehe 1990).

Wiehe (1990) includes prolonged tickling as a form of abuse employed by siblings. Although tickling is not usually considered a form of abuse, there are instances when it ceases to be harmless fun and becomes torment. These instances occur when the one who is being tickled wants the behaviour to stop or is genuinely unwilling to participate, but the perpetrator ignores her or his wishes and fails to respect the integrity of the victim. Victims may be forcibly restrained or held down. The tickling may even become painful. This kind of behaviour may be particularly prone to dismissal by parents as "just playing." Such dismissal invalidates the victim's experience and may be that much more detrimental in the long run.

Sibling abuse can also be perpetrated by one child against another or it may take the form of serial abuse, which involves a perpetrator violating one sibling after another. Research on serial abuse is inconclusive at least partially because it is so difficult to conduct such studies and to interpret findings. Serial sibling abuse does not pertain only to sexual abuse; it may pertain to the other forms of abuse as well (Wallace 1996).

Adolescent Abuse

Adolescent, or teen, abuse is often overlooked. Some researchers in the field suggest that adolescents are generally considered to be deserving of whatever violence they may experience in the family, partly because of the stereotypes surrounding teen behaviour (that is, teenagers are "mouthy" or display otherwise obnoxious behaviour, they are rebellious against parental authority and give their parents a good deal of grief) and partly because teenagers are believed to be capable of defending themselves (Health and Welfare Canada 1995; Gelles and Cornell 1990; Garbarino and Gilliam 1980). There is a greater likelihood of parents using more extreme forms of violence (for example, physical beating, or using a knife or gun) against adolescents if they can defend themselves. In addition, teens who are having a particularly hard time separating from their parents may for this reason behave in more extreme fashion and generate a higher level of conflict or violence.

Background

Historically, there have been times when adolescence has carried a certain degree of stigma. Because of their lack of maturity, adolescents have been considered foolish, irresponsible and unreliable.

Erikson noted in the 1960s that adolescence was a time of great change in all areas of the individual's life; that is, changes take place physically, sexually, psychologically and socially as young people grow into adulthood. However, up to the early part of this century, many adolescents had adult responsibilities, sometimes because adults in their family died at younger ages and children picked up the slack or because it was common for adolescents to work. There were no child labour laws and most occupations did not require extensive formal education. The teen years may have been better defined to some extent and less confusing, since teenagers were not as likely to be in some "in-between" stage of education and occupation. Parents have absorbed conflicting attitudes towards adolescents, on the one hand expecting that they will behave with a higher level of maturity and control, while on the other hand expecting them to remain obedient and childlike. For many parents, adolescent sexuality is and has been problematic. Parents must learn to come to terms with their children's increased sexual maturity (Garbarino and Gilliam 1980).

Even today, adolescents themselves may not know how to deal with the conflicting expectations of our society. Because there are no real guidelines for parents on how to handle these years, and few rites of passage to mark adulthood (beyond getting a driver's licence, graduating from high school, the "age of majority" and having the right to drink alcoholic beverages), parents are probably at a loss as to when exactly to give their children increased responsibilities and how many to give them. This ambiguity makes this stage much more difficult for both parents and teens since negotiation is largely without guidelines and conflict is likely to be the usual outcome (Garbarino and Gilliam 1980). Parents may see the behaviour of their teens as reflecting on their parenting skills, making them that much more sensitive to the vicissitudes of adolescence. If teens challenge their authority to a great degree, parents may feel that they have failed in their duties. This sense of failure may exacerbate existing conflict between parents and their adolescent children (Gelles and Cornell 1990).

The Experience

Once again, statistics on adolescent abuse differ. Gelles and Cornell (1990) cite studies that have revealed that, of known victims of abuse, adolescents between twelve and seventeen years of age make up 47 percent, while another study indicates that 25 percent of reported cases of abuse have adolescent victims. Yet another study holds that 54 percent of ten- to fourteen-year-olds have been struck by a parent and 33 percent of fifteen- to seventeen-year-olds have experienced the same treatment from their parents. The diversity in these findings is probably because of the way the studies were conducted. The findings will vary depending on the definition of "violence" or "abuse," the measurement used and the sample. In addition, because this type of abuse has only recently been placed on the research agenda, there has not been sufficient time to replicate previous studies or use similar definitions and measurements to verify findings. Only with further research will social scientists be able to achieve more reliable statistics.

Certain instances of adolescent abuse constitute "child abuse grown older" while others appear for the first time when children reach the adolescent years. In both cases, however, the circumstances may be similar: intrafamilial strains and lack of resources combined with extrafamilial pressures and challenges over which individuals have little or no control due to the power structure in society. Intrafamilial strains may include changes in the parent-child relationship, psychological problems, teens' difficulties in separating from parents or addiction to drugs or alcohol. Extrafamilial pressures may be due to occupational demands, long-term unemployment or underemployment, geographical location or social isolation. Many individuals and families are incapable of adapting to these strains and pressures. What may lead to abuse within the family is an accumulation of internal and external stressors. However, in families where abusive treatment of members has been ongoing for an extended period of time, there may be other factors at work in addition to the underlying circumstances (Garbarino and Gilliam 1980).

Researchers have suggested that girls are more likely to be abused as they grow older because of the greater anxiety many parents have over their daughters' sexuality. Their fears compel them to place greater restrictions on the daughter's movements at the very stage in her life when she is feeling the need to acquire more freedom and responsibility; restrictions may lead to the escalation of conflict and the potential for violent behaviours. Conversely, parents tend to worry less about their sons' sexual activities; this lower level of parental anxiety, coupled with the fact that boys usually get bigger and stronger as they go through adolescence, frequently results in less violence directed at teenaged boys (Burgdorf 1980 as cited in Gelles and Cornell 1990).

Garbarino and Gilliam (1980) argue that there is a qualitative difference between teens who have suffered long-term abuse (that is, since childhood) and those whose maltreatment began in adolescence. This characterization specifically excludes sexual abuse. Teens who have only suffered short-term maltreatment are more likely to report it (22 percent versus 13 percent). Such reporting may indicate that these teens are not willing to tolerate their parents' treatment. Long-term abuse may convince teens that they deserve their maltreatment so they are less likely to report themselves as victims.

A manifestation of the problem of long-term adolescent abuse is the population of runaways and homeless teens, often referred to as "street kids." Janus et al. (1994) document the "substantial amounts" of physical abuse these adolescents have experienced in their lives. The study was conducted in Toronto, Ontario, using teens who had voluntarily referred themselves to a shelter and also volunteered to participate in the study, having been assured strict confidentiality so that their responses would not jeopardize the services they were receiving. Of the teens using the Toronto shelter, 16 percent agreed to be interviewed. The average age of respondents was eighteen years old, they were mostly Caucasian, and there were 113 males and 74 females. The authors indicate that the sample was representative of the shelter clientele. Seventy-four percent had run away from home more than once and had been on the street for more than a year. Females tended to leave home for the first time at the age of thirteen, while the males had left for the first time early in high school. More than two-thirds had left single-parent homes for the first time. Females reported that the main reasons for leaving home involved conflict with both male and female adults in the home, physical and sexual abuse and feeling unloved. They also reported more abuse across all categories except the denial of food. The abuse that was reported was recurrent, not a single incident. That street kids tend to be long-term sufferers of family violence is supported by information given to one of the authors by workers in a resource centre in St. Catharines, a small city (population 130,000) in southern Ontario.

In addition, the median age of onset of abuse in the Janus et al. study was twelve years or younger. Some teens had experienced being intentionally burned at about age six, while others had been struck hard enough to leave a mark when they were seven years of age. A number had been abused as early as the age of five and almost all had experienced some form of abuse by the time they were fifteen years of age. Abuse of females tended to begin earlier than for males. The abuse typically lasted from four to six years. Once again, there was a propensity for females to suffer abuse longer than males and their abuse was more secretive.

Mothers as abusers were cited most, and more often by female adolescents. Mothers also abused their daughters more than their sons. Fathers were more likely to have abused their sons. The reason for mothers appearing more often as abusers may be simply because more of the adolescents came from single-parent families, which are usually mother-headed (Janus et al. 1994). Proportionally speaking, the rate of abuse by mothers may not be greater than by fathers, once single-parent families are controlled for. Also, since the socially prescribed role for mothers is that they are loving, caring nurturers, behaviours by mothers which do not strictly conform to the social prescription may be less tolerated by adolescents than similar behaviours by fathers.

Abusive treatment for street kids continues after they leave home as well (Janus et al. 1994). So-called "friends" whom they meet on the street are also possible abusers. These friends range from drug dealers and pimps to lovers and even police and hostel residents. The most shocking and saddening finding is that 58 percent of the respondents cited persons in various types of institutions, including those in authority, as having abused them. The youth workers in St. Catharines reported that there were numerous types of individuals who preyed on street kids, like "old guys" who open up their homes and rent rooms to the teens, charging them exorbitant rates of rent and offering to "take care of them." Such "care" often means sexual and other forms of exploitation. Janus et al. propose that abused adolescents run away from home as a way of coping; they continue to suffer at the hands of non-family members once they are on the streets because they do not know how to protect themselves from others. In addition, years of maltreatment may have rendered them unable to distinguish between real friends and predators. The St. Catharines workers suggest that long-term abuse has conditioned the teens to expect only maltreatment from everyone; these adolescents do not know how to deal with any other type of treatment and they mistrust kindness. Some of them will phone the centre and talk to the workers, but they are too suspicious to actually come in.

Some street kids who use the resource centre in St. Catharines demonstrate a great deal of affection for one another, hugging every time they meet, even if their last encounter was only a few hours before. They also refer to some of the mature female workers as "Mom" and want to hug them as well. One worker stated that she believed that most of the kids would have "given anything" to be able to go home to their mom, even to the extent of tolerating some maltreatment, but were not wanted at home. These teens are not runaways but "throwaways." They are not rebellious or even necessarily running away voluntarily but simply unwanted by their parents. The St. Catharines workers reported that the teens will turn to each other as substitute family in the absence of any real family; family-type relations are still important to them. The importance of family ties is further demonstrated by some of the female street kids who bring their babies with them to the centre.

A great deal of anger is displayed by some of the adolescents who attend the resource centre in St. Catharines. The workers told of teens who punched out concrete walls, tearing up their hands. One youth had taken a burning cigarette and put it out on the inside of his forearm. The workers speculated that this was because he felt "dead inside" and needed to feel something, even if it was pain. Another possible explanation is that self-inflicted wounds help externalize the inner psychic pain that such teens endure, thus relieving some of their internal suffering.

Parent Abuse

While sibling and adolescent abuse receive little attention, the thought that children could abuse their parents is so far beyond the pale for most of us that we would quite likely dismiss such a notion as outlandish rather than give it serious consideration. Yet, parent abuse does exist.

We might point out that parents are the ones with power in the family; they control most of the resources. How, then, is it possible for them to become the victims of abuse? Gelles and Cornell (1990) state that it has been argued that violence is a means of control or power for anyone and that it is always present as a resource whenever anyone believes it should be used. It is perhaps just a cultural prejudice of ours that we believe that it is the dominant who are more likely to use violence as a resource than the subordinate.

Researchers have argued that these abusers are children generally between the ages of ten and twenty-four years and are usually dependent upon their parents and live with them in the same home. Such a definition distinguishes this type of violence from that perpetrated against the elderly by their children: that is, in this case, the "children" are quite young rather than middle-aged (see Wilson 1996).

Early reports estimated that "almost 10% of children between the ages of three and eighteen have attacked their parents" (Wilson 1996: 102). More current research sets the rate of child-to-parent abuse somewhere between 7 and 13 percent. Gelles and Cornell (1990: 97) place the range as being from 5 to 12 percent. Approximately 3 percent involves severe violence, such as using a knife or a gun against parents or beating them. The variation may be due to the type of violence (milder forms being more prevalent) or it may depend on the instrument used to measure the behaviour (Wilson 1996).

Since parent abuse by children is so hard to fathom, understanding what kind of children would do such a thing may be that much more difficult. Wilson (1996; see also Gelles and Cornell 1990) reports on some of the demographic traits that have been associated with abuse of parents in the literature. Gender has been found to be relevant in some research, while in other research the rate of violence by males and females has been relatively similar. It would appear that visible minority adolescents are less likely to abuse their parents than Caucasians. Some researchers have posited that the discrepancy may be due to stricter discipline and less tolerance for insubordination among minority parents or possibly because some minority groups tend to have stronger religious ties, which mitigates the amount of violence they are likely to display to family members. Age also is a factor. Older children are more violent towards parents than younger children. Several studies have shown that the peak age for aggression among adolescents is fifteen to seventeen years of age; others have found a peak age of seventeen to eighteen years for females but none for males. However, it has been asserted that, as males age, they are less likely to display violence towards their mothers and more likely to display violence towards their fathers. Size and strength of the adolescent has no bearing on whether she or he will perpetrate abusive behaviour towards her or his parents (see also Gelles and Cornell 1990).

It has been stated that socioeconomic status has no correlation with parent abuse (Wilson 1996). However, Wharf (1994), in his study of families in crisis in downtown Victoria, British Columbia, found that poverty was a "primary factor" in these families because they have few resources to begin with and what little they have diminishes over time, creating more problems for them. He cites the breakdown of the relationship between the parent and the child as a factor in parent-teen conflict — a breakdown possibly caused by the necessity of both parents working just to keep the family surviving. Working parents can increase the isolation of the family members from their neighbourhood, friends and each other because family life is dominated by work, which is usually low paying and stressful, and leaves little time and energy for family life and relationships.

Although the research is somewhat contradictory about the kind of family where parent abuse occurs, there are some common variables. One example is the presence of other forms of violence in the family. If children have witnessed violence between their parents or have themselves experienced violence within the family, they are more likely to participate in violent behaviours. Some studies have indicated that family relationships are distant and "disengaged" where parent abuse takes place; others have found that family relationships are overly involved and abusive adolescents are looking for a way to distance themselves when they abuse their parents. Still other studies have shown that adolescents abuse their parents when the spousal bond is not strong. Possibly, when the spousal bond is relatively weak, parents do not present a united front to their children so a potentially abusive child may believe that she or he can successfully commit violence against one or both parents. There are researchers who assert that adolescents abuse parents when the family has become chaotic, the result of parents abdicating their control over matters; these adolescents are attempting to restore order to the family by taking control (see Wilson 1996; Gelles and Cornell 1990).

Adolescents who abuse their parents usually have little interest in school and have frequently experienced truancy or expulsion. They tend to have low self-esteem. Often they have been involved with some facet of law enforcement or social services and have experienced violence in their homes. Their emotional needs may be better served by their friends, who are more likely to have deviant or delinquent values and who may be assaulting their own parents. Substance abuse is often prevalent among these adolescents, and some studies have found that alcohol use is correlated with parent abuse (see Wilson 1996; also Gelles and Cornell 1990).

There may also be the problem with independence/dependence. Adolescents are at a stage in their lives where they are receiving all kinds of familial and societal messages about appropriate behaviours. They are expected to take certain responsibilities, but they are restricted from taking others. They may be unhappy with the responsibilities that are being forced on them and frustrated because they are barred from taking on the responsibilities which they would choose. For example, adolescents have to deal with burgeoning sexual desires; they are told that these are appropriate and that they must deal with them, but, conversely, it is not socially sanctioned for them to participate in the practices which would most effectively satisfy such desires. In other words, adolescents are becoming sexual beings but they are not supposed to have sex because they are considered to be too young to properly deal with the consequences of sexual involvement.

Wilson (1996) argues that adolescents who have gained control of their families through their utilization of violence both desire and fear independence because, as much as they would like to break away from their parents, they are afraid that their parents will not be able to take control and function without them. Worry for their parents causes resentment in these adolescents. As much as they like to have the power to make the decisions, they feel anger towards their parents for relinquishing their responsibilities and also because adolescents think their parents are not concerned about them when parents do not attempt to place restrictions on them.

Parent abuse is hard to detect because of the reluctance of victims to report to authorities. Many parents deny that their adolescents are abusing them, often because of their desire to protect their children, but also because they may be ashamed to admit that their children are violent towards them. They may fear that they will be blamed for their own victimization, probably because they will be seen as "bad" parents. It is frequently not until the abusive behaviour of their adolescents is so severe that it can no longer be denied that parents will admit that it is happening to them. Another reason for the reluctance of parents to admit that they are being abused is that they may fear that their adolescents will be taken away from them and that their family will break up if such behaviour is detected by authorities (Wilson 1996; Gelles and Cornell 1990).

To the best of our knowledge, there has been no research done in Canada with regard to parent abuse[1] and it is evident that Canadian researchers need to do a great deal more study. We need to have national prevalence studies in order to understand the parameters of these problems and create social policy to deal with them. Relying on American data is always dubious, since the two countries' social and legal systems differ greatly. Nevertheless, because Canadian researchers do cite heavily from American studies, a portrait of sibling, adolescent, parent and elder abuse is incomplete without the U.S. research.

The last form of abuse to be investigated, that perpetrated against elderly people, is another matter entirely. Although much work still needs to be done to establish a comprehensive body of knowledge, Canadians have made substantial contributions to the understanding of violence against senior citizens.

Elder Abuse

Elder abuse, as a concept, has not been in existence for very long, although the behaviours commonly believed to constitute this phenomenon may have been with us for generations (Hudson 1988). According to Podnieks (1988), gerontologists have been aware of elder abuse for a long time, but it is only recently that it has come to public attention. As a concept, the abuse of senior citizens gained a certain amount of prominence in the 1980s (Gelles and Cornell 1990). Leroux and Petrunik (1990) mark the emergence of attention to this problem in the United States as being a response to the 1978 study by Steinmetz on parent battering and in Canada as a response to Shell's 1982 study on elder abuse.

Background

One reason for the emergence of elder abuse as a social issue is the previous "discoveries" of child and wife battering. Another, related reason is the growth in the number of professionals and experts who deal with the elderly and their concerns. These professionals and experts may be found in the health and social service sectors as well as in academic settings. Demographically, we live in what is known as an "aging" society. With longer life expectancy and the decrease in the birthrate, there is a much larger proportion of elderly people in the population than there ever has been before (Gelles and Cornell 1990). Elderly people enjoy a certain amount of political power so public officials have reason to address their concerns (Gnaedinger 1989).

Furthermore, another reason given for the emergence of elder abuse as a social problem in Canada is that old age itself has become a social problem. Many people view the elderly as frail, unwell and dependent; such a view generates a sense that there is a need to focus special attention on them (see Schlesinger 1988). Leroux and Petrunik (1990) state that being "elderly" has become a master status, dominating and obscuring all other statuses, and that people who are labelled with that master status are being segregated from the remainder of society. This is similar to the case of "battered women" raised by Jones, who argues that these women lose all other facets of their identities when they are viewed as victims of abuse. When an individual becomes a "senior citizen," all other dimensions of her or his life fade into the background as the cultural baggage surrounding the status moves into the spotlight. In addition, the desire to care for senior citizens takes precedence over the recognition that old people are adults with full legal and social rights and privileges. Social policy has tended to be formulated on the basis of this well-meaning, but rather misguided, attempt to help the elderly.

There is a danger that thinking of senior citizens as dependent and needing care can lead to the assumption that they are not capable of legal and social competence. The consequence of such an assumption could be the development of experts and advocates who, with the best of intentions, may violate the rights and dignity of the elderly with intervention policies that do not consider the wishes of the elderly themselves (Leroux and Petrunik 1990). An illustration of such a violation is to be found in the similarities drawn by Steinmetz between elder and child abuse. To equate elder abuse with violence against children is to ignore the essential fact that senior citizens are adults, not children; they have full legal status and civil rights.

In some sense, we may think of this phenomenon of viewing aging as a social problem as creating a greater "market" for services relating to the elderly and, therefore, more room in which advocates of various types may focus their attention on them. Leroux and Petrunik (1990) effectively argue that changing social trends and the "professional agenda" of the individuals who work in the field or are carving out a professional niche for themselves are largely responsible for putting family violence, including elder abuse, on the social agenda.

The point made by Leroux and Petrunik (1990) is further emphasized by the suggestion that little or no impetus came from the elderly population itself. In addition, mobilization around the issue of elder abuse has occurred due to the efforts of interest groups of professionals/advocates which have called for legislation regarding legal guardianship, abuse, mandatory reporting, shelters and even registration of people who have been identified (presumably by these professionals themselves) as abusers (Leroux and Petrunik 1990: 657). Provincial governments have responded more decisively than has the federal government, probably because health and social services fall under the jurisdiction of the provinces. However, the legislation dealing directly with elder abuse is less specific than that for woman and child abuse. The call for specific legislation is complicated by the conflicting findings of so many studies and the many problems associated with definition and measurement of the phenomenon itself, which makes comparisons impossibly difficult (Leroux and Petrunik 1990).

Although it is provincial governments which have enacted specific laws dealing with elder abuse, the federal government, in establishing the Family Violence Division of Health and Welfare Canada, has funded projects addressing elder abuse that have helped to shape our understanding. At the community level, groups have formed for the purposes of social and legal advocacy; education programs have been established to train special groups, such as the police (*The Spectator* (Hamilton) March 17, 1995: A2) and home-care workers; and techniques for detection and reporting have been developed in social and health service institutions and agencies.

In the United Kingdom, after an initial upsurge of interest in senior citizens and their concerns, including incidents where they were abused, there was a period of dormancy during which elder abuse disappeared from public awareness. Recently, however, British research in the field has experienced something of a renaissance and has been gaining some of the ground that American studies have already covered in the United States. Canada occupies a kind of middle ground between our American and British counterparts. Research in Canada has been growing steadily over the past decade or so, although it still lags significantly behind research in the United States. However, regardless of where research is conducted, it may be stated that elder abuse enjoys less legitimate concern than wife and child abuse.

McDonald and Wigdor (1995) provide a brief history of the background of Canadian research. What they refer to as the "first phase," the period when elder abuse was brought to the attention of the Canadian public, came to an end in 1992. That year the American *Journal of Elder Abuse and Neglect* devoted an entire issue to showcasing the most recent work done by Canadian researchers in the field. The first prevalence studies (studies which attempt to establish the extent to which types of abuse are present within particular populations) in Canada took place in Quebec, Manitoba, Nova Scotia, Alberta and Ontario, and came out in the early to mid-1980s. Podnieks et al. published their national survey in 1990. McDonald

and Wigdor state that the 1990s is the "new era." Canadian researchers are no longer attempting to find evidence to establish elder
abuse as a social problem; now they are focusing on informing
interventions, policy and legislation.

Connidis (1989) suggests that the study of multigenerational families has only recently become a possibility in the western world. Until
this century, most people did not live long enough to make multiple
generations cohabiting in the same home a common experience.
Therefore, there is not a great tradition of caring for the elderly within
the family, despite prevailing myths about multigenerational families
constituting a "golden" past. Three-generation households sometimes meant that the older parents were in control of assets, such as
property, or, more frequently, were widowed and dependent upon
their children for support because there were no government programs to provide them with income assistance. Therefore, multigenerational households historically were formed out of necessity. The
same is often true now: elderly people, especially those who are
classified as "older" senior citizens, tend to move in with family
members when their health is deteriorating.

The Experience

Much research suggests that the most likely victim of elder abuse is
a very old woman who is dependent on her caregiver. Steinmetz
(1993) has been a great proponent of the notion of victim dependency
being the primary factor in cases of elder abuse. Her research demonstrates that older senior citizens, especially those who are suffering
from physical and mental impairments, can be a source of great stress
for their caregivers, who are usually members of their family and
frequently their children. Caring for an elderly person can also involve financial stress in terms of medical expenses and the costs of
having one more person in the household. Schlesinger (1988) found
that the elderly person is frequently blamed for her or his condition,
both physical/mental and economic, making her or him that much
more of a target for violence. Further stress results from the fact that
children often do not expect to have to care for their parents. There
may also be problems such as substance abuse, mental or marital
difficulties within the caregiving family, which increase the risk of
abuse (Gelles and Cornell 1990; Schlesinger 1988). Finally, lack of
privacy when an elderly person resides with the family may increase
tensions.

In contrast to this approach of victim dependency, Pillemer (1993) suggests adopting a new position in the research on elder abuse. He counters Steinmetz, stating that it is not the elderly who are dependent on their caregivers in many cases, but the caregivers who are dependent on the elderly. He concedes that dependency may be a factor in cases of elder abuse, but that research to date has not been able to elucidate the direction of the dependency. Caregivers may perpetrate violence because they themselves are powerless and dependent (Gelles and Cornell 1990).

Dependency is not the only pertinent factor in elder abuse. Any elderly person is potentially a victim, but patterns have emerged from some studies that suggest there are risk factors. Social and geographic isolation of both victims and their families is linked with elder abuse. Vulnerability and powerlessness of the victim are also significant factors. Both isolation and vulnerability/powerlessness are often associated with widowhood (more prevalent among women because they live longer than men and tend not to remarry) and health problems of a physical or mental nature. These victims are unable to care for themselves, often live with their abusers, and are unwilling to report abuse, fearing institutionalization because they have no alternative shelter. Living with someone else has also been noted (Pillemer and Finkelhor 1988) as a risk factor involved with abuse. Co-residents are often abusers of the elderly, whether these co-residents are adult children or spouses, although elderly people tend to reside with spouses more frequently than with adult children. In fact, Pillemer and Finkelhor's finding that the risk of abuse for elderly men was twice that for elderly women was linked to the fact that these men tended to be co-residing with spouses more often than elderly women tended to. Elderly men do not usually outlive their spouses and, when they do, they are more likely to remarry.

Another important risk factor in the profile of victims is a lack of support services. Victims have no one else to turn to, other than their abusers, so they are isolated, vulnerable and powerless or, at least, perceive themselves to be. They are frightened of being abandoned. Without friends, other family members or community services to provide them with alternatives to their abusive situation, they end up being victimized. The same may be true for those victims who are institutionalized. If they have no one else to rely upon for alternative support, they may feel that they have little choice but to accept their victimization. A history of abuse is also strongly correlated with elder abuse, so victimization is an established pattern in the older person's life (Gnaedinger 1989; National Clearinghouse 1986).

The literature to date tends to profile the "typical" abuse victim as being over seventy-five years of age, female, isolated, co-residing, and dependent for care due to mental/physical disabilities. She may feel powerless to do anything about her situation, possibly because she has internalized the identity of "victim" from past experience. Or she may not have access to support services. Future research may confirm this profile or discover other factors contributing to abuse.

Naming the Issue

Scarcely a study of elder abuse does not start with a discussion about the problem of the lack of universality in definitions. Similar to other types of family violence, elder abuse takes the forms of physical, emotional, psychological and verbal abuse. Under psychological abuse, Hudson (1988) adds that if an elder's room is not kept clean and tidy, bedclothes are not changed appropriately or there are no curtains on the windows, the environment in which she or he must spend a good deal of time will not be conducive to good mental health. Verbal abuse includes "infantilization," where an elderly person is treated like an incompetent child (Hudson 1988). This is similar to what Podnieks (1992: 38) refers to as "paternalism"; well-meaning professionals or family members intervene in an elder's life and make decisions for her or him because they believe they "know what is best" for the older person. Sexual abuse has also been committed against the elderly, specifically rape or attempted rape (Vadasz 1988).

In addition, the elderly often suffer from neglect. Neglect may be passive (without intent) or active (with intent). It can also be thought of as "abandonment." Behaviours involved in this form of abuse could be withholding of food or personal hygiene (as in not bathing an elderly person or not allowing them to clean themselves) or other kinds of assistance (National Clearinghouse 1986). Material or financial abuse is the most widespread form of abuse found in the literature on elder abuse. This abuse entails the elderly being coerced or tricked into giving up their money or possessions, or control over them, to their abuser. In their Canadian survey of elder abuse, Podnieks et al. (1990) found that this was the most widespread kind of abuse perpetrated against the elderly. Beaulieu (1992: 14) adds two other categories to the repertoire of elder abuse: "violation of the freedom of right," which is "restricting someone from having normal control over his or her life, imposing medical treatment and physical or chemical restraints;" and social and collective abuse, which she characterizes as "social indifference."

Some American researchers include self-abuse and self-neglect in the typology of elder abuse, arguing that, when senior citizens fail to care for themselves by abandoning personal hygiene, not eating or even committing suicide (*Toronto Star*, December 4, 1984: E4), they are doing so as a result of the failure of family members or the community at large to look after their needs. This issue is a contentious one for two reasons. The first is that broadening the definition of elder abuse to encompass scenarios which have no actual "abuser" may result in very high estimates of abuse. In other words, there is potential danger in overestimating the incidence of abuse to the point where the problem may take on overwhelming proportions in the mind of the public and governmental agencies. The second reason is that including such situations may make the entire issue lose meaning in terms of social consciousness. When everything that elderly persons encounter in their lives can be taken as abuse, then old age becomes the problem. Senior citizens may become more marginalized as a result. Research aimed at understanding the dynamics of elder abuse may be hampered by such a broad definition because factors relating to the problem will be difficult, if not impossible, to pinpoint. Studies will be harder to compare than they already are if self-abuse and self-neglect are included. It has been noted by certain researchers that broader definitions of elder abuse result in larger estimates of incidence (Gelles and Cornell 1990). Determining whether elder abuse is increasing or decreasing over time also becomes problematic.

Characterization of the Elderly

The elderly are often categorized as being "younger" or "older." "Younger" senior citizens are between the ages of sixty-five and seventy-two years; "older" are over seventy-two years of age (Koch and Koch 1980 as cited in Gelles and Cornell 1990: 100).

The British terms "grannybashing" and "granslamming," found in some of the earlier material on elder abuse, highlight how stereotypes have prevailed in the field (see Schlesinger 1988 for an example). One characterization of the problem was that women were more likely to be dependent on their families because their traditional role as homemakers meant that they had small pensions when they entered old age. Generally, they tend to be depicted as old, frail, sick and dependent.

This kind of portrayal of the elderly is in stark contrast to the vital, independent and socially active people to which Connidis's study (1989) made reference. Although she does not necessarily ignore the fact that seniors often have health concerns, her general portrait is a much more positive one. More specifically, Connidis is interested in examining the significance of family ties to the process of aging, concentrating on four dimensions: the availability of family members; the amount of contact with these family members; the type of relationship that emerges among family members; and the quality of such a relationship. She demonstrates that family ties shape people's lives and continue to shape them into old age. The way an elderly person lives is affected by the availability of family members, particularly a spouse. The amount of support she or he receives is also affected by such availability, something which is particularly important if the elder suffers from ill health. Connidis challenges the stereotype that elderly people who were never married are destined to live their lives in isolation and loneliness, illustrating that they often have aged parents and siblings, nieces, nephews and cousins with whom to share their lives. Her attention to sibling relationships makes her study noteworthy since it is frequently forgotten that elderly people have other close family ties besides those to spouses, offspring and grandchildren. The depiction of the elderly which emerges is a much more optimistic one than what it is generally held to be and makes elderly persons seem less likely to be hapless victims and nothing more.

On the other hand, Goldstein and Blank (1988) state that older persons may be demanding, used to having their own way, angry at being dependent on a family member or institutional caregivers. They may be intolerable to live with and display "passive-aggressive" behaviour. They may accuse their caregivers of being neglectful of their needs or even be abusive towards them. This characterization of the elderly as cranky and curmudgeonly is probably the flipside of the old, frail and sick stereotype, and equally problematic.

Podnieks (1992), in her interviews with elderly women who had been abused by their husbands, expected to find that they would express feelings of powerlessness or helplessness. Instead, she discovered that these women were actually hardy and resilient. Having these qualities meant that they were able to cope with their lives, including the abuse, because they felt that they were exercising control. They remained emotionally healthy in the face of stressful lives because they were able to choose how to handle their stress, allowing them to cope. Some of the factors Podnicks examined were their sense of self, their inner-strength and independence. In essence, we might say that they had rejected the label of "victim." Podnieks's findings are more interesting in light of the fact that demographically these women fit the stereotypical pattern of abuse victims: they were older elderly, dependent, widowed, had a history of abuse, and were institutionalized. Moreover, they were unwilling to report that they were being abused within the institution because they feared reprisal or relocation to another place.

Living Arrangements

Elderly people may prefer to live on their own if they are able to do so (Connidis 1989). With more women going into the paid labour force in recent years and the advent of government pensions and income supplements, senior citizens are in a better position financially and are more likely to have the option of independent living. When they are forced to live with their grown children, the elderly may be angry and resentful, leading to strains in their relationships with their children. In turn, because of increased longevity and medical technology, older people are more likely to live longer and require extended periods of care. Having fewer siblings may place the burden of care on only one or two children, giving them very little respite. Children who must care for elderly parents will have to take on obligations that are likely to last much longer than they might have in earlier years. Coupled with their other family obligations, such long-lasting and onerous caregiving relationships may put enormous strain on adult children (Duxbury and Higgins 1994). Conflict or even violence may result from these strains.

Such responsibilities could lead to role strain, making it difficult for caregivers to perform in other roles as well. Role strain is a term which designates the experience of having multiple roles, each of which demands time, energy and commitment; these manifold demands create strain to the point that it interferes with the ability to perform all or any one of them. Caregivers who must care for children or elderly parents or both and who work outside the home display common problems, such as absenteeism from work, lateness and having to leave work early, all of which may threaten their jobs (Duxbury and Higgins 1994). Losing a job due to caregiving responsibilities could lead to more stress and possible violent repercussions for those who are dependent upon these caregivers for their care. Since an estimated one-quarter of workers over forty had elder-care responsibilities in 1991 and demographic trends indicate that the number of elderly in the population will continue to grow, there will probably be many more people suffering from role strain in the future (Duxbury and Higgins 1994: 32). The possible repercussions of such increased responsibilities and role strain could mean higher levels of various types of family violence.

Yet, despite all the difficulties involved in caregiving, in 1988, the Bureau of National Affairs indicated that 80 percent of the care needed by the elderly is provided by family members, typically daughters or daughters-in-law (see also Harman 1995; Gelles and Cornell 1990). A 1989 report by the same agency notes that tasks involving elder care take approximately ten to twenty hours per week. Lifestyle changes are required to accommodate these extra responsibilities, a potential source of conflict (Duxbury and Higgins 1994: 32; Wharf 1994 also deals with economic problems).

Harman (1995) states that women are usually the caregivers in families. It is generally left to women to keep the family together, to smooth out problems and to care for family members who are suffering in one way or another. When the family unit begins to deteriorate, it is often blamed on the woman. Therefore, when, for example, economic problems arise, a common problem for many Canadians, the toll such problems take on the family could be instead viewed as the failure of the woman to fulfil her role. The implications of this insight are that various forms of family violence may be attributed to women, directly or indirectly. As a result, women may experience greater pressure to care for their family members and suffer from more stress and strain. Blame may be wrongfully attributed to them, not only by a misinformed public, but by the purported victims as well.

Not all elderly people live with their children; a small percentage of the elderly population lives in institutional settings, like nursing homes and senior citizens' homes. Most elderly people prefer to live with family members, if at all possible, when they are unable to live independently. This preference may be due to the depersonalized environment of institutions.

In her research, Canadian researcher Gnaedinger (1989) found that 97 percent of staff members in institutions were female. Of these, 10 percent admitted to abusing elderly residents physically while 40 percent admitted to psychological abuse. These results are apparently similar to those of a Quebec survey conducted by Belanger (1981, as cited in Gnaedinger 1989). It should be noted, however, that the sample is gender biased because staff members in most institutions are, in fact, women. Therefore, it is difficult to discern whether females are truly more responsible for institutional abuse than are males. Gnaedinger also discovered that residents sometimes abuse each other, particularly if they are mentally impaired.

The study done by Americans Payne and Cikovic (1995) consisted of a content analysis of reports of abuse to a publication called the *Medicated Fraud Reports* from 1987 to 1992. Most of these reports cited physical abuse, although they concede that this finding might be because physical abuse is the easiest type of abuse to detect and prosecute. Sexual, monetary or "misperformed" occupational duties (such as changing the dressing of a wound using a sharp instrument) were the other types of abuse noted. The abusers were found to be mostly nurses' aides but, again, since these are the staff members who generally have the most patient contact as well as being the most numerous, it is not surprising that they would most often be cited as the abusers. More males were accused of abusing (almost 63 percent) and more were also victims of abuse (almost 57 percent), a rather surprising finding. Reasons for abusing were stress, job interaction and provocation, the last being specifically that patients hit or abused staff members first.

Pillemer, one of the foremost researchers of elder abuse in the United States, in his study of institutional abuse with Moore (1990), did a survey of nurses and nurses' aides, the majority of which were females, whose average age was thirty-nine years. Almost half (48 percent) had had postsecondary education and stated that they had chosen their occupation because they were motivated by a desire to help and to be meaningfully, as well as gainfully, employed. Because of the growth in the number of nursing homes due to government funding and the fact that they believe the number will continue to grow, coupled with their concern that the kind of care that the elderly receive in these institutions is poor, Pillemer and Moore were anxious to examine the levels and types of abuse old people may be suffering and what factors contributed to them.

Pillemer and Moore's study demonstrates the complexity of elder abuse, specifically with regard to an institutional setting, but its implications can be extrapolated to the non-institutional setting as well. Their findings indicate that almost half of the staff had been insulted or sworn at ten or more times in the preceding year by elderly residents, 41 percent had been physically assaulted in some way ten or more times, 70 percent had been hit or had something thrown at them, of which 61 percent had experienced this kind of assault ten or more times, and 47 percent had been kicked or bitten during the preceding year. Therefore, there is evidence, according to Pillemer and Moore, that working in an institution that cares for elderly residents is a very high-risk occupation in terms of experiencing violence on the job. The implications of these findings are that, in a non-institutional setting as well (that is, caring for an elderly person at home), caregivers may have to endure a certain amount of abuse from their elderly charges, increasing the stress level associated with caring for them.

In addition, Pillemer and Moore found that 81 percent of the staff members they studied had witnessed at least one instance of psychological abuse, most commonly angry yelling by a staff member at an elderly resident. Of physical assault witnessed, excessive restraining was most often observed, then pushing, shoving and pinching. Ten percent of respondents admitted to physically abusing a resident; again, the most common act of abuse consisted of restraining. Forty percent reported psychologically abusing residents, with the majority of the abuse (33 percent) consisting of angry yelling. The candor of respondents may be due to the way the questions were couched or it might reflect genuine concern on the part of respondents over their own and fellow staff members' behaviour. At any rate, Pillemer and Moore associate staff–patient conflict and staff burnout with physical abuse, and burnout and patient aggression with psychological abuse. Furthermore, younger staff members and those with more negative attitudes towards patients were more likely to psychologically abuse elderly residents. The implications of this study are that high stress levels for caregivers which, in the institutional setting are linked with low wages, low numbers of staff, and insufficient training to handle interpersonal conflict with elderly residents, are correlated with both physical and psychological abuse.

The overall findings from the Pillemer and Moore study are significant in that they indicate that caring for elderly people is a highly complex and possibly volatile task, one which requires a good deal of training in terms of dealing with the situation and sufficient resources. It is not a vocation which should be entered into lightly because of the high level of stress, but one that, on the unofficial level, probably is. Therefore, the study indicates the need for a great deal of support for caregivers, both in terms of services and of emotional resources. Caregivers need to have a better understanding of what they may be undertaking when they agree to care for an elderly person and older people themselves may need to be informed that their caregivers are under a good deal of strain because of their responsibilities.

Detection of Abuse

The actual statistics relating to elder abuse indicate that approximately 2 to 4 percent of the elderly population suffer from some form of abuse (Podnieks 1990; Gnaedinger 1989; Pillemer and Finkelhor 1988 for the United States). Although this is a small percentage, in terms of raw numbers, there are still many individuals enduring maltreatment. Furthermore, there is no way of knowing the dark figure, meaning the number of cases which never come to the attention of officials.

Some researchers claim that abuse is difficult to detect when it comes to the elderly because they tend to be more isolated from society and less tied into social networks. Gelles and Cornell (1990) suggest that isolation makes the continuation of violence more likely, presumably because the abuse is easier to hide and less subject to social control. Furthermore, they state that the elderly are confined to their homes and dependent upon their caregivers/abusers, so they are far less likely to report being abused. In fact, it is generally a third party who reports elder abuse (see also Schlesinger 1988).

There are other reasons advanced by Gelles and Cornell (1990) for which elders are unwilling to admit to being abused. One is embarrassment. It may be very difficult to admit that they raised a child who could abuse them. Another reason is that they assume the blame for the violence they suffer. In addition, their love and loyalty for their abuser may be stronger than their desire to escape the behaviour. Similarly, senior citizens may be more concerned about the welfare of those who perpetrate violence against them than about themselves. They may also fear possible repercussions if they report abuse. Also, the alternative to abuse in their homes by their caregivers may be less appealing to the elderly; that is, they might prefer to suffer abuse than to be institutionalized. Indeed, they may also resist being labelled victims. Finally, they may also be unaware of where in the community they can turn for assistance, or community support may be inadequate. The portrait of the elderly by Gelles and Cornell tends to suggest that senior citizens are rather helpless and very much dependent on their caregivers. As has already been noted, the work done by Connidis (1989) generates a vision of the elderly as vital, independent, vigorous individuals who maintain social networks, interests and active lives to their fullest capacity.

Despite these difficulties, elder abuse can be detected. Emergency staff in hospitals are often the ones who report elder abuse because they are in a position to see physical injuries and to detect other types of harm that may have been suffered. Mandatory reporting laws mean that these staff members are under the obligation to report suspected abuse. However, reporting may still be problematic because of unclear definitions of abuse, the fear of wrongful accusation suits and the possibility of removal and subsequent institutionalization of the older person, even against her or his will. There is a very real possibility of trespassing on the rights of the victim in the case of abuse of the elderly. On the other hand, there is the very real concern that, if reporting were not done, vulnerable people would be left without protection, crimes would not be reported to the proper authorities, and the public good would be sacrificed in the name of rights, or of individual good. Mandatory reporting lightens some of the burden for professionals of making the decision to report (Gnaedinger 1989).

In addition to physical manifestations of abuse, there are other possible indicators. These include self-abuse or self-neglect, such as poor hygiene, dishevelled clothing, no emotion or poor communication between the elderly person and the caregiver (National Clearinghouse 1986). However, these indicators are not self-evident in that they may be present for other reasons besides abuse. Without the opportunity for prolonged observation, staff members in an emergency room or in another institutional setting may not have sufficient information to make an accurate decision about abuse. Therefore, they may be quite hesitant about reporting.

Two factors further complicate the detection of abuse: (1) many elderly people in Canada do not speak either official language well enough to communicate their situation to a third party or even to know what their rights are; and (2) in an institutional setting, nurses or other staff members may be quite reluctant to report friends or colleagues who may be responsible for the abuse. Even though the Canadian Nurses Association code of ethics requires members to report cases of abuse, personal feelings and fear of wrongful accusation may make reporting extremely difficult (Gnaedinger 1989).

Researchers have discussed detection of abuse in generic terms. There has been very little work done on ethnic variation with regard to elder abuse and its detection, even in the United States. A study done by Anetzberger (1987, as cited in Tinsdale et al. 1994) on Appalachian communities in and around Tennessee attempts to deal with cultures in specific geographical locations. Anetzberger found in his study that factors relating to abuse were isolation, living in a rural setting and being poor and having little education. In addition, when parents had abused their children, there was a very great possibility of these children abusing their parents at a later stage. Also, there was an increased likelihood of a child abusing a parent if there was a long period of co-residency of the parent and child. These findings do not differ greatly from those of other studies.

Conflict Factors/Potential for Abuse

Canadian researchers Tindale and associates (1994) suggest four factors that can generate conflict and may lead to intergenerational abuse within families. They are co-residency, gender and intangible support, perceived parent–child inequities, and perceived sibling inequities. Tindale et al. arrived at these factors from a small study they undertook involving only twenty families, from which they obtained seventy interviews. The respondents consisted of ten Anglo-Canadian families and ten Italian-Canadian families. Although they concede that this is a very small sample and, therefore, should not be taken as representative of the Canadian population as a whole, or even of the two ethnic-Canadian groups included, their study yielded interesting preliminary findings about the conflict factors and their potential for intergenerational abuse.

The first factor, co-residency, refers to adult children returning home to live with their parents. Despite the fact that none of the parties to the study endorsed this option, Italian-Canadian parents did not mind their children returning home to live with them. Tindale et al. discovered that what was paramount in this situation was not so much whether adult children actually resided with their parents, but the expectations about these children returning home. In other words, the potential for conflict stemmed from what kinds of expectations the parties had about adult children residing with parents. If the expectation was that adult children should not do this, then conflict was more likely to be generated were such a situation to arise.

The second factor is gender and intangible support, which was defined as emotional support. Anglo-Canadian sons did not provide intangible support to their parents. As a result, intangible support fell to daughters, which Tindale et al. believed increased the possibility of abuse. Both Anglo-Canadian daughters and daughters-in-law gave more of all kinds of support than did sons. For the Italian-Canadian families, the support provided by sons and daughters was considered to be equal. Furthermore, Anglo-Canadian fathers did not recognize receiving support from their children, which might make Anglo-Canadian children feel unappreciated and fathers feel unloved because they themselves do not recognize receiving emotional input. Communication blocks could occur, increasing the potential for abuse.

Regarding the third factor, perceived parent–child inequities, the researchers found inequalities in the amount of support expected by Anglo-Canadian parents from their children or given by parents to their children. In the latter case, parents might be seen as taking a sense of autonomy away from their adult children. Such a situation can lead to a breakdown in parent–child relationships and open a space for the potential for abuse.

Finally, Tindale et al. found inequities among siblings in the giving of support to parents. These inequities were among Anglo-Canadian families only, although there was a division of labour along gendered lines for the Italian-Canadian families in the sense of what parents expected from their children. Conflict among siblings could arise due to these inequities because some siblings might perceive that they are doing more, or are expected to do more, for parents than other siblings. Again, the potential for abuse could be generated by such a situation.

The conclusion from this study is that it is not conflict itself or even the circumstance of the conflict that is associated with the potential for abuse, but the history of the family relationships. In other words, what must be examined whenever abuse is found or suspected are family communication patterns, the quality of affection among family members and problem-solving skills. There is evidently some ethnic variation, but with such a small sample size and only two ethnic groups involved, it is not prudent to make any conclusions about patterns of abuse in different ethnic groups.

Profiles of Caregivers/Abusers

The literature in both Canada and the United States suggests to a great extent that caregivers who abuse their elderly charges suffer from a high degree of stress. The stressors in their lives could stem from mental problems, alcohol/drug abuse, a history of violence, unemployment, too many responsibilities or from the caregiving situation itself (that is, a difficult or abusive elder or being sandwiched between their elderly charge and their children). Alternatively, their stress could be due to their own sense of dependency on the older person. It may also stem from the caregiver being older and having her or his own needs to meet while having to meet the needs of the elderly charge (Gnaedinger 1989; Hudson 1988; Goldstein and Blank 1988; National Clearinghouse 1986).

In addition, Goldstein and Blank (1988) suggest that caregiver stress levels may be increased by friends, relatives, medical or health care professionals and society in general criticizing the quality of care the caregiver is providing. She or he may begin to feel frustrated that her or his efforts are not being appreciated or may fear being unable to manage the elder's care. This fear could lead the caregiver to experience guilt over the possibility of having to place the senior citizen in an institution, something which may be against the elder's will. The caregiver's ability to cope may become diminished over time in light of this sense of inadequacy. Coping skills may also be strained over time as the elderly charge continues to decline as the years go by (Gnaedinger 1989).

The profile of the institutional caregiver is similar in many ways since the kind of care she or he gives to her or his charges will be affected by personal stressors and problems as well as attitudes towards the elderly (Hudson 1988). The institutional caregiver's stress may be further increased by a lack of adequate staff in the institution, low pay, difficult charges and criticisms from supervisors. In some cases, staff members may be "damned if they do and damned if they don't," which refers to the situation where residents are abusive to their caregivers, yet when the caregivers attempt to deal with them or handle the abuse, they themselves are accused of being abusive (Goldstein and Blank 1988). This kind of circumstance can be very frustrating, particularly if the staff member has no intention of being abusive, and can create a very high level of stress.

Therefore, stress is the major characteristic in the profiles of caregivers/abusers. Stress may come from many different sources, as we have seen. Future research must be done to discern the link between stress and abuse, however, to indicate how stress leads to an actual situation of abuse.

The stereotypical abusive caregiver is the victim's adult child. Sons are cited as more likely to abuse elderly parents than are daughters (Schlesinger 1988). However, a recent report cited in the *Niagara Falls Review* (April 5, 1997: A1) found that daughters are the majority of perpetrators of material abuse against the elderly. Pillemer and Finkelhor (1988) found that it was spouses more often than children who abused the elderly. The study conducted by Podnieks et al. (1990) discovered that, in terms of material abuse (2.5 percent of the sample), it was distant relatives or non-relatives who were more likely to be the abusers than close relatives. With regard to physical abuse (found in 0.5 percent of the sample), the majority of the abusers were spouses of the victims. More research needs to be done in elder abuse, using similar definitions, measurement instruments and sampling techniques to provide for maximum uniformity; in this way, we may be able to gain enough comparability among studies to enable us to provide more accurate profiles of abusers with increased confidence.

Conclusions

Although the study of elder abuse is the most developed of the various types of family violence cited in this section, it is far from being a cohesive body of literature. As has already been mentioned a number of times, there is very little consensus on what behaviours constitute abuse of the elderly. Existing stereotypes regarding elderly persons may taint the research that is being done. Researchers debate the issues involved in this form of violence, some insisting that it is the result of the dependency of the elderly on their caregivers, others arguing that it is the caregivers who are dependent upon the elderly and this is what produces the abuse. Canadian research is not as advanced as American research. In short, there is still a great deal of work to be done in this particular field of family violence before we can draw conclusions with any assurance.

The same is true for the other types of abuse discussed above. They are all very recent additions to the research agenda and, particularly in Canada, there have been very few studies undertaken to date. Therefore, it is impossible to make generalized statements that would give a concise but comprehensive overview of sibling, parent, adolescent or even elder abuse. If the reader is left in a state of confusion over the sometimes conflicting findings of the studies which have been done or is frustrated at their inconclusive nature, it is quite understandable. What has been done to date is preliminary work only; it represents an attempt to establish the terrain of these types of violence. Coherence and conclusiveness may only be achieved in the future, after years of study.

Notes

1. This cautionary note is not meant to imply that the data gathered for this study are completely invalid, but just to call attention to problems with sampling and the possibility of distortion. Wiehe (1990: 6) himself points out that the study is exploratory and meant primarily to open the field to discussion and future research.

5

Looking for Explanations: Exploring Theoretical Perspectives

Canadian society is filled with conflict and violence of various types. Family violence does not occur in a vacuum. Even though the actions take place between *individuals*, individuals learn how to behave and think in certain ways from the society in which they live. To put it another way, the social context in which people live shapes how and why they act. Accordingly, family violence takes place within a social framework. As a result, we must examine the diverse social aspects which facilitate its occurrence and recurrence to fully comprehend its complex dimensions.

The Social Reasons for Violence

Many aspects of western society promote violence, but capitalism may be chief among them. Capitalism is a hierarchical structure based on the exploitation of workers. Thus, it is inherently abusive. The culture of capitalism promotes a "dog-eat-dog" ethos and causes the social bond to deteriorate because of competition, self-interest, efficiency and rationality. Furthermore, in the contemporary economic climate, where the proverbial "pie" for workers has become so much smaller, fewer people enjoy economic prosperity. That means that they suffer the violence of economic deprivation and marginalization. With the dismantling of the welfare state, more and more people are descending into poverty. This further breaks down the social bond as those desperately clinging to what they have are fearful that those below them will try to take what they have; a kind of mean-spiritedness takes over and they become resentful of anyone receiving anything "for free." Those trapped in poverty may feel abandoned and betrayed by society and may not care if they harm others.

Economic conditions play a crucial role in family conflict and violence. "Economic conditions" does not mean simply the level of income of the family, although this is also a salient factor. Rather, it refers to the economic conditions that prevail in contemporary Canadian society. The decade of the 1990s has been marked by severe recessions in this country, a fact which has had enormous impact on people's lives. The loss of jobs throughout the country due to downsizing and closures in industrial sectors means less stability and security in terms of an individual's employment and income.

Harman (1995) demonstrates that poverty is a widespread phenomenon in our society. Even those people who work most of the year are not exempt from impoverishment. In fact, 27.7 percent of poor families in 1990 were those termed the "working poor" (Ross 1992 as cited in Harman 1995: 239). People whose incomes remain above the poverty line but are still close to it are not necessarily in less dire financial straits, Harman argues, because "poverty lines" are arbitrary constructions. Due to the recessions of the 1990s, many middle-income families, traditionally considered beyond the problems generated by poverty, have also found themselves experiencing economic hardships. Unemployment rates have been on the rise and downsizing has meant the loss of many mid-range white collar jobs. Single-parent, mother-headed families have also meant higher numbers of families enduring financial difficulties, since women have historically earned less income than men and their work has tended to be part-time (Harman 1995; Duffy and Pupo 1992). Studies of family violence have repeatedly demonstrated a high correlation between abuse and neglect and low socioeconomic status.

More women having to work to supplement family income may contribute to various types of family violence. Siblings unsupervised by adults may have greater opportunities to perpetrate abuse on one another. Children may abuse their mothers or fathers because they feel neglected when both parents are working long hours outside the home. Elderly people suffer some forms of abuse because caregivers are not home to look after their needs or are too tired to do so once they get home (Harman 1995; Wharf 1994).

Neo-conservative governments, with their emphasis on cutbacks to social services and their focus on deficit reduction, are eroding the social welfare state and depriving Canadian society of the "safety net" of earlier days. This erosion has made life more difficult and stressful for more and more people. Not only does this deprivation create people who live in impoverishment, but it may also, in the long run, create "impoverished people" in the sense that economic and social deprivations often lead to heightened conflict within the family and with other members of society. The social bond breaks down as people suffering from deprivation seek to gain something for themselves, once again at the expense of others. Conflict is heightened as people struggle against one another for scarce resources in the zero-sum game of competition. Such conflict may lead to an escalation of violence, which damages adults and children alike in various ways. Damaged children grow up to be damaged adults. A vicious circle is created and perpetuated in this way. Therefore, violence in the family could continue for two reasons: impoverished social contexts and impoverished people within those contexts (see O'Neill 1994).

The social ethos of neo-conservatism produces a higher level of competition among individuals and pushes them to believe that those unable to support themselves are those who do not deserve to do so. This attitude serves to make those who are already suffering feel worse about themselves and their situation. Poverty becomes a moral issue. Self-esteem suffers; shame and anger grow. This dangerous cocktail of destructive emotions may contribute to family violence as well, as people turn to drugs or alcohol, their mental states deteriorate, and their intimate relationships become the dumping ground for all their negativity. For these reasons and others, family violence is a major social issue and one that encompasses all of us.

Conflict and violence are endemic to the Canadian social context, as this discussion has shown. They are not peripheral or alien elements; they are, in fact, part of our everyday lives in some form. Most of us cannot successfully escape them. The implication for individuals is that we have all internalized conflict and violence. And many people indicate that they believe that a life without conflict, including family life, is not possible — or even desirable. A certain level of conflict is considered to be healthy. Such an attitude may be attributed to a set of ideas in operation in Canadian society that promotes the acceptance of conflict. There are other ideas that have become so ingrained in Canadian society and the consciousness of individuals that they are rarely viewed as anything other than what might be termed "the natural order."

Ways of Thinking

There are two ways of thinking that enjoy dominant (or hegemonic) positions in Canadian society: liberal democracy and patriarchy. These can be referred to as "structuring" ideas because they have been instrumental in the creation of social structures and form the basis of culture.

Liberal philosophy emerged in the eighteenth century as a defence for the development of industrial capitalism, which brought about the separation between private and public spheres as production moved into factories, away from the home (Lynn and O'Neill 1995: 287). Since then, western societies have cherished the notion of a split between the "public" and the "private" spheres; that somehow human beings move from one world to another. It is believed that somehow these two worlds do not overlap or, indeed, that they are not one and the same. Feminists have strongly challenged such notions, stating that "the personal is political." Their argument is that such a division is not only arbitrary and artificial, it is also oppressive for women and children, who are often relegated to the private sphere.

Miller (1990) argues that the cherished image of the private sphere depends on an image of the public as being dangerous and full of treachery. As long as people believe that it is the street, the world outside of home, hearth and family, where they will be mistreated and where they must always be on guard to ensure that some predatory stranger does not assault them, they will be more likely to view the family as being diametrically opposed. In other words, they will hold the opinion that the family is a sheltered sanctuary, a much-needed "port in the storm," where no harm can befall them. Miller notes that the rhetoric of the family is remarkably resilient and enjoys a great deal of authority as both "a natural and a moral order"; furthermore, the moral authority of the family influences how we view other spheres (1990: 264-65).

"What is the problem with that?" it may be asked. The problem is that such thinking could very well blind people to the reality of their experience. If they adhere to the myth of the family as haven, they may be more likely to ignore what is happening to them. When their partners slap them during the course of an argument, they tell themselves that they "provoked" the behaviour. Perhaps their partners come home drunk and beat them. In this case, they decide that alcohol was to blame for their partners' behaviour. Or they might explain the violence by saying that something had "come over" their partners, this was not "usual" behaviour, she or he was behaving "like a different person" (Miller 1990). These explanations are attempts to make sense of the anomaly of abuse within the haven of the family, where relationships are supposed to be loving and caring; the acceptance of such explanations ensures that the myth lives on. Miller (1990) describes this process as a redefinition of the act of violence so that it fits in with this way of thinking. This is rather ironic: the action is redefined to fit the set of ideas rather than the set of ideas questioned as a result of the action. It demonstrates how powerful this way of thinking really is. It also implies how dangerous it is for those who are the victims of the violence.

Of course, sometimes the people who experience abuse have little choice but to redefine it and continue to maintain an idealized picture of the family. These people are the children who suffer everything from a spanking to broken bones, insults to forced sexual activity. Because they are so dependent upon their parents, they very rarely have alternatives. Children are a "captive audience" because they can do little to prevent their abuse at the hands of their parents or other family members. In addition, because they may have nowhere and no one to turn to, they are often forced to deal with the aftermath of their own emotions and their knowledge that they still want the love and attention of their abusers. Those who finally reach a point where they can no longer tolerate the violence sometimes take flight from their homes and families, preferring to live with the brutality of the streets than to return to the hypocrisy and pain of their home life. At this point the myth of the family as a haven has at last disintegrated, unable to support the reality of the behaviour. Keeping the myth of the family alive means that family violence remains vested in certain individuals and particular families in the popular imagination. In a sense, it is a kind of tolerance. By adhering to the family myth, we are sticking our heads in the sand, ignoring the reality that violence in the family is a pervasive problem that stems from social causes, not psychological ones.

The development of this idea of the family as a haven can be traced back to the nineteenth century when Protestant evangelical religions arose and redefined family roles (Bradbury 1996: 70-72). Wives were sentimentalized and moralized in middle-class families. As was already true for working-class families, home and work were becoming more and more separate from one another. This separation was in great contrast to earlier times when the home was also the

farm where the family worked to produce both subsistence and sur-
plus, or when the home was also the craft shop where goods were
made for sale. With industrialization and the rise of factories, it
became commonplace for people to leave their homes to go to work
in another location. Middle-class wives were now increasingly
charged with the responsibility of making the home a warm, cosy
and appealing place for their husbands. In addition, wives were to
encourage their husbands' virtue and godliness. Legislation was enacted beginning in the 1850s to ensure that husbands bore the responsibility of supporting their wives after the marriage had broken down,
even in the event of breakdown due to the husbands' abuse.

Moreover, the idea that men and women should marry for love —
and, by extension that the family should be based on love — grew
in acceptance. People also came to believe that marital partners
should be good companions. Previously, marriages had been based
on necessity or economic considerations. Once again, the responsibility for nurturing the loving relationship was placed squarely on
the woman's shoulders; if the marriage failed, the fault was with her.
Working-class marriages were subject to the same changed notions,
even though maintaining a loving marital relationship in the face of
poor economic conditions was extremely difficult. Women of this
class were frequently forced to remain in bad marriages because of
low wages; it was rarely possible for women to survive on their own,
without a man's wages. The breakdown of working-class marriages
was quite public because a wife's only recourse, however rare, was
the courts and charities. Middle-class people then, as now, were more
capable of hiding their troubles because they could draw on greater
family resources (Bradbury 1996: 73).

In tandem with the increasing significance of the family sphere,
the myth of the family grew. This myth promotes a particular kind
of family: the nuclear family. There is actually no consensus on what
constitutes "the family," certainly in terms of the reality of family
life in Canada. "The family" is a way of thinking charged with moral
overtones, one known as "familialism." That means that the family
is often assumed to be a heterosexual couple with a male head of the
household who enjoys power and authority over his wife and children
(Luxton 1988). Lynn and O'Neill assert that children are considered
to belong to their parents; they are subject to their parents' authority.
In fact, "[p]hysical abuse of children is not considered assault if done
by parents" (1995: 277). The fact that loving relations are increasingly difficult to obtain outside of family relations as people move

from place to place and job to job strengthens the ideas of the family and makes people cling to the family more tenaciously than they might otherwise do. Because this exclusivity and tenacity undermine the potential for community-based love and caring, the result is that the family becomes more prone to conflict and violence and, at the same time, more resistant to admitting to such problems (Luxton 1988).

Another element that contributes to the myth of the family is our determination to cling to the notion of privacy. Such intransigence is one reason family violence ends up being tolerated to some degree. It is also why it might arise. The argument is that the family is considered a private sphere, a place where public officials dare not trespass. People are afraid to interfere. Privacy is considered sacred. When this is coupled with the idea of the nuclear family, we have a dangerous situation. If men are supreme heads and women and children are their property and under their power and authority, and if we believe that public officials have no right to poke their nose into the family without invitation, then we have a situation where abusive relations can go on virtually unchecked. Social control, for example, through community disapproval, will be ineffectual to a great extent because it will not be able to reach the individuals in question. Therefore, we must rely on individual self-control, a shaky proposition at best in light of the many stresses and strains of modern life.

Liberalism and democracy have fused together in western thought to form a unified way of thinking. It is the foundation for the Canadian way of life, from the way that governments legislate to how men and women comprehend their day-to-day lives. This fused set of ideas has an enormous influence on the emergence of violence within the family context and on the manner in which family violence is treated both publicly and privately.

The Liberal Democratic Perspective

Liberal democracy is the philosophy that accompanies capitalism. Many argue that liberal democracy *justifies* capitalism as an economic system. As a way of thinking, it has shaped our Canadian context in profound ways. Liberal democratic principles hold that people have choices and equality; they also emphasize the individual over society (Himelfarb and Richardson 1991: 81). Freedom is also a key component of liberalism. We are imbued with notions of equality and freedom, and, more importantly, the goodness and rightness of such notions, to the point where it becomes difficult to see the harm such notions can bring to ourselves and our social relations.

The ethos of competition is endemic to liberal democracy (see O'Neill 1994). It is premised on the notion that everyone is equal and thus has equal capacity to compete for scarce resources. "Scarce resources" is another idea fundamental to liberal democracy. It proposes that things that are most sought after are finite in nature; they are limited — therefore, some people will enjoy them while others will not. People must compete with one another to obtain the things that they desire; if they do not, they must not expect to have them. This is referred to as "zero-sum" competition: what one individual acquires is at the expense of others. People must take what they desire before someone takes it from them. It is apparent how this type of ethos decreases the importance of social ties and social responsibility.

What may not be quite so evident is how such an ethos may influence family ties. As another type of social tie, the belief in zero-sum competition for scarce resources has the same effect on family relations. It is unrealistic to think that people learn a set of social values regarding how they should behave in the public sphere but that they are somehow able to shed these values the moment they walk into their homes and begin to interact with their families. Members of families must not only compete outside the family, they must also compete within the family. Furthermore, family ties may actually impair their ability to compete for scarce resources outside the unit, so the importance of such ties may diminish. For example, within the family, members may compete against one another for love, attention, approval or material goods (as in sibling rivalry); parents may struggle against each other to ensure that they are obtaining all to which they feel entitled. Such struggle and competition against kin and loved ones may decrease the sense of connection they feel towards each other. As self-interest gains priority over family bonds, family members might find it easier to engage in conflict and might violently abuse one another.

Furthermore, Kaufman (1987) asserts that the economic rationality that accompanies capitalism does violence to (male) workers as they become mere extensions of machines. In addition, workers are often exposed to dangerous chemicals and substances and to physical harm. Not "violent" in conventional terms, this type of exposure is still an abuse against workers whose health may be severely damaged. Dangerous jobs may result in the ultimate abuse: death of the worker. The logic of this argument is that, violated at their place of employment, men internalize this violation; they then go on to violate others, including those whom they love.

Liberalism also presupposes that individuals are "disembodied, degendered and defamilied" (O'Neill 1994: 41). In other words, individuals are regarded as atomistic units, without deep-seated ties to anyone or anything, and are somehow able to disengage themselves from their sense of being male or female. According to this assumption, human beings are free-floating, attaching themselves to someone or something only so long as it serves their interest, moving on when it no longer fulfils that function. This sort of ideational position contributes to the common belief that, when family relations become abusive, the one being abused should simply leave. These ideas fly in the face of the reality that women, children and the elderly have very little recourse to such an action. Even if these people, often the ones who are abused in situations of family violence, had the material resources to leave the family, what is not taken into consideration is the fact that they have emotional ties that bind them to their abusers. Or they have profound moral beliefs in gender roles, family life and kinship ties that do not allow them to simply leave. Therefore, it could be argued that liberal democratic theory also presupposes that individuals are without feelings or desensitized.

Liberal democratic beliefs structure our society, our experiences and, perhaps most significantly, our thoughts. They engender a way of thinking that frames our view of society and how it operates and that provides ways of understanding our experiences. When we believe that experience is underscored by the need to compete for resources that are finite in nature and must be grasped quickly and decisively before someone else takes them from us, conflict becomes a way of life and a way of comprehension. When this sense of constant struggle is joined with notions of freedom of choice and equality of opportunity for all, then it is possible for family violence to become entrenched. That is, violence appears in relationships but it becomes trivialized as a matter of individual "choice" (of action and tolerance) and "equality" (in terms of who hits whom). In this way, people who remain in relations characterized by violence do so because it is their "choice." Men who display violent behaviour are excused, to some extent, because there are cases where women are violent as well; this is construed as some sort of "equality," which implies that violence is not a serious public issue. Entrenchment makes it quite difficult to envisage violence in the family as a social problem that concerns every member of society. It becomes hard to view family violence as an issue relating to social context rather than idiosyncratic tendencies. It becomes easier, however, to be insensitive to the pervasiveness of its harmful effects and simply retreat into a disgusted kind of blindness.

Liberal democratic principles are shaped by patriarchy and, in turn, help to shape the way that patriarchy manifests itself in Canadian society. Patriarchy is indeed a way of thinking but, more significantly, it is a structure that pervades the social milieu. Many people are aware of the overt effects of patriarchy but they are frequently blind to its more insidious covert aspects.

Patriarchy

Patriarchy is so deeply engrained in Canadian society that it is readily overlooked. Not only does patriarchy mean that males are privileged and dominant, it also means that males occupy the upper levels of the public offices that control and deal with family violence. It is a hierarchical system that often puts women and children in the hands of men. According to many analysts, it is not possible to understand family violence without a comprehensive understanding of patriarchy as well.

Patriarchy, of course, has a long history, far too long to chronicle here.[1] Family violence has a similarly long history. Their histories are united in the longstanding moral obligation of men, as commanded by the Church, to ensure that their wives and children behave themselves properly. Male violence may be legitimately employed to ensure such behaviour. It is the patriarch's Christian duty to "save their souls." Thus, violence against women and children was sanctioned by important social institutions and fortified by dominant ways of thinking (Lynn and O'Neill 1995).

Accompanying this sanction to control women and children through violence is the socially constructed definition of masculinity in terms of power and domination. Men are "supposed to" be the strong ones, the ones who go out into the social jungle and conquer the enemy (usually other men), thus protecting their dependent wives and children and providing for their needs. Pleck argues that "men's social identity is defined by the power they have over women and the power they can compete for against other men. But at another level, most men have very little power over their own lives" (1995

[1974]: 10). His position is based on the idea that masculinity has, over the years, become equated with the breadwinner role. This equation has meant substantively that, because men generally get little psychological return from the work that they do, they trade their job satisfaction for satisfaction with their masculinity. Men gain a sense of privilege and power having women wholly or partially dependent on them economically and a sense of pride in not having to do "women's work" in the domestic sphere (that is, not having to do unpaid work). This portrait of hegemonic masculinity (which will later be discussed in greater detail) demonstrates that patriarchy is not just an attitude, but the structuring agent for ideas about gender. Patriarchy structures these ideas concerning gender in such a fashion that a particular way of being male is held up as being the definitive masculinity; only this way of being male is socially rewarded, while other ways are denigrated. The form of masculinity that enjoys hegemony is the one which fits the contemporary needs of the social order. At this historical moment, the social order requires unemotional, rational, competitive workers for corporations and aggressive, obedient, hierarchically oriented soldiers for armies; therefore, these are qualities that are given priority in hegemonic masculinity.

Patriarchy also establishes a basis whereby men come to believe that they are the foundation of the family and, therefore, have a right to exercise their power over it. Violence is a byproduct of such a family system. Men are charged with the responsibility of maintaining the unit economically. Hegemonic masculinity ensures that they take measure of their masculinity in this way. This makes masculinity a precarious situation that can be easily threatened (see Conway 1993).

Another unfortunate aspect of such ideas about gender is that many men are reluctant to face the fact of family violence. Perpetrators, as well as some men who are not abusers themselves, deny responsibility, personally and collectively, for this brutalization (see Kuypers 1992). Their reluctance stems from at least two sources: first, because men are in charge of society, due to patriarchy, the subject of family violence is extremely sensitive, handled usually in a particular fashion. Shame plays a role in maintaining this silence and avoidance of responsibility. Second, boys also experience abuse in various forms from other males. Because being a victim is not consistent with the idealized masculine role, it is difficult for men to admit having endured violence and domination. Women assist in the preservation of patriarchy as well as men. Many women are just as

reluctant as men to face the realities of violence in the family (Lynn
and O'Neill 1995). The unwillingness of women may stem from
similar sources as that of men: dependency upon men means that
many women will not wish to examine too deeply the truth about
men and violence for fear that they will have to face the possibility
of being in danger in their own intimate relations. And, those who
are victims of abuse are ashamed to admit that their family relations
do not live up to the ideal.

Finally, it should be mentioned that there is also a myth in our
society concerning control: people are expected to exercise control
over themselves and their own destinies. If they fail to do so, they
are often blamed for whatever happens to them. Such a characterization is common in cases of woman abuse, for example. The
belief that we should be able to control ourselves and what happens
to us can make it difficult for us to recognize the multidimensional
nature of family violence. In the alternative, having the sense that we
are in control of our lives can help us deal with almost any situation.
Podnieks (1992) discovered in her interviews of elderly women who
had been abused that, even if they chose to remain in their abusive
situations, feeling that they were in control of their lives and could
make their own decisions was empowering. They felt a degree of
satisfaction because they were able to choose their own destinies to
some extent.

These are just some of the prevailing myths in Canadian society
that are pertinent to family conflict and violence. Each one of them
has an important role to play in setting the context for family violence; together they create powerful conditions for relationships between family members to lead to violence. Such myths are neither
random nor purely arbitrary. Rather, they are rooted in reality as
structures of power in society which privilege some individuals and
situations over others. They are powerful forces; many people support some of them, even when they are contrary to their true interests,
while attacking others which may serve them better. Myths also
create foundations upon which identities are formed. Individuals
internalize these myths as ideals, which help to form their motivations for behaviour and become their justifications for what they do.

There has been a long history of violence in the family, violence
which was largely tolerated because of the lack of power of women
and children. This was so until the late 1960s, when the power
balance began to shift with the rise of the civil rights and women's
movements and eventually the children's rights movement. As these

groups made headway, their views gaining more and more acceptance in society, alternative ways of thinking became more prominent. Feminists are largely responsible for putting family violence
on the public agenda and changing the consciousness of the general
population. This shift has been accompanied by changes in definitions of family violence. Now spanking children, which once was
normative, is debatably considered a form of child abuse. It has been
defined by many as violence against children and, therefore, inex-
cusable as a form of discipline. One of the ways in which definitions
are changed and promoted to the general population is through the
various mass media.

The Role of the Media

The role of the media is central to the debate over ways of thinking
because, for the most part, what is conveyed through the media is
generally the most conservative of these ways of thinking, those that
attempt to preserve the status quo. However, as groups with alternative ideas gain more power and power relations shift, they are more
able to gain some access to media and, hence, to people's consciousness.

Furthermore, the mass media not only play an important role in
the promotion of dominant myths but also in the conceptualization
of "social problems." A social problem does not spring forth full-
blown onto the centre stage of media reports. Rather, the media give
the problem its shape and content.

There are many social-problems-in-the-making at any given time.
Few of these, however, make it to the front page of the newspaper
or the top of the news program on television or radio because members of the media can only highlight a limited number of them. Most
receive intense, but short-lived, coverage and then pass into the
dreaded zone of old news. A few manage to remain in the spotlight
for extended periods of time, constantly being redefined and recast
over time. In order to remain in the public eye, these stories must
promote easy identification for audiences.

Media characterizations of family violence tend to rely on "common family experience" to tap the emotional sensibilities of their
consumers. They take actions out of context, truncate interactions so
that consumers get only a fragment of the interaction and not the
sequence of interactions which led up to the situation. Since the
contexts tend to be private, media must rely on external sources, such

as social workers, police officers and court officials. The myth of journalism is that only the objective facts are presented, without any kind of subjective undertones. However, the exigencies of capitalism are such that the most dramatic examples of abuse will be covered in the media since they generate the most sales. This coverage makes it seem as if these extreme cases are the norm. Hence, the result is sensationalization of both the cases and the social problem itself. Further, the media almost invariably point to "personal responsibility" of the individuals involved in family violence. That is, they tend to ignore or downplay social factors and strongly imply that abuse can be reduced to personal choice and culpability (Johnson 1989; Voumuakis and Ericson 1984).

There are programs on our television sets that show how damaging family violence can be and the terrible toll it can take on human lives. However, in these instances as well, the media still tend to preserve the status quo by presenting the most sensational cases as the basis for human interest stories. Once again, the tendency is to suggest that violence in the family is due to individual or family-specific pathologies and that the victims are individuals or particular families rather than society as a whole. This once again trivializes family violence and makes it seem that it is not a social problem but a psychological or, at best, a kinship-relations problem. The media in this way continue to divert the popular consciousness away from the larger social context of violence and its connection with what goes on in families (that is, the effects of violence on families). People continue to believe that family violence happens only to others, that it has nothing to do with the configuration of the family in our society, that it does not relate to structured power differentials within social relationships.

The effect of the media is to segregate perpetrators in the popular imagination, and so, as in ancient times with lepers, those who are segregated appear to deserve it because there is something wrong with them (see Foucault 1979: Chapter 3). This means that the general population does not feel it needs to take responsibility for family violence. It is "their" problem, "they're" sick or "they" need to be taken care of either by psychiatrists, police or prisons. It is not "our" problem. Family violence doesn't have anything to do with "us."

Thus, the role of the media is of enormous importance in terms of family conflict and violence. The media have the power to shape the issue and to shape the consciousness of Canadians. By sensationalizing and trivializing cases of abuse, the media create a segmented public vision of victims and perpetrators, conjuring up notions of an "us/them" polarization; they are then able to push "them" to the periphery of public consciousness and dismiss these people as pathological. In this way, the social nature of the act is ignored. Similarly, by taking acts of violence within the family out of context and out of their interactional sequence, the media are able to generate big "news" without disturbing the status quo *vis-à-vis* power relations.

Psychological, Sociological and Feminist Theories

While enormous strides have been made in researching the dimensions and patterns of family violence, theoretical explanations are still in the early stages of development. In the rest of this chapter, we outline the broad parameters of the three major approaches: psychological/social psychological, sociological and feminist. While efforts will be made to identify the distinguishing characteristics of each of these approaches, there will be overlap between them. The same or similar arguments often appear in several different perspectives and frequently theorists (analysts) acknowledge the value of at least some aspect of a competing approach. Indeed, it is often difficult to fairly determine which category best represents the work discussed since there are certainly feminist psychologists and sociologists as well as feminists who employ psychological and sociological methodologies (Yllo 1993: 48). At the same time, there is also considerable direct disagreement and rancor between advocates of diverse perspectives as they struggle for recognition and dominance in identifying the roots of (and, therefore, the solutions to) family violence.

A diverse and rapidly expanding literature is emerging that attempts to explain violence in the family. Some of this literature has been developed by clinicians working with abusers and attempting to eliminate certain behaviours. Much has been articulated by feminist activists and researchers working with victims of abuse. Finally, sociologists have been developing their explanations in the rapidly growing literature on family violence. The following overview gives an introduction to some of the major theoretical approaches being used in the field of family violence.

Why Do Men Batter?

Psychological[2] and Social Psychological Explanations

Not surprisingly, much of the early thought on abusive males came from a psychological, even a psychiatric, perspective. The emphasis was on explaining why these particular men were pathologically violent or prone to behaviour problems such as alcohol and drug addiction. The focus was on how their personalities differed from "normal" men and on disturbances in their early upbringing — domineering and rejecting mothers, distant and ineffectual fathers and so on. The solution was some form of psychotherapeutic intervention.

More recent advances in social psychological theorizing about abusive men have placed more of the onus on the social roots and connections. In this approach, abusers are still separated from "normal males." Donald G. Dutton, a British Columbia psychologist who is one of the leading authorities on the psychology of abusers, argues, for example, "most men remain nonviolent toward intimate female partners over the course of their lifetime" (1995a: 17). He also suggests, as do other analysts, that batterers are not a homogeneous group and that some are indeed psychopathic (1995a: 25; 1995b: 120-60). These "psychopathic batterers" exhibit no pangs of remorse for their brutal attacks and are cool and composed in the midst of vicious and violent assaults. Indeed, these men are so psychologically flawed, their violence is generalized as antisocial behaviour and they are extremely difficult to treat. The relatively more common "cyclical abusers" are the focus of Dutton's work and their violence, he argues, is treatable (1995a).

In Dutton's analysis, the batterer's violence towards his partner is traced back, in part, to shaming and rejecting fathers. He writes that "if I had to pick a single parental action that generated abusiveness in men, I would say it's being shamed by their fathers" (1995a: 83). Ambivalent and angry mothers are also implicated. The abuser's mother, according to Dutton, mixes rejection and affection in a manner which leaves him as an adult drawn to and fearful of women (1995a: 106). The solution is to create a therapeutic context in which abusers may understand and come to terms with these patterns of responding and relating and create new behavioural alternatives. For example, by working on managing anger, the abuser learns to be more sensitive to his own inner world of feelings and desires and to articulate these feelings rather than suppressing them. In group sessions, he charts his anger in a diary, examines each episode to discover the trigger, learns to recognize the physical reactions and inner dialogue ("the bitch tape") that escalate the anger and learns to "talk down" the anger and soothe himself (1995a: 170).

This theoretical perspective and its therapeutic approaches is currently preeminent in efforts to understand the abuser's psychology and to provide appropriate counselling. It is important to distinguish this approach from others but to also note that there are linkages. The focus here is clearly on the individual male and on the personal/familial roots of his actions. In particular, the key premise is that his behaviour is not "normal" and only through counselling and therapy can it be brought into more normal parameters. However, this psychopathological framework does not completely ignore the sociocultural environment which makes the creation of violent men more likely, which establishes a social context (the privacy of the family) in which this violence may be displayed and which makes women (and children) the likely victims of this violence. In Dutton's work, for example, there is considerable recognition that abusers' actions are often, at least partially, rooted in "normal" social experiences and normal patterns of behaviour in Canadian society. For example, he notes that male gender socialization normally sets men up for emotional insensitivity and mother(woman)-blaming, which may become key ingredients in abusive episodes (1995a: 44, 88, 120-22). Alcohol is a socially acceptable way in which the abuser can suppress his uncomfortable feelings and a socially legitimate rationale for "losing it" (1995a: 54). Dutton also acknowledges that society provides both "negative attitudes towards women" and "an acceptance of violence as a means of resolving violence" (1995a: 121). Finally, Dutton and others working from a social psychological perspective often incorporate a social learning approach pointing out that abusers often grow up in a violent home, particularly where the father abuses the mother (1995a: 123).

Ultimately, however, Dutton and other psychologists argue that the emphasis must be primarily on the etiology of personal pathologies in the individual abuser. They seek to tease out the complex relationships between early childhood experiences and later acts of violence. They are quick to point out, for example, that most boys, regardless of male socialization patterns do not become abusers, that even boys with violent male role models typically do not grow up to abuse their wives and that females, despite their female socialization and societal subordination, do sometimes abuse their partners in lesbian relationships. The answers to these complexities, they argue, lie not so much in history, social institutions and dominant ideologies as in the psyches of the abusers.

Sociological Theories

Sociological theories have several distinguishing characteristics. First, American sociologists have tended to approach the basic question Why is there violence between intimates in families? in gender-neutral terms. Secondly, since they examine the societal roots of abuse and the connections between family violence and social institutions, sociologists often explicitly reject the psychological and pathological model. Richard Gelles, who, along with Murray Straus, pioneered American research on family violence, points out, for example, that psychological defects (such as mental illness) and psychological explanations cannot account for 90 percent of abusive family incidents (Gelles 1993: 41). Thirdly, some sociologists have distanced themselves from feminist analysis. Gelles, for example, acknowledges the value of feminist insights but argues that ultimately the framework must be rejected on the grounds that it focuses too narrowly on violence towards women and has little useful insight into child, elder or sibling abuse or abuse by women (1993: 42-43). Similarly, Canadian sociologist Mark Liddle argues that feminists, while making valuable contributions to our understanding of violence against women, are now bogged down by unclear conceptualizations of violence (and related terms) and by a failure to examine the implications of the heterogenity of masculinities; that is, that not all men are violent and not all men support violence against women (1989).

These distinctions between the sociological, psychological and feminist perspectives appear to be particularly prominent in American sociology. Canadian sociologists, while rejecting psychological explanations, often focus on gender analysis and frequently explicitly identify themselves as working from a feminist perpective. As a result, the line between Canadian sociological and feminist theorizing is less clear.[3] However, Canadian work is often influenced by or responding to American sociological theories, and it is therefore important to outline some of the main developments in the United States.

In seeking to create explanations for intimate violence, sociologists have employed some of the basic theoretical orientations in sociology — socialization, systems theory, conflict theory, subculture analysis and so on. Most closely associated with social psychology and one of the intuitively most obvious explanations of wife abuse is the theory that abusers (and their victims) are socialized into violence in their family of origin. According to this *cycle of violence* or *social learning* approach, abusers learn from watching their fathers that violence is an appropriate and acceptable method of asserting their will in the home. Similarly, girls who witness abuse of their mothers may be learning to expect and accept the violence.

It is not surprising that this perspective has become popular. Unfortunately, it is at best only a partial explanation of violence against women in intimate relations. While it makes a great deal of intuitive sense, analysts must still account for two key research findings. First, as indicated in the Canadian Violence Against Women Survey (CVAWS), the majority of abusive men did not witness violence in their family of origin and secondly, the majority of men who did witness violence do not behave in a violent manner towards their wives (Johnson 1996: 177; see also, Gelles and Cornell 1990: 76). The relationship between violence in childhood and adult use of violence is clearly a complex phenomenon that implicates institutions far beyond one's family.

Sociologists have gone beyond these social psychological perspectives and suggested that socialization into subcultural patterns of values helps explain some of the complexities and inconsistencies in wife abuse. For example, the frequently repeated finding that abusive men are more likely to come from the lower socioeconomic ranks has led some analysts to argue that one key to understanding the batterer is the *patriarchal subculture of violence* amongst working-class males (Smith 1990a; 1990b; Hotaling and Sugarman 1986; Gelles 1993). Smith found that there was indeed a relationship between wives' reports of their husbands' adherence to traditional patriarchal ideology, attitudes supportive of wife-beating and actual violence. For example, men who were violent towards their wives were more likely to agree with this statement: "Sometimes it is important for a man to show his wife/partner that he is head of the house." The men who endorsed patriarchal and violent beliefs were also more likely to be unemployed and poorly educated, so there is the possibility of a connection between lower-class subcultural values and violent behaviour. Some analysts suggest that since "lower-class" men experience limited power and authority in the public domain they embrace values that legitimate their control and primacy in the home (Messerschmidt 1993). However, this relationship between social class, subcultural values and violence is complex and far from fully understood since many men (as evident in Smith's research) who are poor, unemployed and non-violent adhere to traditional patriachal ideas and yet are nonviolent.

Canadian sociologists Lupri, Grandin and Brinkerhoff recently reexamined the proposed link between socioeconomic status (SES) and wife abuse. Using male self-reports from a representative national sample of males eighteen years of age and older, their findings raised questions about the notion that wife abuse is particularly common amongst working-class men. In part, this reflects their methodological decision to focus on psychological abuse as much as physical violence. Since they found psychological violence is higher amongst men who are better educated, it is logical to assume that research based primarily or exclusively on physical manifestations of abuse will generate an inaccurate picture of the SES patterns of violence. When an operational definition of violence that includes physical, psychological and sexual abuse is used, the results suggest that chronic abuse is widespread and widely based throughout the social classes (1994: 62, 67).[4]

Finally, *sex role theory*[5] is also used to locate violence against women in society. Feminist sociologists point out that prevailing notions of masculinity and femininity generally mean that boys are brought up to be more aggressive, tough, competitive and unemotional, while girls are encouraged to be softer, more emotional and more passive. These gendered patterns of behaviour and emotionality tend to separate males and females and set them up for patterns of conflict and violence (Mackie 1991: 231-32). Recent research into male socialization and masculinity suggests that it is not simply the direct social messages supporting violence, aggression or sexism which are relevant but also the lack of clarity and security about male identity (Thorne-Finch 1992; Kuypers 1992).

In contrast to these individual-level theories, sociologists have also developed explanations that emphasize the institutional and societal levels of analysis. The general systems approach focuses on the family as a system of interrelated parts. This system is inherently subject to stresses and upset because of the intensity of the relationships, age and sex differences. Any number of probable factors such as pregnancy, childrearing, relations with extended family and family finances are likely to generate marital conflict. From this perspective, violence is then one of several strategies available to family members as they seek to deal with upheavals within the family system (or, presumably, as imposed by other social institutions, such as the economy or the education system).

Problems result when some family members in some families resort to violence as a strategy for coping with an upheaval. For example, unemployed parents may find their parental authority challenged by their employed teenage children. One mechanism for reestablishing the family system's status quo would be to use physical violence to reestablish control over the children. If this strategy is successful, that is, if there is positive feedback, then it is likely to be repeated (and vice versa) (Johnson 1996: 19-20; Gelles 1993).

This general systems approach is easily combined with the resource theory that states that those family members with considerable resources will have little need for violence to achieve dominance. However, when resources are absent or are removed, individuals may resort to other resources, such as physical violence (Gelles 1993). This theory is consistent with the view that levels of violence vary between social classes and various ethnic groups because of varying access to power resources (Johnson 1996: 18).

One of the other general trends in sociological thinking on woman abuse is the elaboration of typologies of batterers. American sociologists Finkelhor and Yllo, for example, proposed three types of marital rapes: battering rape in which the husband rapes the wife as part of a larger pattern of physical violence and abuse; force-only rape where there is little or no abuse, relative equality between the partners and only as much force as necessary to force sex; and obsessive rapes in which the male is bizarrely preoccupied with sex and pornography and the sex involves obsessive, sadistic practices (1985). More recently, Canadian sociologists Lupri, Grandin and Brinkerhoff proposed from their research that there are three types of wife abusers: silent attackers (who use physical but not emotional or psychological violence); threateners (who use a variety of psychological aggression but not physical violence); and severe abusers (who use both psychological and physical violence against their spouses) (1994: 58-59). These typologies are in their earliest stages of development,[6] particularly, in terms of explaining the social factors (social class, age and so on) which may account for differences amongst violent men. However, this line of analysis has important immediate implications. If abusers differ significantly from one another then it is unlikely that one course of remediation is useful for all. Since in each of the above examples (see also Dutton 1995a)[7] a significant minority of abusers are presented as characterized by severe psychiatric problems it follows that psychiatric/psychological explanations (and treatments) are at least partially endorsed.

Sociological theory can be justifiably credited with generating a rich variety of explanations for violence against women. And many of these theories have been incorporated into feminist analyses and have created a "wider explanatory framework" for psychological and social psychological explanations. However, by their very nature, these complex, multidimensional explanations have not been particularly helpful in identifying either therapeutic or policy directions (Gelles 1993: 43). For these and other reasons, feminists have cultivated an alternative perspective.

Feminist Theories[8]

According to feminist analysis, in patriarchal societies, every social relationship is conditioned by the pervasive inequality between men and women. Further, the function and structure of every social institution — from family to religious to political — are embedded not only in differences between men and women but in the dominance of men as a group over women as a group. The economy, for example, is dependent on women's "free" reproductive and productive work in the home. If women refused to do the bulk of the work (housework, childcare, emotional support), which daily and generationally prepares workers for employment, the economic system would grind to a halt. This inequality between men and women is understood as neither natural nor inevitable; it has evolved historically and currently serves the interests of many[9] men as well as those with power in society (Yllo 1993: 54). It is, however, susceptible to change and social action.

The feminist approach is also often distinguished by its methodological approaches. The research emphasis is on recording and accurately presenting the experiences of women. Often sociological (survey research) and psychological (clinical) research and theory are criticized for reinterpreting and re-victimizing battered women. For example, research that only tallies the number of physical blows or counts the number of victims fails to consider the effects on women, both as victims and as members of a society in which victimization of women is widespread. Similarly, research that relies on data about who hit whom and how often disregards the personal and societal context in which violence occurs (Johnson 1996). Feminist research is also constructed as advocacy work "for" women; that is, the goal is to work towards an end to both woman abuse and patriarchy, not simply an abstract advance in scientific knowledge (Bograd 1988).

Within these general parameters of feminist theory, there are significant divisions. Radical feminism, which has been deeply involved with the violence against women issue, emphasizes the role of patriarchy. From this vantage point, violence against women is embedded in every aspect of society and male-female interpersonal relations. Ending violence depends upon a societal transformation that will end male dominance. Socialist feminists, while in agreement with the need for a social revolution, emphasize the role of economic forces (notably capitalism) in disempowering women. As Coomaraswamy notes, for socialist feminists "violence is a result of economic exploitation and only secondarily a function of the male–female relationship" (1995: 19). Liberal feminists adopt a narrower view of the problem and advocate institutional (more shelters and so on) rather than systemic change. Lastly, ecofeminism links violence against women with the general patterns of exploitation and destruction of the natural order endemic to the military industrial complex that currently dominates the world order (1995: 20). Each of these perspectives is an important aspect of contemporary feminist theory. Although we refer to feminism as a generic category, we recognize that within feminist theory there is a rich diversity of perspectives.

By the 1980s feminists, particularly radical feminists in the shelter movement, had developed their major theoretical initiative: the *power and control approach* to family violence (MacLeod 1994). According to this perspective, male violence in the family must be located in the larger context of male power both within the family and in the larger society. When men use violence they do so knowing that they live in a society in which violence against women — in the form of sexual assault, sexual harassment, wife battering — is part of the taken-for-granted reality that spans the generations. They do so knowing that the societal response, including the criminal justice response, is one which often blames the victim for the violence and which frequently treats the victimizer leniently.

Conversely, women's response to male violence must also be located in these societal patterns of power and control. A woman does not react solely to the specific violent incident; she responds in the context of a lifetime of relevant experiences — a friend who is sexually harassed at work, a cousin who was the victim of date rape, media images of male violence and so on. His aggression and violence along with her fear and hopelessness cannot be understood outside the context of their gendered experiences of violence and power.

According to feminist theories, both within the family and in the larger social order, men use violence as a strategy for male control. For example, sexual harassment keeps many women out of certain sectors of employment and establishes these sectors as distinctly male. The Canadian and American military have been repeatedly criticized for turning a blind eye to female sexual harassment. For example, in 1992, sexual harassment forced Cpl. Glenda Grenier to quit the Canadian Armed Forces. After ten years of service, she could no longer endure the sexist slurs, comments and harassment as well as the lack of official support in combatting the problem.

Domestic violence is a comparable "control tactic" within the family. According to the Domestic Abuse Intervention Project of Duluth, Minnesota, physical and sexual violence can be conceptualized as a wheel in which the spokes (intimidation, isolation, emotional abuse, threatening or co-opting the children, economic abuse, coercion and threats, male privilege and minimimizing, denying and blaming) all serve to connect violence to its hub of power and control (Yllo 1993: 54-55). According to this feminist framework, men do not use violence because they disagree with their wives or because their wives are too demanding or the men are feeling stressed; rather, men want to dominate and control women. Growing up and living under patriarchy, men have been conditioned to believe that this is both right and appropriate. Physical and sexual violence can be used to achieve control of women.[10]

One of the more recent feminist theories on violence is Dee Graham's societal Stockholm syndrome (1994). The original thesis of the Stockholm syndrome originated in 1972 to explain the surprising reactions of four bank employees held hostage by two ex-convicts. Despite the fact that the ex-convicts endangered the hostages' lives, the hostages seemed to bond with their captors. As Graham explains, it seems from this and other hostage incidents that four elements set the stage for this unexpected sense of community between captors and their captives: a perceived threat to one's life, some expression of kindness by the captors, isolation from perspectives other than the captors' and perceived absence of escape possibilities.

Graham applies the theory to women. She argues that women in general are subject to the Stockholm syndrome. First, all women, whether they are directly victimized by violence or not, are conditioned by the knowledge and fear of male violence. Researchers have extensively documented the fact that women, more than men, express fearfulness about violence. For example, the CVAWS found that 60 percent of Canadian women reported they felt worried about their personal safety when walking alone in their area after dark (Statistics Canada 1993: 8). Despite the fact that men are much more likely to be the victims of violence committed by a stranger, it is women who express fear (Maxim and Keane 1992). Secondly, Graham points out that men as a group are socialized to perform specific ritualized expressions of kindness (chivalry, opening doors, "placing women on a pedestal"). Thirdly, she argues that the male perspective and male dominance in society (such as male-premised religious ideologies) are part of normal female socialization. As a result, women (and men) have difficulty conceiving of a world in which their lives are not structured by the possibility of male violence. Fourthly, women as individual victims of violence, such as victims of woman abuse, along with women as a group often define the violence as inevitable and inescapable.

In response to these four societal conditions, women as a group, Graham argues, respond in much the same fashion as the Stockholm hostages. Despite (or due to) their fear of violence, women adopt the psychology of subordinants by bonding to (becoming romantically attached to) men while often rejecting such perspectives as feminism that challenge male dominance. From Graham's theoretical position, women's stereotypic behaviour, for example, "femininity," is simply an expression of the psychological attributes that typically characterize subordinants such as members of minority racial/ethnic groups. Taking care of and being responsible for the emotional needs of the dominants and carefully attuning to their emotional state (feminine intuition and sensitivity) are, according to Graham, outgrowths of the societal Stockholm syndrome. "Being nice, caring, intuitive, sensitive and flexible help ensure that interactions of subordinants with dominants go smoothly" (1994: 191).

Feminists who use this approach understand woman abuse as one fragment of a larger overall pattern. All women bond with and adapt strategies to survive. Abused women's "bonding" with their abusers and their perception of violence as inescapable are simply part of a larger continuum of subordinate behaviour in which almost all women participate. Graham's provocative conclusion asks, "Could it be that all women in patriarchy are battered and that our feminity is both our strategy for surviving and proof of our oppression?" (1994: 197). From this perspective, violence and abuse against women must be understood as normal, not pathological, and as embedded in the social structure, not in individual psyches.

Why Do Abused Women Stay?

First and foremost, before addressing this issue, it should be noted that many feminists and social activists find this popular question inherently offensive. To them, it implies that somehow the victimized women are to blame for and should explain the violence. The implication is that by staying in the relationship after the first sign of psychological or physical violence, the woman herself is part of the problem, perhaps because she is abnormal (masochistic) or weak. Clearly, the popularity of this question is a classic example of victim-blaming.[11] Victims, aware of this public response, are inclined to blame themselves and to withdraw further. In very real terms, the question, if it implies a defect or weakness in women who stay in abusive relationships, serves to perpetuate the violence.

Furthermore, this line of inquiry is factually flawed because it assumes that, by leaving, the woman can end the violence and abuse. As noted in Chapter 2, almost half of abuse victims do leave. However, many discover that leaving, or even threatening to leave, escalates rather than ends the violence. The CVAWS reports that for about one-fifth of abused women the violence and intimidation continued after separation and of those cases about one-third experienced an escalation in the abuse (Johnson 1996: 170). Indeed, evidence suggests that abused women who leave may be particularly at risk of lethal violence. Wilson and Daly report that married women who separated from their husbands had murder rates three times higher than women who were living with their husbands (1994: 7).[12]

With these facts in mind, we can examine the literature from the victim's perspective. Analysts have in fact much to tell us about why women stay, and the answers are helpful not only in understanding the violence but also in articulating useful responses.

Psychological and Social Psychological Explanations

As with psychological and psychiatric approaches to the batterer, there are analyses that explain the abuse of the victim in terms of the victim's self-esteem issues, dependency needs, depression and anxiety. The notion that abused women are masochistic, that is, that they desire to be physically abused and derive pleasure from it, has enjoyed some popularity (Gelles and Cornell 1990: 72-74). However, these psychological assessments have been subject to thorough critiques and are today less popular as explanations of abused women's actions (Caplan 1985).

One of the most prominent psychologists working in this area is Leonore Walker, who clearly treads the line between feminist and psychological perspectives. In the 1970s, she first suggested that abused women's actions are conditioned by the particular psychological dynamic in abusive relationships. The relationship, she argued, tends to follow a *cycle of abuse* in which an episode of violence is followed by a honeymoon stage wherein the abuser apologizes for his violent behaviour and makes promises to reform. This period gradually (or quickly) gives way to a period of mounting tensions, which ultimately produces another violent episode. The cycle then repeats itself. The result, according to Walker, creates a psychological condition of *learned helplessness* in the abuse victims. Much like experimental animals who are subject to unpredictable patterns of reward and punishment, the women face an uncontrollable pattern of violence. As a result, victims become personally disorganized, depressed and unable to effect change (Walker 1979, 1993).

The sociopsychological notion of *traumatic bonding* as developed by Painter and Dutton (1985) paints a similar picture. They argue that relationships between batterer and victim (or hostage/captor, abused child/abusing parent) are characterized by two traits: a power imbalance and intermittent (perhaps, cyclical) abuse. These kinds of relations produce a contradictory sense of helplessness and potency. The victim may feel powerless to leave the relationship yet may also feel that she, in some sense, causes the violence and, therefore, by changing her behaviour can control it. Together these psychological dimensions lock victim and victimizer together.

Some feminist activists are embracing these and other psychological perspectives on woman abuse. For example, Marilyn Goodman, who works in a Rhode Island shelter for women, rejects the "male-dominated society" approach as too simplistic and argues that a more psychological strategy is appropriate. She believes that when a woman is unable to leave an abuser or has a series of abusive relationships she must be recognized as having a problem of her own. While she is not responsible for the violence against her, Goodman argues that a dysfunctional childhood is likely to blame for the woman's vulnerability to violence. Needless to say, the solution she advocates entails considerable psychological counselling (1990).

Sociological Theories

Certainly, there are mainstream sociological approaches that have some applicability to the plight of women victims. For example, the CVWAS reported that the majority of women (70 percent) who left their abusive spouses returned at least once. Their reasons are a testimony to the traditional *sex role socialization* as well as the economic inequalities between men and women. The most frequently reported reason for returning was "for the sake of the children" (31 percent), followed by "wanting to give the relationship another try" (24 percent), the husband promised to change (17 percent) and lack of money or a place to go (9 percent) (Johnson 1996: 189). It certainly appears that the ideologies of maternalism and romance are alive and well and are a potent combination when linked to economic inequities.

Feminist Theories

Feminists, despite their well-founded critique of this type of question, have in fact provided considerable insight into the plight of abused women. As noted previously, they've drawn attention to the importance of recognizing the larger social context that conditions and informs women's responses to violence. Just as male violence is structured by societal patterns of male dominance, women act and react within the parameters constructed by their social realities. Rather than accepting[13] sociopsychological explanations (such as the cycle of violence and learned helplessness), which explain women's staying in terms of psychiatric defects, weakness or immaturity, feminists argue that women often stay or leave based on a rational evaluation of economic factors, the prospects of escape, the possibilities of support, the availability of alternative shelter and threats to other family members (Bowker 1993: 158-60). This perspective is more consistent with the experience of shelter workers who find that abused women often do not experience an intermittent cycle of abuse, but rather, state that the abuse is constant. It is more consistent with the feminist framework that is inclined to normalize rather than pathologize the violence and that focuses on the larger sociocultural context of abuse, "A woman's decision to stay appears to follow logically from power disparity and the cultural rules she has learned about marriage, the family and woman's role as traditionally defined" (Hoff 1994: 42; see also 32, 47).[14]

In recent years, feminist analysis has sought to more accurately and fully encompass the lives of diverse groups of women. In terms of violence against women, this has meant developing a *diversity approach* that focuses attention on the racial/ethnic, poor/wealthy, lesbian/straight, abled/other-abled, old/young, immigrant/native, rural/urban differences amongst women (Chalmers and Smith 1987; Stevens 1995; Boyce 1995; Murray and Welch 1995). Reflecting the double jeopardy of women who are lesbians, members of minority groups or other-abled, the violence they experience has often been essentially invisible and unrecorded (see, for example, Renzetti 1992). It is important not only to give voice to these women's experiences but also to understand the ways in which the social construction of their abuse differs from that of many other women.

Differences amongst women in Canada — for example, women who cannot speak English or French or who are poorly educated or who are subject to racism — have often meant that some women found it more difficult to challenge their relative powerlessness and dependency in an abusive relationship and to locate external sources of support. Minority group women may be accustomed to experiencing the police as a hostile community presence. The economic vulnerability of single mothers is heightened due to overt and covert discrimination in employment practices. Similarly, women who are geographically isolated may have greater difficulties ending the violence and escaping the relationship than urban women (Struthers 1994).

Aboriginal women's experience of incest reflects both the impact of sexual victimization and patterns specific to their lives as Native women. For example, they report, as do many adult survivors, that they feel guilty and shamed, vulnerable and fragmented. However, these feelings are intertwined with their experiences as Aboriginals. They grew up being devalued and belittled as "fat squaws" and "dirty Indians." Some, as a result, feel flawed from birth, believing that "they deserved to be abused." As children, they were aware of mainstream society's stereotypes of "dirty drunk Indians ... all sluts and bitches." It is difficult to disentangle the impact of these experiences of "feeling worthless and undeserving of help" from the shame inflicted by the abuse itself; the two coexist and support one another (McEvoy and Daniluk 1995). Understanding the abuse means examining the social and historical context in which it occurred.

Considerable recent research and analysis has also looked at lesbian battering. Abuse in lesbian relationships is conditioned by a homophobic societal context. Victims of lesbian battering may be loath to call upon the police and court systems, expecting both an unsympathetic hearing for themselves and an oppressive reaction to the assailant. Similarly, they may fear making the abuse public for fear of feeding into negative stereotypes of lesbians (Card 1995). In short, their experience of violence is conditioned by the broader social realities which they have encountered as lesbians (Murray and Welch 1995).

Other directions are also being explored in feminist analysis. Not surprisingly, some feminist theorizing is moving to a more complex and multifaceted approach. A recent example is the *feminist relational view of battering* laid out by Virginia Goldner, Peggy Penn, Marcia Sheinberg and Gillian Walker (1990). Their work seeks to integrate social learning, sociopolitical and systemic levels of analysis; in other words, they strive to create an analytical framework that is useful at the individual, interpersonal and societal levels. As one of the leading American feminists in the field, Kersti Yllo, comments, "These researchers are trying to explore the full subjective experience of batterers and the women they abuse without losing sight of male dominance in relationships and in society" (1993: 57).

According to the relational view, the individual roots of violence are laid by socialization patterns that establish both the social and personal differences between men and women and the inequalities between them. In the process, the separateness of men's and women's psychological and social worlds is established along with contradictory feelings about masculine and feminine identities. Men, for example, learn to repress their emotions (big boys don't cry) yet still seek emotional connection through love and sexuality. A man who comes from a family with deeply traditional gender norms may experience conflict over seeking emotional connection with a woman while still clinging to his sense of manliness. In this context, male violence against female intimate partners may hold two contradictory elements. The man may use the violence not only to establish control over the woman (the power and control paradigm) but also to diminish his fears and contradictory feelings about emotional connections with the "other" — the woman. Violence may be both a rational response to control this woman and limit her power over him and a regressive, emotional response ("losing it") to his panic over his masculine identity and gender insecurities.

The woman's role in the violent relationship is similarly constructed in the context of her female socialization. Her sense of self-worth and identity are likely moulded in terms of her ability to build and maintain the caregiver role (wife/mother). In other words, traditional socialization creates deeply personal structures in which dependency is central. When confronted with a controlling, abusive and violent male, the woman will find it difficult to "reclaim ... a sense of her independent subjectivity and establish ... or re-establish ... her capacity for agency in the world" (1990: 349). She will be subject not only to her own inner sense of her identity as a woman but also to the cultural messages that reinforce male dominance.

Gender socialization and gendered psychological structures are seen to be deeply embedded in societal structures that are constructed around and depend upon the gender schema of both difference and inequality. Indeed, the key social institutions (the economy, the family, the education system and the military) are premised on gendered social realities (the division of labour, occupational segregation and so on) and in this sense the social system itself rests firmly on a gendered foundation.

With these formulations, Goldner et al. (1990) are seeking to establish an analytical framework that does not pathologize or privatize the violence, that locates violence amidst the normal processes and structures of our society and that can move back and forth from the intimate, personal and therapeutic to the public, structural and social policy levels of analysis. Creating such a theoretical framework is crucial to developing appropriate therapeutic interventions, focused research questions and viable public actions or policies.

Why Do Parents Abuse Their Children?[15]

Mainstream Theories and Models

As public awareness of and academic interest in child abuse have grown exponentially in the last two decades so too have efforts to create explanations for abusive parents. The theoretical frameworks have tended to develop in response to two distinct interpretations of the question Why do parents abuse their children? Many mainstream analysts have developed theoretical formulations that target the implied question. Why do *certain* parents abuse their children? In this body of work, the emphasis has been on explaining the patterns of abuse; in particular, the greater reported rates of abuse in poor, single-parent, minority families. Other theorists have tackled a much more challenging and broadly framed issue: Why does our culture condone any violence and abuse against children? Rather than focusing on specific groups of families, these analysts question the normative patterns of childrearing in our society and call into question basic, cherished values. Typically working from a feminist or cultural perspective, their work is amongst the most contentious and unsettling to emerge from the family violence literature.

As with wife abuse, early theorizing drew heavily on a psychoanalytic or psychological perspective. Many analysts applied a *psychopathological explanation* to child abuse, arguing, for example, that abusers were suffering from depression, poor impulse control or some other mental disorder. However, the deluge of research in the past two decades has firmly established that psychological illness is of limited utility in explaining most violence against children; indeed, research has failed to document any consistent relationship between a specific psychological disorder and a particular type or expression of abuse. Most analysts today appear to agree that psychopathology explains a very small proportion (4 to 10 percent) of all maltreatment of children (Lenton 1990: 159; Gelles and Cornell 1990: 112). Consequently, theorizing has tended to move away from this individualistic approach.

Once again, one of the most popular approaches has been the *social learning theory*[16] (Swift 1995: 96). According to this perspective, children who grow up in a violent household learn to model the rage and violence that they witness (Tower 1996: 71). These childhood lessons include not only the use or non-use of violence in interpersonal relationships but also justifications for any use of violence. As Alice Miller comments, "The way we were treated as small children is the way we treat ourselves the rest of our life. And we often impose our most agonizing suffering on others" (Miller 1984: 133).

While the social learning perspective is appealing, it has its weaknesses. Specifically, some abusive parents (along with wife abusers or elder abusers) have not been abused as children and conversely, many victims of abuse do not grow up to be adults who use physical violence either in their marital or parental roles.[17] There are in all probability as many exceptions as there are one-to-one relationships.[18]

The social learning approach is strongly related to the *social-situational model* of child abuse. From this perspective, there are two main elements in the child abuse situation. One concerns the societal norms and values concerning violence, child discipline and childrearing that are learned at home. This factor intersects with the second: structural stress. Various families throughout society will be subject to diverse stresses such as economic deprivation, illness, divorce.

Families subject to considerable stresses such as poor families coping with marital and addiction problems and living in a culture that legitimizes disciplinary violence against children would be, according to this perspective, at greatly increased risk of child abuse.

The social-situational approach does allow for more complexity than social learning perspectives and seems to explain some of the variations amongst families in terms of reported abuse. However, the conceptualization of stress is difficult; not all families or most families on welfare physically abuse their children and while we tend not to hear as much about middle- and upper-class child abuse, we know from numerous celebrity cases[19] that it exists. One of the ground-breaking personal accounts of incest in Canada, Sylvia Fraser's *My Father's House*, locates the violence in a relatively comfortable middle-class world (1987). Perhaps stress, in the form of economic problems, marital difficulties or addiction, does figure in instances of child abuse amongst the middle-class and the well-off. However, such an amorphous concept provides little insight as to why severe abuse appears in some families subjected to stress and not in others.

James Garbarino's *ecological model* seeks to address precisely the complex interrelationship of factors that result in child abuse. Just as any organism must constantly adapt to numerous aspects of its environment, the family develops in the midst of a complex of neighbourhood/community, institutional and societal/historical relationships. As C. Wright Mills pointed out forty years ago, the individual must be viewed in a societal (the complex interplay of institutions such as the economy and the state) and historical (the legacy of beliefs, values, power structures that characterize our society) context. We recognize this interplay between the individual level of analysis and the societal level when we understand that many seemingly extraneous factors — an argument in the office, a sermon at church — may influence the ongoing development of our family life. Larger social events — a declaration of war, changes in economic policy — are likely to have an even greater impact on the day-to-day development of our family (Garbarino 1977).

Garbarino does not, however, suggest that all these influences are equally relevant to family violence. Rather he targets two *necessary* factors: ideological support for the use of physical force against children and inadequate social support systems for the family (1977: 728). If the family emerges in a social context that both legitimates the use of force in disciplining children and provides little support for the family, child abuse is likely. For example, if there are few quality daycare centres, if kinship connections are weak, if there is a lack of parent education, if social services are scarce or short-term, or if neighbourhoods are victims of social decay, high-risk (poor, stressed) families are at greater risk of child abuse. At the individual level, various *sufficient* factors such as parents under marital stress, struggling with addictions or dealing with an unwanted child may tip the balance in the creation of an abusive situation. However, in the absence of the *necessary* conditions noted above, these difficulties will not produce child abuse.

Garbarino's work has been particularly important[20] because it explicitly challenges the psychopathological approach and suggests that research must incorporate the complex interplay between individual, institutional and societal elements. This line of analysis is consistent with policy and practice that attacks the ideological foundations of abuse, that fosters community and neighbourhood development and that targets improved social services for the impoverished.

Feminist and Other Approaches

Each of the preceding perspectives, however helpful, appears to focus on variations in child abuse rates — particularly, why are poor and lower-class, Native or minority families more likely to abuse their children? As discussed previously, the research on this point remains problematic. Even nationally representative surveys based on self-reports, such as Gelles and Straus (1986), tend to define "severe abuse" in what is probably a class-specific fashion; that is, as "physical violence." The research record does seem to document that working-class families are often more likely to spank and physically discipline their children. They, along with minority families, are also more likely to be reported for neglect by social welfare agencies. However, as with patterns of wife abuse (Lupri, Grandin and Brinkerhoff 1994), middle- and upper-class families may be more inclined to use psychological forms of abuse. As pointed out by victims of wife battering, the humiliation, shame and denigration of psychological abuse may be at least as damaging as physical violence. Further, numerous analysts have made the point that poorer families are more subject to the scrutiny of welfare workers than well-off families. Finally, middle- and upper-class forms of parental neglect — sending children to boarding schools, summer camps and leaving them with an endless series of caregivers — are defined as socially legitimate actions. Mainstream theories may be seeking to explain differentials in child abuse that do not exist, are not significant or are more complex than currently acknowledged.

Feminist theory takes a much more comprehensive perspective on the issue of child abuse and seeks to answer the question Why does our society support the parental abuse and mistreatment of children at all?[21] As with wife/woman abuse, feminists identify patriarchy as the key ingredient. Patriarchal social structures presuppose notions of hierarchy (superiority and inferiority), of otherness (us and them) and power. Our first lessons in separating the world into dominant and subordinant parts (husband/wife; parent/child) are learned in the family as are the earliest lessons about power and control (Firestone 1973). Contemporary notions about parental authority and rights are rooted in the historical rights of men to own, control and discipline women and children. Patriarchal traditions mean that fathers have played the pivotal power role in the family. The adage "wait till your father gets home," with its implied threat that father will dispense final justice, speaks to both the power and control men have had in their families over the generations.

From the position that patriarchy is key to the organization and content of family life, explanations of specific aspects of child abuse follow. Neglect, for example, is part of the construction of women's impoverishment. Since neglect and poverty are complexly interlocked, it is not surprising that women, who are more likely than men to be single parents and poor, are more likely to be charged with neglect. The latest poverty statistics reveal striking male/female inequalities. Throughout their adult lives, women are typically more likely than men to be poor (National Council of Welfare 1997: 34). Women's vulnerability to poverty is further heightened if they become single mothers. In 1995, single-parent mothers under age sixty-five and with children under eighteen years of age had a poverty rate of 57.2 percent while only 12.6 percent of comparable couples were poor (1997: 17). When single motherhood is combined with youthfulness, the overwhelming result is poverty — the poverty rate amongst single mothers with children under seven is 82.8 percent (1997: 2).

Similarly, the physical and sexual abuse of children is conditioned by the male/female patterns. These forms of abuse are generated by the belief that children are the property of fathers and, secondarily, mothers. Given that men[22] are conceptualized as the sexual actors and dominators under patriarchy, it is to be expected that men will be most likely to undertake the sexual exploitation of children. Girls' early socialization to be obedient, pleasing to others and "attractive" sets them up for childhood sexual victimization.

Most feminist theorists do not, however, suggest that patriarchy translates into "the overwhelming majority of child abusers [being] male" as suggested by some analysts (Conway 1993: 81). While inequality between men and women sets the stage for child abuse, abuse does not necessarily or usually take the form of some threatened patriarch lashing out against challenges to his prerogatives. Rather, feminist analysis often acknowledges that mothers abuse their children, perhaps as much as fathers (Washburne 1983: 291). However, the societal sources of fathers' and mothers' violence against children differ. While fathers "batter their children because they have power," women batter "because they have little power" (Cole 1988: 523). It follows that women's violence against their children must be understood as an outgrowth of the basic inequalities between men and women.

We live in a society where women are expected (even required) to have children;[23] once a woman becomes a parent, it is she who is required to assume the primary caregiver role. This translates into educational, career and occupational choices that are sculpted to fit mothering responsibilities; it also often means reduced career choices and opportunities, restricted economic independence and limited pension funds. Despite these sacrifices, women still receive few social rewards for their efforts and little in the way of societal support for managing the process of parenting. Finally, despite much commentary on changes in the family, the division of domestic work, including childrearing, is still far from equally shared between the average husband and wife (Pupo 1997). It is this socially structured pattern of personal frustration, overwork and dependent vulnerability that sets many women up to be abusive. Some, of course, are lashing out at their children in response to their own victimization. Others, however, are expressing their alienation and misery by lashing out at the only available victim with less power than them (Cole 1988; Washburne 1983; Gelles and Straus 1986: 247-48).

It follows from feminist analysis that the ultimate solutions to child abuse hinge on revolutionary social change. The social order premised on inequalities between men and women and socially constructed male violence would need to be fundamentally altered. The change would be so profound that it is difficult to conceive of "family life" without the gendered inequalities currently taken for granted. Since the contemporary family is complexly interrelated to all other social institutions and their patterns of gender inequality, no aspect of social existence would be untouched. In the absence of such a transformation, feminist analysis suggests that men and women, for differing reasons, are "quite likely" to continue to abuse their children (Cole 1988: 530).

Feminist analysis does not stand alone in this general critique of our social structure and its implications for violence against children. Amongst the most influential criticisms has been the work of Alice Miller. Although for over twenty years Miller practised psychoanalysis, since 1979 she has developed a far-ranging sociological analysis of childrearing that challenges both psychoanalytic and mainstream approaches. Though she does not base her work in feminist writings, she joins feminists in arguing that child abuse is rooted in our historical traditions, endemic to our social structure, and that normal, average parents are likely to mistreat their children.

According to Miller, we are socialized into accepting a "poisonous pedagogy" in which as parents we come to believe (despite contradictory experiences as children) that as parents we have the right and responsibility to control and dominate our children. Consider, for example, the embarrassment and anger of parents whose young children are "acting up" and being disobedient in a public place. Children, for their part, are required to learn not only to accept but to value domination by parents as being in their "best interests." In this process, children learn to repress their true feelings and submit. While the product of such "cruel" childrearing practices may be functional to any social order dependent on an obedient, repressed citizenry, it is hardly functional to the children themselves, who are forced to give up their vitality, curiosity and exuburance. Further, Miller argues that such children will in all likelihood repeat the abusive pattern with their own offspring (Miller 1981; 1984).

Trocme's review of child abuse cases in Ontario tends to lend some credence to Miller's position. He found that 85 percent of substantiated physical abuse cases involved punishment or discipline-related issues (1994: 70). In other words, it appears that the perpetrators explained (or rationalized) their abusive behaviours as efforts to punish or discipline their children. Either significant numbers of parents cannot appropriately draw the line between physical abuse and good parenting or the line we, as a society, have established is murky at best. In this vein, it is also interesting to note that crosscultural comparisons of childrearing approaches reveals American practices to be amongst the most severe (Stephens 1963: 370-71).

It is, of course, the broadly framed perspectives such as Miller's and feminists that are the most challenging and, possibly, disheartening. These analyses suggest that the entire social order is in need of change. The task is certainly daunting and, many will argue, unnecessary. Advocates of social learning or psychological frameworks believe, for example, that counselling and treatment that specifically target offenders will eventually resolve the child abuse issue. However, from our perspective, the evidence of the last two decades suggests such narrowly conceptualized analyses cannot adequately account for the sheer volume of violence and abuse which is being made public. Many popular social commentators on family violence today argue that most[24] families are dysfunctional. If this is an accurate assessment, then the implication is that there must be something profoundly amiss in our society and our culture.

Why are Siblings, Adolescents, Parents and Elders Abused?

Although a number of theories have been advanced to explain violence in the family, these have limited value in accounting for sibling, adolescent, parent and elder abuse. They do, however, offer some insight into why these types of abuse exist and advance interpretations at both the individual and societal levels of analysis. Many of the former explanations stem from the symbolic interactionist, or social psychological, paradigm, which deals with such things as socialization, role-playing and personal interpretations.

Why Do Siblings Abuse One Another?

The foremost response to such a question is given by *social learning theory*: children have learned violence in their family. They may have witnessed this violence between their parents, or they may have experienced violence at the hands of their parents, or both parent/parent and parent/child relationships in their family might be characterized by abusive treatment. The violence children have experienced might even be something many people consider quite benign: spanking. In any case, through viewing and/or experiencing abusive relationships, children learn that family relations, which are supposedly loving relationships, may also be characterized by violence. Concomitantly, these children learn that resorting to violence is a way of dealing with conflict. An effective resolution for conflict involves hitting or verbally abusing the person with whom conflict is experienced. Therefore, when siblings interact and their interactions produce conflict, the children involved may resort to violent behaviours.

Feminist issues of power and control go hand-in-hand with the notion of learned violence in the family. It has been shown that generally it is one sibling who abuses another, not necessarily all siblings equally abusing each other. When one sibling is being abused by another, the victim may then go on to abuse another. There is also some suggestion in the literature that an abusing sibling may serially abuse others. At any rate, some studies have shown that a sibling becomes abusive to another in an effort to assert power and control over the sibling targetted for abuse. There may be jealousy between them; the abusing sibling may feel that the one she or he is victimizing is the child who is favoured by the parents. She or he cannot control her or his parents' emotions, and for that reason, the abuser may experience the desire to assert her or his authority over the favoured one in an attempt to gain a measure of control. Alternatively, it may be her or his own insecurity that drives a sibling to abuse another. The abuse, as a way of asserting power, may be a means to bolstering low self-esteem (Wiehe 1990).

According to *sex role theory*, gender socialization may play a role in sibling abuse. Since males are generally socialized to be the more powerful members of society, while females are generally taught to be submissive, a brother may abuse his sister, particularly when sexual abuse is involved, in order to actualize his socialization. In other words, he may try to act out the gender role he has been taught at the expense of his sister. This may be a form of rehearsal for anticipated adult relationships. He is learning to engage in dominance and control of women. He may also be mimicking the way he sees his father treating his mother.

In some cases, *social exchange/control theory* may apply: a sibling may abuse another, in effect, because she or he can get away with it. If parents have a benign view of sibling conflict and refuse to define abusive behaviour for what it is, the sibling may simply be allowed to get away with maltreatment of another.

To conclude, although there is no well-developed theory pertaining to sibling abuse, we can see that there are some at least tentative ways to explain such behaviour.

Why Do Parents Abuse Adolescents?

Typically child abuse declines as children get older largely due to the fact that the child develops in size and strength, so she or he can fight back, and also possibly because older children are more able to get away from their parents (Gelles and Cornell 1990; Steinmetz 1977). But this is not always the case. Abuse of children may continue even when they are well into adolescence. On the other hand, abuse may begin in adolescence due to the very peculiarities of the age (i.e., that teenagers are more rebellious against authority and likely to assert their independence from their parents) and, *because* they are bigger, parents feel the need to discipline more vigorously. Such discipline might result in violence because of the greater effort parents employ to control their teenagers. Also, the issue of adolescent sexuality, particularly female sexuality, may cause parents considerable anxiety. They may wish to exercise much greater control over female adolescents to keep them from engaging in sexual activities, which can lead to escalating levels of conflict and the use of violence.

Once again, many researchers propose that a history of violence in the family contributes to the phenomenon of adolescent abuse. *Resource theory* suggests that parents without adequate resources to deal with family conflict caused by both intrafamilial stresses and those external to the family, such as isolation or poverty, may find themselves abusive when faced with adolescents who are troublesome and questioning their authority. Resources, when already at a premium, and tested by greater demands from teenagers, may contribute to violent behaviour because parents are unable to cope.

Finally, it has been proposed by some researchers that, as they grow into adolescence, boys are more likely to be abused, even twice as likely. Higher levels of abuse may be due to the belief held by parents that they must treat their teenaged sons harshly in order to prepare them for the violence parents believe young men will encounter in their lives. This is known as *linkage theory* (Straus 1971). Such a theory, however, does not explain why adolescent girls would be the victims of parental violence at all. Neither does it deal with the fact that women are likely to experience violence as well, particularly sexual violence, in which case one would assume that parents desiring to prepare their offspring for adulthood would treat their teenaged daughters with the same degree of harshness. It is a very limited and weak explanatory model.

Why Do Children Abuse Their Parents?

Other violence in the family is often affiliated with this type of abuse. Once again, *social learning theory* suggests that children learn abusive behaviour in their family and, in turn, use it against their own parents.

Exchange theory suggests that family life may become chaotic when parents do not assert their authority and take charge of the family. Overly permissive parents who do not set proper limits for their children would fall into this category. Adolescents step in to fill the void and assert their own authority. They feel that someone must be in charge of the family and, since their parents are not doing so, they must take that role. Once again, we see the feminist issues of power and control in this explanation. Ineffective parenting means that children must fill the role of the parents but, because they are really not equipped for the role — being emotionally immature and dependent — they lash out angrily at their parents for putting them in such an untenable position. The violence may even be a way, inappropriate as it might be, for adolescents to attempt to force their parents to respond and regain control over the family, although they may paradoxically resist every effort (Wilson 1996).

Exchange theory may also help to understand the suggestion that parent abuse is a way for children to gain their independence from their parents (Wilson 1996). This appears to be a rather extreme method for accomplishing such a goal, but the kind of abuse employed must be taken into consideration before dismissing this explanation. An adolescent who is highly dependent on her or his parents may use verbal abuse or even milder forms of physical abuse to gain some distance from her or his parents. If conflict escalates between the child and her or his parents because of the former's efforts to gain independence, more serious types of physical abuse against the parents may result. However, it is not real independence in that the adolescent is not developmentally mature enough to handle it; the result is continuing emotional dependence. In any event, the adolescent may be attempting to break off the old exchange with her or his parents in order to establish a new, less dependent, more equal one.

A perhaps more serious problem is that the cycle of violence and abuse is continued when the adolescent resorts to such behaviour as a problem-solving mechanism. The use of violence may lead the adolescent into further delinquency and future criminal involvement. For the family as a unit, an adolescent becoming abusive toward parents perpetuates domestic violence and continues the cycle of abuse (Wilson 1996).

A final explanation for why children abuse their parents might be a weakened parent/child bond (Wharf 1994). The bond could be weakened by parents working long hours and having little time left to devote their attention to the needs of their children. Children may become resentful towards parents because they feel neglected or irrelevant. On the other hand, if parents are not able to meet the material needs and desires of children due to low income, the children may feel angry and deprived, taking out their negative feelings on their parents. They may believe that their parents are not good enough because they cannot provide them with what other children have. Such scenarios are conflict-producing in themselves; coupled with the weakened bond between the parents and children, the outcome could be parent abuse.

These explanations seem to rely heavily on the notion of adolescent anger motivating the perpetrator to abuse her or his parents. They also suggest that the condition of adolescence is at the heart of parent abuse. The insights of *exchange theory* may be helpful in understanding why this would be the case; that is, the adolescent may be using violence to repair the inequality of the parent/adolescent relationship.

Why Do Elders Become Victims of Abuse?

There has been much more theoretical work done in this particular field of abuse, at least partly due to the fact that elder abuse, as a social issue, enjoys a good deal more legitimacy in the eyes of both government and the public than do sibling, adolescent or parent abuse. As a result, much more literature is available in the area of elder abuse.

Theoretical explanations for why elders are abused may be grouped into four main paradigms: *symbolic interactionism, situational, exchange* and *feminist* theories. It would appear that there is some overlap among these theories, especially in terms of the variables they consider, but there are distinctions among them which warrant examining them separately.

Symbolic interactionist theory is mainly concerned with how individuals learn certain behaviours and patterned interactions (Pittaway et al. 1995; Tindale et al. 1994; McDonald et al. 1991). It is also referred to by some researchers as "social learning theory" (Johnson 1996; Gelles and Cornell 1990; Schlesinger 1988), the "development framework" (National Clearinghouse 1986), or the "intergenerational transmission of violence theory." According to this theory, a caregiver may abuse an elder because the former was abused her/himself. In other words, there is a history of abuse in the family so the caregiver has learned to resolve conflict or to deal with the elderly person by using violent methods. It may be seen as a continuation of family patterns of interaction. The implication is that the abuser has internalized the use of violence as a method of dealing with other members of the family and will, therefore, almost automatically resort to this kind of behaviour. The onus is placed on the psychosocial characteristics of the abuser.

Also associated with *symbolic interactionism* is the means by which relationships are developed by family members and the explanations that are created through this interaction. The theory allows for a different understanding of violence by each member of the family and the consequences of these various understandings as family members interact with one another (Tindale et al. 1994). For example, a well-known explanation of violence within the family is that it is a means by which loving, responsible parents discipline errant children in order to mould them into better citizens. Sibling rivalry is a phrase frequently used by parents to explain violence between their children, thus trivializing it into behaviour quite common to, and acceptable from, brothers and sisters, in moderation. Similarly, verbal abuse from her husband may mean violence to a wife but to him it is just teasing.

Another possible explanation for elder abuse which could be placed under the heading of *symbolic interactionism* is the *filial crisis approach,* which argues that elder abuse is a continuation of parent/ child conflict. A weak attachment between parents and children means that a positive model for good relationships is missing. Adult children and their elderly parents may not be able to negotiate and exchange support in an appropriate manner, hence abuse of the elderly parent may result when the child is in the caregiving role. Open communication and a sense of balance in their exchanges may be absent because of the weak attachment between parents and children. Such a pattern may be passed on to subsequent generations as well, since the children will not have a positive model for family relations (Tindale et al. 1994).

Finally, learned helplessness (Podnieks 1988) of the elderly person may be included under this type of theoretical framework. The senior was perhaps abused at an earlier stage in her or his life and has learned to be a victim. One study has shown that 40 percent of abused elderly people studied suffered abuse prior to age fifty-five

(Pittaway et al. 1995). Other researchers have suggested that the elderly may develop traits such as being too demanding and wanting everything done their way, or displaying "passive-aggressive" behaviour, because they are frustrated by their lot in life and their own dependency. These traits make them very difficult for their caregivers to deal with, so they may be at greater risk for abusive treatment (Goldstein and Blank 1988).

To summarize the *symbolic interactionist* approach to explaining elder abuse, both abusers and victims enter the situation with internalized behaviours learned from previous relationships, including the use of violence as a way of resolving conflict; they interact with one another on the basis of social status such as age and gender, and on the basis of roles such as caregiver or spouse, and their interactions develop a pattern; they learn how to behave in those patterned interactions and they give meaning to those interactions based on their previous learning and the interactions themselves. Either or neither of them may characterize their situation as an abusive one, based on the meanings or explanations they have created. It may require a third party to identify the situation as being abusive. In any case, this approach implies that the root cause of the abuse is to be found in the individuals themselves. It is a more sociological alternative to the psychological models, which attribute the abuse to the pathology of the caregiver, which might include sociopathy, mental illness, or the abuse of a substance such as alcohol.

Situational theory, also known as "caregiver stress theory" (Podnieks 1988) and the "environmental framework" (National Clearinghouse 1986), considers the significance of stressors with which the caregiver must cope, implying that when these stressors become too great, the caregiver will abuse the elder in her or his care. The dependency and disability of the senior citizen are clearly visible. Being sandwiched between children and elderly parents or being older and perhaps in ill health is also considered stressful for the caregiver. Other stressors may consist of problems with alcohol, drug use, psychological difficulties, work responsibilities, financial concerns, unemployment or poverty, and social isolation, to name a few (Johnson 1996). Thus, stressors can be personal, internal or external to the family. Resorting to elder abuse as a way of countering stress is an inappropriate coping mechanism.

Such an explanation does not, however, lend any insight into why some caregivers who are faced with stressors do not abuse their elderly charges. It is a rather mechanistic explanation implying that there is either a threshold of stress beyond which caregivers will resort to violence or that stress somehow automatically predisposes a caregiver to become an abuser. Neither alternative offers any predictive power; that is, neither suggests *when* a caregiver will turn to abuse so that such a turning point could be avoided.

Exchange theory examines how power differentials in relationships which are based on rewards and punishment might precipitate abuse. Dependency is an important factor, according to this theory. Discussions of dependency dominate the literature on elder abuse, most focusing on the dependency of the elder. The explanation is basically that the financial, physical and emotional dependency of the senior on her or his caregiver results in a great deal of stress on the part of the caregiver. Unable to cope, the caregiver might lash out at the elder in her or his care (Pittaway et al. 1995; Tindale et al. 1994). Because of the unequal nature of the relationship, the caregiver may feel that she or he is reaping very little reward while the elder is receiving more than her or his fair share. Dependency of the elder means that the caregiver cannot easily terminate the relationship; that is, the dependency of the elder effectively renders the caregiver powerless. Therefore, abuse of the elder may be a way for the caregiver to balance the reward and punishment equation more in her or his own favour by punishing the elder.

Newer research, however, suggests that it is not elder dependency that is significant in the abusive situation but *caregiver* dependency. The theoretical approach could still explain elder abuse in this case by asserting that the inequality of the exchange works to make the caregiver resentful of the power that the elder exerts over her or him because she or he is dependent for support on the elder; therefore, to restore balance in the power differential, the caregiver lashes out at the elder. Another term used for this type of theoretical approach is "web of dependencies" (Tindale et al. 1994).

The upshot of the social exchange explanation is that inequality of power in the relationship is the dynamic which leads to elder abuse.

Feminist theory is mainly concerned with gender inequality, citing the unequal distribution of social power as being at the root of elder abuse (Pittaway et al. 1995). When an entire social category of people (i.e., women) is devalued, it is this group that is more likely to be the target of abuse. Some researchers hold that elder abuse, in many cases, is "spousal abuse grown old" (see Aronson et al. 1995). Men abuse women because they are socialized to see themselves as powerful and dominant, particularly over women. They believe that they have a right to control women and have no compunction about using violence to do it. Sometimes women retaliate, which may explain some of the findings of Pillemer and Finkelhor's (1988) study, where men, who tend more than women to be married in their senior years, were more at risk of being the victims of abuse. It is possible that the wives of these men were retaliating for violence they had suffered in their lives.

If the same ethos of societal devaluation and inequality is applied to senior citizens as a group, then feminist theory can explain elder abuse as a product of a society in which they are held in low esteem and denied services devoted to their care. Stereotypes about older people depicting them as making no contribution to society — incompetent, burdensome, infirm or senile — are thought to make it easier for caregivers to abuse them and ignore their needs (National Clearinghouse 1986).

In conclusion, there are a number of theoretical paradigms which have been used in one way or another to attempt to explain the phenomenon of elder abuse. None of them addresses the problem in its entirety nor grants the power to predict when elder abuse will occur. Part of the problem with these theories may be due to the fact that none of them has been developed specifically for elder abuse; they have all been borrowed and adapted from other disciplines and fields of study.

Notes

1. For a detailed and cogent discussion of patriarchy, see Johnson (1997).

2. The discussion which follows is from a "psychological" perspective in that it focuses on the individual and his or her psyche. However, in this context, psychoanalytic theories (which address conscious and unconscious behaviour patterns) and psychiatric frameworks (which focus on the treatment of mental illness) are referred to.

3. Michael Smith points out that in recent years both American and Canadian feminist social scientists have called for a more collaborative relationship with mainstream approaches to research (1994: 123).

4. Based on these results, Lupri et al. have proposed a "dispersion theory" of wife abuse. According to their perspective, wife abuse manifests itself in a variety of ways, including physical and psychological abuse. Patriarchal ideology which supports violence against women is dispersed amongst all classes in society. Wife abuse "is a manifestation of men's power to control women, regardless of class position" (69). This framework is clearly tied to feminist theory.

5. Also referred to as *gender socialization theory*.

6. In a recent review of the research literature, Wallace proposes a list of sixteen abuser traits including employment problems, isolation, authoritarian personalities, moody, wall-punchers, excessive attachment to wife, traditionalist (1995: 174). From the overlap and ambiguities of many of these terms, it is evident that typologies would be a useful line of further research.

7. Dutton suggests from his work that there are three types of abusers: psychopathic, overcontrolled, cyclical/emotionally volatile (1995). Significantly, as with other typologies, a significant minority (20 percent) are characterized as so psychiatrically impaired that they are impervious to counselling methods typically used with abusive men.

8. The line between sociological and feminist theorizing is often fuzzy (Yllo 1993). In general, feminists distinguish themselves by rejecting any suggestion that intimate violence is gender-neutral and any psychological and social psychological theorizing that explains woman abuse primarily in terms of psychological pathologies. Rather, feminists argue that woman abuse is rooted in and cannot be understood outside of the patriarchal structure of society.

9. Feminist analysis does not necessarily suggest that all men are more powerful than all women. Rather, the focus is on men and women as social groups. Clearly, there are women who are more powerful (in terms of wealth, corporate position and so on) than some men. However, there are social patterns in society which suggest that men as a group are privileged over women as a group. For example, women comprise about 9 percent of the directors of Canadian corporate boards while men comprise 91 percent (McCuthion 1997: E3). The old feminist axiom "where

power is, women are not" is not always true, but a power differential between women and men as groups is apparent throughout
our society.

10. Wife killings are typically precipitated by real or imagined in-
    subordination by the wife. The husband accuses her of sexual
    infidelity or confronts her unilateral decision to terminate the
    relationship or he simply wants to control her. In contrast, wives
    often kill husbands in defence against their aggression (Wilson
    and Daly 1994: 4).

11. Victim-blaming refers to the tendency in society to hold victims
    accountable for their victimization rather than laying the blame
    firmly at the feet of the perpetrators. For example, rape victims
    are often, implicitly or explicitly, blamed for wearing the wrong
    clothes, for being in the wrong place, for not taking adequate
    precautions. Blaming the victim serves to take attention away
    from those parties who are actually responsible for the violence
    or abuse.

12. As Wilson and Daly point out, it is not clear if the act of
    separation triggers the lethal violence. It may be that the violence
    becomes so intolerable that the woman leaves, but whether or
    not she leaves, she might be killed.

13. Walker argues that her notions of learned helplessness and bat-
    tered women syndrome (BWS) are in fact consistent with femi-
    nist theories (1993: 144). She argues, for example, that BWS is
    consistent with the feminist view that normal women are victim-
    ized by batterers, that normal women may stay in abusive rela-
    tionships and that the violence is not women's fault (145). Other
    feminists reject Walker's approach on the ground that is overly
    psychological and focuses too much on personality while putting
    too little emphasis on the relevant structural and cultural factors
    (Bowker 1993).

14. Ironically, while the decision to stay may be based on a rational
    calculation of the alternatives, by staying the woman often is
    providing her husband with a "license to hit" (Hoff 1994: 44).

15. Theoretical work on child abuse tackles a wide variety of ques-
    tions. For example, models have been developed to explain the
    treatment stages characteristic of child sexual abuse (Orenchuk-
    Tomiak, Matthey and Christensen 1989). While the emphasis

here is on the central question — Why do parents abuse their children? — it should be noted that theorizing has pursued a variety of avenues.

16. Social learning theory is also often termed socialization theory, social psychological theory or the cycle of violence approach.

17. It should be noted that some victims of physical abuse may deploy other abusive actions (such as psychological or sexual abuse) as adults. It would be inaccurate to conclude from this lack of a necessary relationship between childhood abuse and adult victimizing that children can escape completely unscathed from an abusive childhood.

18. For example, the social learning impact of being exposed to wife assault may vary depending upon the child's ability to distance her/himself from the situation, her/his self-esteem and proclivity to internalize the conflict (Moore et al. 1988: 81).

19. Amongst the numerous celebrities who have come forward to describe themselves as abuse survivors are Sinead O'Connor, Roseanne, Brian Wilson, Gary Crosby (son of Bing Crosby), LaToya Jackson, Marilyn Van Derber Atler (former Miss America), and Christina Crawford (daughter of Joan Crawford). Many of these people grew up in affluent surroundings.

20. For a recent Canadian application of the ecological model, see Krishnan and Morrison 1995.

21. Needless to say, feminist analysts have addressed a much broader range of issues than suggested by this one question. For example, Karen Swift's work on which child neglect examines the ways in child welfare work processes construct certain mothers (notably, low-income, single parent mothers) as neglectful (1995).

22. There clearly are many ways in which one can "be a man." Contemporary masculinities range from Phil Donohue's sensitive male to Arnold Schwartzennegger's robotic fighting machine. However, not all masculinities are equally valued and legitimated by our society. As many analysts in male studies now point out, there is a "hegemonic masculinity" which represents the prevailing image of what a "real" man should be.

23. To gauge the social pressure on women to have and raise children, consider social stereotypes of women who explicitly choose not to have children or the societal stigmatization of women who give up custody of their children in divorce. As Cole (1988) points out, reproductive policies which make it difficult or impossible for women to terminate unwanted pregnancies also function to compel women to become mothers.

24. John Bradshaw suggests that 96 percent of all families are to some degree emotionally impaired (1988).

Looking for Solutions

As evident throughout the preceding chapters, family violence is a pervasive social problem. The cost to Canadian society is incalculable in terms of human suffering and lost or wasted talents and abilities. However, researchers have attempted to estimate some of the more concrete costs to underscore the fact that it is profoundly inefficient and shortsighted for Canadians to ignore or accept family violence. For example, analysts calculate that sexual assault and physical abuse of women and girls cost Canada $4.2 billion a year to cover medical costs, workdays lost and so on (Priest 1996: A1). The Centre for Research on Violence Against Women estimates battered women who are unable to work because of assaults lose $7 million a year in earnings and the welfare system spends $1.8 million a year to support women who have left abusive relationships (Gurr et al. 1996: 6) Clearly, even economic costs underline the need to search for solutions.

Woman Abuse

Personal Interventions: Counselling and Related Strategies

Personal interventions, such as counselling and therapy for the victim[1] or abuser, are tremendously attractive since they seem to respond so immediately to the needs of the individual victim. As a result, it is not surprising that considerable effort has been directed at these kinds of solutions. Based on a psychological and socio-psychological understanding of the issue, therapists and counsellors have sought to heal the violence one individual at a time. However, such an approach is expensive and time consuming. Many sociologists and feminists would question whether such an approach can ever address the societal dimensions of family violence. Further, and more troubling, this strategy addresses the problem after the fact. However, it is at the same time difficult to ignore the personal plight of so many.

The first concerted response to the plight of abused women was to provide them with safe and secure shelters. In this way the women's movement hoped to ensure that all women, regardless of income, had somewhere to go and someone who cared. Initially, this meant finding a house that could accommodate a number of women, locating funding to sustain the shelters and training volunteers. It was immediately apparent, however, that additional efforts were required. For example, telephone crisis counselling for women who could not leave but who needed support and information became a high priority. Women's security also became an important consideration. While efforts were made to keep the location of shelters secret, this was not a successful strategy and enraged men showed up at the doors of some shelters. Additional funding was needed to secure the premises with such additions as bullet-proof glass and television monitors. Counselling became more sophisticated as efforts were made to respond not only to victims but also to their children.

By the 1990s the shelters had evolved into a national network of approximately 400 houses scattered across urban and rural locations (MacLeod 1994). On May 31, 1995, across Canada, 2,300 women and 2,300 children were living in shelters for battered women. In the preceding year, 85,000 women and children had been admitted to shelters and, on an average day, Canadian shelters received 3,000 outside requests for their services (Statistics Canada 1996: 36). Shelters today provide a selection of services to women and their children. Counselling, often premised on feminist therapy[2] and provided through volunteers as well as paid staff, is typically available in a variety of forms — the 24-hour crisis phone line, individual counselling and group counselling along with referrals to other agencies. Specific support is also available to women who choose to go through the criminal justice system. Most shelters are also able to refer "clients" to various community resources including lawyers and therapists. Services for children include childcare and counselling support. In addition, most shelters provide public education to their local community. This entails producing educational pamphlets on wife abuse and related issues along with presentations to various community groups such as schools, clubs and workplaces. Many shelters also pay particular attention to women with special needs, non-English speaking, immigrant, Aboriginal and minority women in their counselling work and education campaigns (Gurr et al. 1996). Finally, most shelters are pursuing these diverse activities 24 hours a day, 365 days a year while also maintaining the two core activities of the organization: fundraising and ongoing training of volunteers and staff. Not surprisingly, many activists in the shelter movement report that it is exhilarating but also exhausting work (Rodgers and MacDonald 1994).

Unfortunately, it is difficult to evaluate these contributions. The counselling, for example, is focused on empowering the woman, ensuring she is fully informed about community services and support systems and supporting whatever decisions she makes. Based on feminist analysis, this approach seeks to re-establish the woman's sense of agency and control. Most shelter workers acknowledge that many women return to abusive situations. However, since leaving the violence is often a long process, this is not interpreted as a failure. Perhaps next time she leaves, she will leave for good. As one counsellor comments, "If a woman is going back to the relationship, we've given her the tools to help herself and a lot more knowledge ... A lot of women return" (Hanes 1994: C1). In recent years, there has been an initiative to extend the counselling process so that the ultimate goal is not simply to encourage women to leave violent relationships and establish independent lives but to help "survivors" move on to become social advocates for abused women (Health Canada 1996).

Abusive men have also been offered counselling solutions. In 1978, Donald Dutton, a psychology professor at the University of British Columbia who has done pioneering work on batterers, launched the first group therapy program in Canada for men convicted of wife assault. Since that time the number of such groups has grown and counselling, with its strong psychological emphasis, has become intermixed with criminal justice approaches. By 1994 there were 123 programs for male abusers across Canada (Health Canada 1994b). Many judges now order counselling sessions for abusers. For example, in a *Toronto Star* examination of 133 domestic violence cases 43 percent of men found guilty were given a probation condition that ordered them to take anger management counselling or that gave their probation officers the option to order such counselling. At that time there was up to a twelve months wait for a spot in a Toronto area counselling group. A counsellor commented in the *Star* series, "it's a program for 120 men and right now I'm seeing 250-300 men ... we're just really hitting the tip of the iceberg" (Daly, Mallan and Armstrong 1996a, 1996b). This problem is not restricted to Toronto; the Health Canada survey of abuser programs found that two-thirds had waiting lists ranging from one week to six to eight months

(1994b). Further, waiting lists are not the only difficulty. According to the *Toronto Star*, men who fail to show up for their counselling are often given an absolute discharge by the courts regardless of their failure to attend the sessions, and some probation officers, seeing this pattern, don't even bother to lay charges when men fail to attend the sessions (Daly, Mallan and Armstrong 1996a: All).

More substantively, it is not clear if the counselling approach is a reasonable and effective solution.[3] Some family violence therapists question whether the twelve- to sixteen-week[4] group sessions are effective mechanisms for stopping years of violence. Although the threat of court action may compel abusers to attend, it is not possible to ensure that they will actively work towards resolving their violence. Family therapists suggest that the anger management approach gives too little insight into the power dynamics and discrimination against women. A group co-leader echoes similar concerns, "I think we know that we're making an improvement, but we're not transforming them ... Four or five out of 20 walk out with nothing. The others at least shake your hand and say, 'Thanks, I got something out of it'" (Daly, Mallan and Armstrong 1996a: A11; see also, Mawhinney 1995: E1, E3). Others have expressed concern that men who learn to contain their physical violence simply turn to "emotional terrorism" and "psychological abuse" to maintain their power in the family (MacLeod 1994: 11; Lindsay, Ouellet, Saint-Jacques 1994).

Institutional Reforms: Criminal Justice Responses

Not surprisingly one of the first demands of the women active in the early shelter movement was for reform of the criminal justice system's response to wife abuse. As extensively documented, violence against women in intimate relations has long been minimized, even trivialized. Just as sexual harassment was once dismissed as "office politics," wife battering was once a joke. As the old ditty goes, "A woman and a chestnut tree, the more you beat them, the better they be." One obvious avenue for challenging the prevailing beliefs and values was the police and courts. If charges were laid against abusers and abusers were punished, beating your wife could not be so easily dismissed as harmless or natural.

One of the first reforms activists demanded was for police to improve their responses to "domestics." Shelter workers complained that police limited their intervention in situations that were dismissed as "just domestics." While the police might have calmed the situation down, they frequently did not lay charges against the abuser and little was done to ensure that the violence did not repeat itself. Even if charges were laid, they were often dropped by the Crown attorney's office or, if a conviction was achieved, the abuser's sentence was unsupervised probation. It was seen as particularly important that police, the first line of response, receive specific education on the issue so that they would, for example, refer women to shelters, fully inform them of their legal options and their implications and carry through with arrests when the woman pressed charges (MacLeod 1980, 1987). One particularly contentious area of police reform was the demand for "mandatory charging," which would require police to file charges against the abuser (when there was a reasonable basis to do so) in domestic violence situations. This initiative would remove much of the police's discretion when called to domestic violence situations and would also frequently run counter to the wishes of the victim who might simply want the violence to end or the abuser removed from the home (MacLeod and Picard 1989; Hannah-Moffat 1995). Indeed the prolonged incarceration of the abuser might cause the victim and her children additional hardship if the economic stability of the family were jeopardized. Mandatory charging was further complicated by the fact that, even if convicted, abusers almost always received a conditional discharge (MacLeod and Picard 1989). At the end of the criminal justice process, the abuser might be back on the streets and be enraged by his wife's decision to lay charges or to testify against him in court.

Further, legal means of protecting the woman from his anger were notoriously inadequate. While courts might, if petitioned by the victim, provide a restraining (non-molestation) order or peace bond[5] against the abuser, police and court responsiveness to breaches of these orders were, at best, uneven (MacLeod 1987; *The Spectator* (Hamilton), April 2, 1988: A4). In particular, the order or bond had to be violated before the police and courts would respond. Women complained that only when they were assaulted again was there any further police intervention. The early 1990s case of a Sydney, Nova Scotia, woman exemplifies the problems. Her husband was convicted of wife beating and given eighteen months' probation. During probation he continued to beat her. Although she then obtained a peace bond against him, he persisted in tracking her down and beating her. He was sentenced to a month in jail for violating the peace bond. Upon his release, he came after her again, and again she applied for another peace bond. At this time she was given a court date three weeks hence at which time she could explain to a judge why she needed the bond. Within three days of her second application, she was killed by her husband.

As apparent in this case and others, judicial responses to wife abuse seemed muted and ineffective. Sentencing practices exacerbated the problem since the courts and judges did not appear to take woman abuse seriously when it came time to sentence convicted abusers. Convictions typically resulted in only probation. Even repeat offenders might receive little or no jail time, which meant they were quickly back in the community. Numerous high profile cases suggest that violence, even deadly violence, against wives was tolerated by the courts. For example, in a notorious case in the late 1980s a Bay Street broker who stabbed his wife to death served only three and a half years before being paroled and returning to the community. Similarly, one of the abusers profiled in the *Toronto Star* series on domestic abuse, who pleaded guilty to assaulting two ex-girlfriends (after charges of threatening to kill one of these women were dropped), received a suspended sentence (Daly, Mallan and Armstrong 1996b: A17).[6]

As the debate surrounding mandatory charging persisted, in 1994, Ontario landed firmly on the side of laying criminal charges. New provincial standards were introduced requiring police to help an abused woman find shelter, to escort her back to her home to get her belongings and to lay charges against her abuser where there were reasonable grounds to do so. As part of the same initiative, police officers were to receive training on issues surrounding wife assault, sexual assault, psychological abuse and stalking. This was to be combined with training to sensitize officers to the specific concerns of Aboriginal, racial minority, disabled and non-English-speaking women.

Unfortunately, in the late 1990s, it appears that various elements in the criminal justice system remain flawed. The Canadian Violence Against Women Survey (CVAWS) found that the majority of domestic abuse victims did not turn to the police. Only 26 percent of women in battering relationships reported to the police. Most, if they told anyone, turned to friends or neighbours. This pattern is not surprising in light of the finding that of those men who were reported to the police only 28 percent were arrested or had charges laid against them (Johnson 1996: 204; Statistics Canada 1993: 7). Other research confirms the lingering impression that the criminal justice system is still struggling to formulate an effective response to wife abuse.

In one of the decade's most ambitious newspaper projects, the *Toronto Star* tracked for one year 133 cases of spousal abuse (all of the cases which appeared before the courts from June 30 to July 6, 1995, in Toronto). The results revealed a profoundly overburdened and inadequate system. Within one year 128 cases had completed their journey through the courts. Only 22 percent of abusers were sentenced to jail. Thirty-three percent were given suspended sentences, or conditional or absolute discharges, and 37 percent of charges were dismissed (typically because the victim recanted her story or failed to show up to testify in court). An additional 8 percent of cases were acquitted or charges were dropped for other reasons. Of the twenty-eight men sentenced to jail, twenty-one were sentenced to fewer than twenty-one days. These results, however meagre, absorbed an enormous amount of court time and taxpayer monies. For example, there were at least 383 court appearances in the cases that ultimately ended in recants and no shows. Nor did the simple fact of having been charged serve to deter these men. Within a year 35 of the 133 men had been charged again (83 percent for attacking the same woman) (Mallan, Daly and Armstrong 1996: E1, 4-7).

The *Toronto Star* series quickly prompted additional pressures to reform the criminal justice approach to domestic violence. In particular, by the end of 1996, there was a push in Toronto to adopt what was referred to as the San Diego approach. Following the police procedures in that city, there is less reliance on victims' testimony. In its place, police are expected to collect a variety of evidence including photographs of the victim's injuries, tape-recorded 911 calls, eyewitness testimony and videotapes of the victim's initial statement. Crown attorneys are urged to adopt a *no-drop* policy; that is, once charges are laid, they are vigorously pursued through the criminal justice system. Indeed recently, Ontario Crown attorneys hailed the first successful conviction of a wife abuser, despite the wife's recantation of statements to police (Gombu 1997: A8). The hope is that these kinds of changes will provide a solution to recants and no-shows and result in more successful prosecutions and fewer repeat offenders.

However, at present, evidence continues to grow that such efforts to "fix" the system have been far from successful. Not only has the mandatory charging policy not resulted in a strong criminal justice response to abusive men, it has alienated many police officers who feel that their discretionary powers are being undermined. Further, the education and training of police officers who are on the front lines of domestic situations has been far from effective. After several decades of public education on family violence, it is disturbing to find that many officers continue to believe that woman abuse is a "family matter" rather than a "criminal matter" and that the victim herself is at least partially to blame for the violence (Hannah-Moffat 1995: 45).

Similarly, Crown attorneys report that the no-drop, vigorous prosecution approach to family violence cases is unwieldy and ineffective. They complain that they often feel caught between political groups that want the full weight of the justice system brought to bear on the abuser and the victim who wants to quickly get on with her life. As a result, they often confront "reluctant, hostile and apparently uncaring witnesses" on the stand. The Zero Tolerance (for Violence) Policy has resulted in charges being laid where there is insufficient evidence, cases becoming backlogged in an overburdened court system and the truly dangerous cases being lost in the shuffle. Ironically, the mandatory charge policy has resulted in counter-charges being laid by some abusers against their victims. Under the no-drop policy, police are compelled to charge the woman as well as the man, which in turn adds to the backlog of cases facing Crown attorneys (MacLeod 1995a).[7] Much as the police, Crown attorneys are also concerned that no-drop policies remove their discretion to make the best decision (to prosecute or not) in any particular situation and obliterate the real complexity and diversity of family violence cases (MacLeod 1995b).

Despite the uncertain progress, there are continuing efforts to reform the police and Crown attorney approaches. These are often coupled with legislative initiatives on woman abuse issues. Although in the last several decades progress in the implementation of the law has been contentious and uneven, major steps have been taken to improve the legal code. One of the first legislative initiatives was to demand a change in the rape law so that it was no longer legal for a man to rape his wife (MacLeod 1980). Prior to 1983 a man who raped or sexually abused his wife, even if they were separated at the time, could be charged with assault only if there were injuries. Reflecting the age-old tradition enshrined by the seventeenth century British Chief Justice Sir Mathew Hale, a wife belonged to and was given in marriage to her husband. Upon marriage, a woman gave her general consent to sexual intercourse and as a result it was considered impossible for a man to steal what he already owned. The law was changed in 1983 and under the reformed Canadian Criminal Code rape was renamed sexual assault with the emphasis on the degree of violence and injury inflicted; wives were not exempted from this new definition (Cote 1984).

The next major legal breakthrough was in 1990 in the case of *R. v Lavallee*. This was the first instance in which the Canadian courts recognized the relevance of the battered woman syndrome in a case where a woman killed her abuser. Although the woman was not being physically attacked at the time she shot and killed her common-law husband, the court ruled that expert testimony concerning the battered woman syndrome was relevant to assessing the woman's state of mind and, therefore, her plea of self-defence. Subsequently, the Supreme Court of Canada supported the decision to acquit the woman on murder charges and revised the traditional masculine conception of self-defence. The battered woman syndrome was firmly entrenched as a relevant consideration whenever women killed their abusive spouses.[8] Since these landmark decisions, the Canadian Association of Elizabeth Fry Societies has sought the release of women presently imprisoned for killing their abusive partners. In 1995, the Justice Minister agreed to appoint an independent panel to review fifteen such cases (Johnson 1996: 191-97; Bindman 1995: A3; Noonan 1993). In 1997, the judge who had been selected to undertake this special federal review reported back that of fifty-five women still serving sentences forty-nine should not have their cases reopened; she also recommended that five women who received lengthy prison sentences for killing their abusive husbands should be given their complete freedom and one woman should be given a hearing to determine whether she is guilty of a lesser crime (Bindman 1997: A2).

The Canadian Parliament has also enacted antistalking legislation (1993). Given that peace bonds and other instruments of the courts failed to provide protection for abused women, the new law was seen as an important advance.[9] Although it covers any individual who is subject to criminal harassment and who fears for her or his safety, it is seen to be particularly important for abused women whose spouses repeatedly follow and communicate with them, watch them in the home or place of work, or confront them with threatening conduct either personally or through their family. While peace bonds and other measures had to be breached before police action could be taken, the criminal harassment law can be acted upon and charges can be laid before an actual attack or confrontation has occurred.

However, ironically, the *Toronto Star* study found that despite new legislation and despite the fact that Crown attorneys are now clearly advised not to use peace bonds in domestic cases, five men in the 133 cases they studied were released on peace bonds, promising to pay an average of $300 if they did not keep the peace towards their spouses. Predictably, four of these men were later charged with a second domestic assault (Mallan, Daly and Armstrong 1996: E1, 4-7)

Recent legislation has also sought to secure compensation for abuse victims. In 1995, a proposal came forward in Ontario to enact a law that would allow abused spouses who are forced out of their homes to collect compensation from their abusers for lost property and expenses incurred (*Toronto Star*, March 18, 1995: A3).

In 1995, Saskatchewan launched a particularly comprehensive and innovative effort with its *Victims of Domestic Violence Act*. The first legislation of its kind in Canada, the Act seeks to allow all victims of family violence — spouses, common-law spouses, children, seniors, disabled persons and any person in family-like relationship — three avenues of action: emergency intervention orders, victim assistance orders and warrants of entry. The legislation, for example, allows specially trained Justices of the Peace to give a victim exclusive possession of the home, direct police to remove the abuser from the home or provide police accompaniment for a victim or abuser who wishes to remove personal items from the home. Warrants of entry can also be ordered that allow a designated person to enter a home to check on (and, if necessary, remove) a victim (for example, an abused elder or abused disabled woman). These legal initiatives were combined with extensive police education both on the new legislation and on the dynamics of family violence. Local shelters were involved in these educational efforts and much of the previous distrust between the police and shelter workers was eroded. Further, Aboriginal groups were involved in both the consultation and implementation processes (MacLeod 1995a: 22-23; Turner 1995). This innovative legislation speaks strongly to both a commitment to end domestic violence and a willingness to explore avenues outside the traditional criminal justice approach.

Efforts are also being undertaken to improve the public's access to information. In 1996 the Ontario government set up a 24-hour telephone hot line so that victims of crime, especially of family violence, could get information on counselling services and, importantly, information on any adult offender in jail or on probation. It is this kind of information that can be vitally important to an abuse victim fearing the release or relocation of her abuser. The hot line also provides information on the criminal justice system itself, the court system and the nature of parole and probation (Wright 1996: A3). Also in 1996, other strong signals were coming from the criminal justice system. For the first time a wife abuser (whose record included ten convictions for assaults on his wife) was ruled by the courts a "dangerous offender" and imprisoned indefinitely.

While in the late 1990s efforts continue to be directed to reforming and improving the criminal justice response to woman abuse, some continue to question the fundamental wisdom of this whole approach. Toronto lawyer Clayton Ruby, for example, asks whether jail time actually reduces the likelihood of re-offending and whether lengthier sentences are a greater deterrent to violence. He argues that no evidence suggests criminalization works to end the violence and that applying the criminal justice system to this issue is enormously expensive as well as ineffective. In his view, the ultimate solutions to woman abuse hinge on broader social changes that will ensure women a dignified, secure existence if and when they choose to leave their abusers (1996: D3).

Others inside and outside the criminal justice system clearly share Ruby's skepticism about the criminal justice strategy. In a move to reform traditional courtroom solutions, Ontario recently set up domestic violence courts (Daly and Tyler 1996). These courts take two forms. The North York model targets first offenders and cases with no significant injuries and where the couple plan to continue living together. If the offender pleads guilty he is ordered into immediate counselling for two months. If he completes the counselling, he becomes eligible for a conditional discharge or, at the end of the initial two months of counselling, the judge may order more counselling for the abuser or couple mediation. Clearly, the program's focus is on remediation rather than incarceration and punishment. There is also some effort to provide the victim with a sense of control over portions of the process since, for example, she decides whether or not the abuser is allowed to return home while he is out on bail. The domestic violence courts are intended, however, as a supplement to the traditional judicial process. If the accused refuses to plead guilty, he is bounced back into the mainstream judicial system.

The second model, initiated at Toronto's Old City Hall, seeks to bring the full weight of criminal prosecution to bear in more serious cases. Once again, there is considerable effort to provide support for the victim through victim-witness programs and by having only one

Crown attorney in charge of each case. In addition, rigorous prosecution means the use of extensive evidence, including hospital interviews, 911 calls and video/audio taped testimony at the scene. Whether these experiments will strike a happy medium between punishment and therapeutic intervention and resolve some of the shortcomings of the current system now remains to be seen. The Ontario government is sufficiently satisfied with this project that it recently announced plans to open domestic violence courts in six other Ontario cities (Mallan 1997b: A10).

Manitoba has already attempted to fundamentally alter its judicial system's response to family violence. Since 1990 family violence cases in Winnipeg — including spousal, child and elder abuse — have been heard in the Winnipeg Family Violence Court (FVC). The first of its kind in Canada, the court seeks to solve some of the problems found in other judicial systems by processing cases expeditiously (averaging three months from first appearance to disposition) involving victims/witnesses more fully in court process so that they are less likely to recant or fail to appear; providing improved sentencing so that the victim is better protected, and where suitable, treatment is mandated for offender and offenders are monitored (Ursel 1995: 170). For example, the FVC includes two victim support programs — one for abused women and the other for child abuse victim witnesses — so that victims are both supported and better represented in the judicial procedures. An early review of this initiative found that the court was successful in expeditiously processing cases as well as providing more consistent and appropriate sentencing. Rigorous prosecution results were more ambiguous in that there remains a problem with case attrition, that is, cases that were stayed because of lack of evidence or trials that resulted in verdicts of dismiss or discharge. However, given that the goals of the specialized court are not so much to "get a conviction" as to "not do harm" and "help to prevent violence," its successes are notable (MacLeod 1995a: 20).

Activists working outside the criminal justice system remain, if anything, skeptical of this kind of institutional reform as a viable solution to woman abuse. It now appears that many of the reforms that feminists lobbied hard to achieve are not effective in protecting or empowering women and feminists are at the forefront in challenging many of these policies. Mandatory charging and a no-drop approach to wife abuse charges may, for example, leave the woman feeling powerless and may intensify the violence she is subject to

(Snider 1995; Stubbs 1995). In particular, concern has been raised that mandatory charging may jeopardize immigrant and visible minority women and, in fact, result in fewer calls for police intervention (Valverde, MacLeod and Johnson 1995: 3). When Statistics Canada recently reported a decline in the number of wife assaults reported to police, women active in the shelter movement countered that the get-tough police policy is not reducing the numbers of women at the shelters (the numbers are reported to be increasing) but simply making women more reluctant to seek help from the judicial system (*The Standard* (St. Catharines), August 8, 1997: B4). Activists are also particularly critical of attempts at judicial mediation since they require the woman to meet with her abuser in a counselling situation. There is concern that after years of abuse she may still be subject to his power and control in mediation, that the mediation process implies couple rather than abuser responsibility and that such contact with her abuser may put the woman at increased risk of violence.

Societal Changes: Feminist Initiatives

Since the earliest days of the modern women's movement, much feminist effort has been concrete and practical in nature. While feminist analysis would call for a social revolution in the structure and values of society, the day-to-day plight of women victims and their children called for shelters, support groups, counselling, reforms to the criminal justice system and so forth. Many feminist activists devote their time and energy to precisely these kinds of efforts. While feminism has this decidedly practical and grounded dimension, it is also clear that feminist analysis emphasizes the need for substantive societal change. Such change implicates every component of society since virtually every institutional arrangement is affected by gender inequalities. Possible steps towards achieving this degree of social transformation are, by definition, numerous.

Graham, who developed the theory of the societal Stockholm syndrome, endorses a variety of general stategies for cultivating the social revolution. For example, she argues that simply by connecting together as women and sharing "visions and "dreams" of "that other world, that world outside the battering environment" (1994: 265), women cultivate alternative social possibilities. Feminist science fiction, for example, keeps alive the image of a social reality unconditioned by male violence. Through shared reflection as well as actions (such as demanding "space for women,"[10] keeping track of the abuses against women and looking out for women by voting for feminist candidates or supporting feminist organizations) women can move towards a social order where they will no longer love men in order to survive but rather "will thrive with love — of themselves and other women and of men who choose to join with us in mutually empowering relationships" (1994: 265).

Graham's rather general prescriptions for societal change can be brought down to very specific social actions. One avenue for societal change is to challenge current ideological systems; that is, to urge the public questioning of the beliefs and values which support current social relations. In terms of violence against women this may mean both drawing public attention to the issue as a societal issue (as opposed to an issue of individual pathology or personality defects) and gaining a public hearing for feminist analyses of this issue. Sociologist Sharon Stone's (1993) case study of the Toronto press coverage of violence against women in the first six months of 1988 suggests that, although the feminist perspective is often absent from most newspapers, a substantial minority (37 percent) did provide access to feminists to "speak out on the general problem" (393). This research suggests that to some degree feminists have been successful in Canada in finding "openings for the expression of their views" and in publicly redefining the issue (Stone 1993: 398).

Feminists have also been able to make some inroads into educational curricula. In the early 1980s, for example, the Design for a New Tomorrow program in the Niagara Peninsula was able, amongst other objectives, to introduce issues of violence against women and gender stereotyping into the local school curricula. Similarly, in 1990 London, Ontario, launched a pilot program in five secondary schools that focused on violence in intimate relationships. Students were informed about rates of wife abuse, the impact of such abuse on children, violence in the media and so on. Since the mid-1980s such efforts were being formally supported for Ontario by the province's Ministry of Education under its family violence initiatives. Under this program the Ministry sought not only to meet the needs of children who were victims of family violence but also to educate all students about family violence issues. By the early 1990s violence was firmly entrenched as a central issue for many schools and children as young as kindergarteners were involved in learning about violence and violence prevention (Mulligan and Mitchell 1992/93).

Public educational campaigns have also become popular mechanisms for both informing the population about woman abuse and challenging some of the beliefs and values that support violence against women. Recently, for example, the Centre for Research in Women's Health identified violence against women as Canada's number one health issue and launched a nationwide advertising campaign to raise funds to study the issue (Armstrong 1996: A18).

Integral to these feminist forays into societal change has been a move towards community-based solutions. One recent effort in this direction is K. Louise Schmidt's (1995) attempt to link the nonviolence movement and feminism in developing a comprehensive response to woman abuse. This entails not only an understanding of the societal roots of violence (as laid out in the nonviolence and feminist literature) but also community-level actions that reject the social roots of violence and hold abusers accountable. The concrete actions include theatre groups that strive to combine "education, action and healing in communities" in their productions (81). For example, a British Columbia group, Saltspring Women Opposed to Violence and Abuse, used art, theatre and dance to educate the local community on the realities of abused women's lives and to present a nonviolent vision of change. A program offered through the Nanaimo, B.C., Nonviolence Society provides six-month educational groups for abusive men which not only hold the men responsibile for ending their personal violence but provide nonviolent alternatives based in ecological, feminist, First Nations, Gandhian, Buddhist and other traditions (82). Schmidt concludes with a call for a wide diversity of actions aimed not only at ending the violence but also at transforming society — heart-sharing groups, nonviolence study groups, parent-support groups, recovery circles, meditation practices and peace-witness groups (119-20). Her work reflects the vitality and diversity of contemporary feminist solutions to woman abuse.

Most recently, in response to increased recognition in feminist analysis of the differences amongst women, activists have sought to develop practical strategies that are sensitive and responsive to the needs of specific groups of women. For example, shelters produce public education material in a variety of languages so that immigrant and racial/ethnic minority women are included. Efforts are made to ensure that counsellors at shelters reflect a variety of racial, ethnic and language groups or that translators are available. Counselling and support groups have been developed that specifically target women who share a cultural background.

Aboriginal beliefs and practices have been particularly influential in the emergent feminist responses to violence. As indicated above, a body of research suggests that various forms of family violence are epidemic in some Aboriginal communities in Canada as well as in New Zealand and Australia. Although early responses tended to be traditional in that they profferred individual counselling, in recent years a much more comprehensive understanding of the problem has emerged and with it, more broadly framed social interventions. Currently, most family violence in Aboriginal communities is understood as embedded in 500 years of colonialization, economic marginalization and racism. Violence against women and children, for example, is seen as rooted in the self-hatred cultivated by a history of oppression and cultural domination (LaRocque 1994).

From this analytical perspective, it follows that any solutions must address the larger societal context. Individuals cannot be healed in the midst of ailing communities; rather, community supports and healing must go hand-in-hand with addressing the plight of victims and abusers. The specific actions are "healing circles" and "healing lodges" that seek to heal the community as a whole by "reclaiming ancestral values and traditions and strive to reintegrate the offender into a supportive community" (Gurr et al. 1996: 24, 27-29). Supported by friends and the larger community, including elders, victims speak to their abusers of the pain of victimization. The abusers are expected to listen respectfully, to acknowledge the harm they have done both to the individual and to the community as a whole. The focus is not on punishment, but on ending the violence and building the community. The abuser is supported in her or his efforts to acknowledge the abuse, to accept the shame and to move on to healing and reintegration.

In this holistic approach, the individual is understood as located in the context of the family, the family in the context of the community and community in the context of the larger society (Gurr et al. 1996: 27). By bringing members of the community together and by locating the violence in the context of Aboriginal oppression and socioeconomic problems such as poverty and welfare, advocates seek to combine the personal and the public, that is, individual counselling and social change.

This general approach has been adapted by other non-Native communities as family group conferencing or communitarian conferencing and advocated as a viable alternative to the confrontational and punishment-oriented criminal justice system. The family, including the victim(s), meet with the abuser(s) and extended family and friends to talk of the abuse and its effect on their lives. The hoped-for resolution of such meetings is a plan to "resolve the harm" and to prevent future violence. The meetings are set up and supported by a local family group conferencing coordinator and a community panel. The coordinator, for example, is responsible for ensuring the victim has someone to support her or him at the meeting, coordinates support from outside agencies and monitors the implementation of the family's plans to prevent violence. Currently, this approach is being tested in selected communities in Newfoundland and Labrador (MacLeod 1995c).

However, it should be noted that this new model has not been uniformly embraced as a "good" solution. Feminists have long rejected the notion of bringing women and their assailants together for mediation on the grounds that a history of violence and abuse makes it impossible for many women to confront their victimizers. Further, such efforts to bring victim and abuser together may jeopardize her safety. Precisely the same concerns have emerged around family group conferencing and although efforts have been made to provide support for the victim and to ensure her or his protection, they have not satisfied some critics. Further, it is not clear, outside of specific groups such as some Aboriginal communities, that there exists a supportive community or family group that can effectively implement and monitor the long-term outcome of the intervention. Presently, it seems likely that some Aboriginal responses to family violence will flourish in Aboriginal contexts, but it is not clear whether they can be effectively applied to many other communities (Stubbs 1995).

Child Abuse

> I can imagine that someday we will regard our children not as creatures to manipulate or to change but rather as messengers from a world we once deeply knew, but which we have long since forgotten, who can reveal to us more about the true secrets of life, and also our own lives, than our parents were ever able to (Miller 1983: xi).

Personal Interventions: Counselling and Therapy

Needless to say, considerable effort is currently directed towards providing counselling and treatment for adult survivors of abuse as well as for child victims. In this respect, much of what was discussed above under wife abuse applies here. For example, children who accompany their mothers into shelters are typically provided with individual or group counselling. Children's discussion groups allow them to deal with issues such as identifying their feelings and building their self-esteem (Moore et al. 1989: 87-88; Pressman, Cameron and Rothery 1989: 88-90). As with adult women who are battered, most therapy is provided on a crisis basis and there is little available beyond the family's stay in the shelter. As a result, whether or not children receive long-term therapy may depend on the family's resources and the accessibility of counselling in the community. While activists are calling for follow-up counselling and support groups for children who have left shelters, it appears unlikely that these services will proliferate in the current economic and political climate.

In the context of child abuse therapy, it should also be noted that there is an important ongoing debate amongst counsellors. Some, especially those working from a feminist position or working in the shelter movement, have adopted an *advocacy* position on counselling and insist on meeting with victims and perpetrators separately. As advocates for the victim, they require that the perpetrator accept responsibility for the violence prior to undertaking counselling with them. There are many rationales for this position. Most notably, it is believed that children may be at risk of re-victimization if their counselling is conducted in a family setting that includes the abuser. A significant aspect of that re-victimization would involve any perpetrator who refused to acknowledge responsibility for the abuse.

Therapists working from the more traditional *family systems position* opt instead to treat the family as a unit. They want to address all the key players together, deal with the family dynamics between members and, ideally, assist the family in moving beyond the abuse. A third alternative, the *reconstructive position*, seeks to strike a middle ground by working through three stages. In the first stage, the victim and abuser receive individual counselling; in the second, the mother (if a non-abuser) and child are treated together and the nature of their relationship is addressed and finally, conjoint family therapy with the abuser (assuming she or he takes responsibility for the violence) is attempted. Steps are taken to assure the safety of the victim and to eliminate re-blaming the victim. The goal is to arrive at a point where the relationship issues between all family members are addressed (Rossman 1994).

Whichever position appears to be the more sensible, it is important to realize that therapists are addressing child abuse counselling from dramatically different perspectives. In particular, feminist therapists emphasize the importance of addressing the needs of the child victim and appear often to be less concerned about reconstituting the family. In contrast, more mainstream counsellors are often more inclined to urge family members to move beyond the violence and re-establish their relationships as a family.

Institutional Solutions: Social Welfare and Criminal Justice

Currently, considerable efforts are being directed at social welfare and criminal justice solutions to intrafamilial child abuse. In many respects, social welfare agencies, such as Children's Aid Societies (CAS),[11] remain the first line of defence. Typically, the CAS workers are the first to investigate suspected cases of child abuse. They may decide to call in the police for criminal investigation or, as in some jurisdictions, police will typically accompany CAS workers as they contact the family.[12] The police may conclude, based on their investigation, that there is sufficient evidence to lay criminal charges. In the absence of a criminal charge, case workers may decide either that the case warrants no further investigation or that there should be further monitoring and exploration. In some cases, workers may conclude that the provision of support services to the family will help to prevent child abuse and they will arrange to provide such services as daycare, homemakers and parenting skills counselling.

In many situations, greater intervention may seem to be warranted. If workers decide the child is in need of protection they will make arrangements for the removal of the child from the home. In some instances, parents will agree to the temporary, voluntary placement of the child with a friend or relative. If parents object to the child's removal, workers may apply to the court to apprehend the child. If the child appears in immediate danger, CAS workers are empowered to remove the child from the home without a warrant and with police assistance.

If at some point, the case results in criminal charges, the offending parent(s) will be tried in criminal court. The court decides on the criminal charge at hand and on the best solution for the child and the family. Judges typically seek to keep the family together. To this end, depending upon the advice of the child welfare worker, they may order the child returned to the home under the continued supervision of family services. Alternatively, parents may temporarily lose custody of the child who is placed with friends or relatives, with a foster family or in a group home. In cases of severe abuse, the child is permanently removed from the custody of parent(s) and, depending upon age, placed for adoption (Federal-Provincial Working Group 1994; see also, Vogl 1996).

While these basic structures of the social welfare and criminal justice systems have been in place for decades, the last twenty years have witnessed upheavals and momentous reforms. These reforms include the introduction of mandatory reporting, the creation of child abuse registers, changes to the Criminal Code and *Canada Evidence Act* to facilitate victim witness testimony, extension of the time limits for laying child sexual abuse charges and the establishment of Native-run child protection agencies.

The most dramatic change has been the introduction of mandatory reporting. Child protection laws in all jurisdictions except the Yukon (and throughout the United States) now require persons who suspect child abuse to report it to a child and family services authority. In some provinces, failure to report the abuse is a criminal offence that may result in a fine or imprisonment. In New Brunswick and Ontario, it is a criminal offence only for a professional (doctor, teacher, psychologist, etc.) to fail to report.

While mandatory reporting increases the visibility of child abuse to public officials, the creation of child abuse registers facilitates the interagency and interprovincial exchange of information on abusers. Registers maintain records of criminal convictions of child abuse offences. This is helpful in keeping track of extrafamilial child abusers (for example, pedophiles) and helps child welfare workers determine whether a family that is new in a community has a prior history of offences.

Changes to the criminal code have facilitated victim-witness testimony in the collection of evidence. For example, children are now allowed to testify behind screens or through closed-circuit television and, in some instances, on videotape. The requirement for corroborating evidence has been removed; for example, criminal charges do not depend upon having a witness to the abuse or physical evidence of abuse. Children are allowed to promise to tell the truth rather than being required to take an oath that they don't understand. In a few locations across Canada, special child preparation programs (such as the Child Victim-Witness Project in London, Ontario, and the Winnipeg Family Violence Court) exist to help reduce children's fear and anxiety and prepare them for the court process (Marshall et al. 1994: 29-36; see also Harvey 1996).

The extension of time limits for laying abuse charges has made it easier for adults to come forward. Until recently, adult victims of child abuse were restricted by the statute of limitations in their recourse to the justice system. If abuse victims failed to initiate civil proceedings four years after the cause arose or within four years of reaching the age of majority (age eighteen), they were forever denied this avenue of redress. Since many adult victims spent years coming to terms with their abuse, these restrictions were transparently unfair. In 1992, the Supreme Court of Canada relaxed these limitations and adult victims were able to come forward and seek justice many years[13] after the original victimization (Vienneau 1992: A1, A36).

One of the more significant efforts at institutional reform has been the effort to create Native-run child welfare organizations. In 1981, the Dakota Ojibwa Child and Family Services was established. Since then, as part of the drive towards self-government, numerous other Native-based agencies have been created. As a result, Native children are much less likely to be placed in non-Native foster or adoptive homes. For example, the Spallumcheen Band in British Columbia not only provides care for Native children but has also assumed responsibility for the supervision of their care in place of the provincial Ministry of Human Resources.

While the Spallumcheen Child Welfare program does not solve the larger issues of poverty and unemployment and the lack of "self-sustaining economic resources," it is an important challenge to the previous approach to child neglect and abuse (MacDonald 1995). Although solutions vary from community to community and in many instances Native organizations work under agreements with the provincial or federal governments, Native children today often remain within or under the control of Native communities (Sinclair, Phillips and Bala 1996).

In addition, there has been considerable effort within the Native communities as well as Native groups in prisons to address the concerns and problems of adult victims of child abuse so that the cycle of violence is broken. Traditional healing methods are combined with increased awareness of cultural heritage and pride to provide a new foundation for adult life. Indeed, as with wife abuse, the Native communities have been amongst the most innovative in developing projects to provide community and educational interventions in child abuse along with counselling for victims (National Clearinghouse 1994).

There is no question that these and related reforms have improved the institutional reponse to child abuse. For example, Carolyn Marshall's review of the justice system's response in Nova Scotia concludes that more cases of child sexual abuse are being reported to police, police are laying more charges, more cases involving younger victims are going to court and younger complainants are being allowed to testify in court (1994: 36). However, despite these and other advances, overall progress remains slow and new problems have arisen.

Although charges are being laid, sentences remain alarmingly light. The *Toronto Star* recently researched seventy child abuse homicide cases that occurred between 1991 and 1996 in Ontario. In fifty-two of these cases, the parent (or caregiver) who was criminally charged received no punishment or a sentence of less than two years. In more than half of the cases, the original charges were plea-bargained down (Welsh and Donovan 1997b: A1, A6).

Mandatory reporting has also been a mixed blessing. Doubtless it has meant an increased case load for many child protection agencies. This is not all positive. There are some concerns that this reform has meant a dramatic increase in unfounded charges which, in turn, take scarce resources away from more serious cases. Trocme reports, for example, that 42 percent of child abuse investigations in Ontario in 1993 were closed as "unfounded" (1994: iii).[14] Other reports suggest that current mandatory reporting guidelines (which vary from province to province) are unclear to many professionals and may undermine client–patient confidentiality and trust (for example, for social workers, psychologists) (Walters 1995; Thompson-Cooper, Fugere and Cormier 1993). Further, it is not clear that child protection agencies, most struggling with cutbacks as well as with increasing cases, can manage the load. An estimated 10,000 children in Ontario alone are admitted into care yearly (Trocme 1994: 74). Already, it is typical for case workers to juggle thirty-five to fifty cases and in many they must struggle with the enormously difficult task of determining whether or not parenting is abusive and whether or not a child is at risk (Swift 1995: 59). Nor are the standards for determining risk clearly detailed. For example, until recent reforms, only twenty-three out of fifty-five Ontario Children's Aid Societies had formal risk assessment plans and those twenty-three used six different plans. Currently, the Ontario government is seeking to establish clear and standard guidelines for child protection work (*Toronto Star*, August 8, 1997: A26).

Making child protection work seems to be enormously difficult. Evidence has mounted that case workers are not always able to protect children, even those with a long history of abuse. Tragically, in a number of high profile cases, case workers have returned children to abusive homes and, despite ongoing supervision, the children have been murdered by their abusers. For example, between 1994 and 1996, nineteen children were murdered while under the supervision of Ontario Children's Aid Societies (Donovan and Welsh 1997: A1; *Toronto Star*, March 26, 1997: A22). Similarly, in British Columbia, a recent task force sharply criticized government-run care of children which failed to prevent the murder of children under government protection (Welsh and Donovan 1997: A2). In 1997, Quebec launched a probe into all deaths of children under age 5, presumably to help gauge the adequacy of child protection services (*Toronto Star*, 1997: A3). Although provincial governments across the country are seeking to significantly reform their systems and to more closely monitor child protection work, it remains clear that there are "major problems in the child protection system" (Donovan and Welsh 1996: A1; Mallan 1997: A1).[15]

In Canada and the United States, these problems have led to some call for limits on mandatory reporting, such as holding citizens who file false reports legally liable or disposing of mandatory reporting completely (Thompson-Cooper, Fugere and Cormier 1993). It has also drawn into question the policy of reuniting the family. Some child advocates now urge a rethinking of this policy (Edmonds 1995: 2A). However, if more children are to be removed from their families, it's not clear that the system has safe, supportive alternative homes for them. Currently, there are complaints that foster care results in many children being bounced around from home to home;[16] adoption of older children is notoriously difficult and some foster and group homes have been charged with sexually and physically abusing the children they are expected to protect (Raychaba 1991: 132).

Further, the child abuse register has been criticized. The Ontario register, which was established in 1978, lists the name of verified (but not necessarily convicted) abusers. The intention is to deter abusers from repeating their offence since their names remain in place for twenty-five years. However, when agencies such as daycare centres, boards of education or various children's organizations wish to confirm that employees are not listed, they are denied access on the grounds of the Charter of Rights, privacy of information, confidentiality of records and Health Act issues (Sweet 1986: F1; Interview—Director of Services, Family and Children's Services, St. Catharines, April 1997).

Nor did the register address the information gaps between child protection workers. Until recently an abusive family could fall through the cracks if it simply moved to another jurisdiction. Amongst the most recent reforms in Ontario has been the creation of a computer database that links every child protection worker in the province (*Toronto Star*, July 3, 1997: A26). This presumably leaves unanswered the fate of abused children who move out of province.

Judicial reforms remain similarly piecemeal and underutilized. Marshall's research in Nova Scotia found that few police were trained in child abuse investigation. Her research found that there were no instances of the use of videotaped testimony; only one-half of child victims were supported during the court process and the Crown attorneys still relied on corroborating evidence even though this was no longer a requirement. Victims and their families also reported that they were often left in the dark, not knowing if charges would be laid or whether the abuser was being released. Finally, in the minority[17] of cases which resulted in conviction, Marshall found that, as in Ontario, sentences were far from harsh. Only one-half of the convicted offenders were incarcerated and most for thirty days or less (1994: 271-74; see also Trocme 1994: 78).

Even the creation of Native-run child protection agencies may have its shortcomings. Critics complain that in some instances provincial child welfare organizations have simply vacated their responsibilities, providing little support, training or guidance to Native organizations. The result, in some cases, has been an inadequate, poorly trained agency that cannot respond appropriately to the needs of the children it seeks to protect. Even in the late 1980s there was documentation of extensive sexual abuse of children in some communities, and today Native children continue to commit suicide at ten times the national average (Teichroeb 1997).

Finally, as with woman abuse, some advocates question whether the institutional approach itself is appropriate and worthwhile as a primary solution to child abuse. Kelly Dunsdon, for example, points out that criminal proceedings may drain the family's resources and victimize the child further by removing the parent. The child may end up living in an unstable, unhappy and impoverished home. Whatever the court disposition of the offending parent, she or he is likely to return to live with the child and, currently, is very unlikely to receive any counselling or rehabilitation while incarcerated. Alternatively, removing the child from the home and placing her or him in a series of foster homes is unlikely to dramatically improve the quality of the child's life.[18] Further, decisions to remove children, as arrived at currently by social workers and judges, tend to be based on "majoritarian, white, middle-class norms and values" (1995: 451). Children may end up in care, in part, because their parents do not fit the appropriate stereotype, regardless of the children's relationship with the parent(s) or desire to remain in the home.

As a result of these various concerns, child protection remains at the centre of a storm of controversy. Many child welfare advocates are today demanding new legislation that will clearly put the rights of children ahead of any concerns with keeping the family together (Pron 1997: A2). Others urge greater powers for CAS workers both to investigate the possibility of abuse and to remove children they deem to be in danger. Finally, there is a growing demand that the child protection system be streamlined so that the movement of children through the system more speedily reaches some appropriate resolutions, whether it be placement for adoption or return to the family (Welsh and Donovan 1997a, 1997c).

If the pitfalls of institutional solutions are to be avoided, we must construct societal changes that prevent violence against children. As most analysts agree, one critical first step towards challenging and changing societal attitudes is education.

Societal Changes: Education and Politics

Not surprisingly, efforts at the societal level have frequently involved efforts to provide better public education on the nature, causes and consequences of child abuse. For example extensive audio-visual resources on child abuse and related topics have been assembled over the past decade. Since child abuse often has long-term consequences on adult behaviour (addictive behaviours, generational family violence, interpersonal difficulties), information campaigns have targeted people in the workplace who want to meet and discuss child abuse issues so that they benefit from understanding the effect of abuse on adult survivors.

In addition, considerable effort has been directed at providing education to children. One of the most innovative campaigns has been developed in the Lincoln County (Ontario) Board of Education. The Board has implemented a comprehensive Kindergarten to Grade 12 curriculum that addresses issues of interpersonal violence and that is directed at preventing child abuse, sexual assault and family violence in general (Moore and Pepler 1989: 91).

Recently, schools in the Niagara region became the first English schools in Canada to introduce the Child Assault Prevention Program (CAPP), under the auspices of the Niagara Region Sexual Assault Centre. CAPP, which was formulated in the United States, seeks through role playing, discussion and drawings to provide children with the skills to handle abusive or exploitive situations that involve family members or friends. Premised on children's right to "feel safe, strong and free," the program challenges traditional rules such as respect for authority and politeness to adults. Advocates argue that such a program in the school will encourage children to fight back or report inappropriate or abusive acts (Hannen 1996/97).

Some analysts, however, are critical of these incremental changes. Bishop argues, for example, that in-depth education is needed at all levels of society; it is ineffective and unrealistic to attempt to teach children to protect themselves. Rather, specific social reforms are needed, including a ban on the exploitation of children's sexuality in the marketplace, a ban on corporal punishment of children as well as the elimination of arbitrary, degrading and humiliating forms of discipline. In this context, the rights of children need to be asserted and community silence on child abuse outlawed (1991).

The kind of changes urged by Bishop go far beyond education since they imply political action in the form of new policies, legislative proposals and public debate. Other analysts also call for political action by challenging the role of poverty in Canadian life. As mentioned previously, it is apparent that a significant root of child abuse is poverty and economic marginalization and that neglect is often synonymous with being poor. Consequently, any economic policy that successfully addressed poverty rates would be the "single most effective way to promote child health and well-being." Specifically, higher minimum wage rates, guaranteed annual incomes and significant child benefits along with "more equitable income, housing, child care and job training provisions" would constitute a significant assault on poverty and poverty-generated ills such as family violence (Aitken and Mitchell 1995: 31; see also Watchel 1994; Tower 1996: 433-34; Callahan 1993).

Unfortunately we may be living in a political era where much of the populace lacks the political will to undertake such systemic solutions and, indeed, much policy appears to be moving in precisely the opposite direction as social welfare, medical coverage, unemployment insurance, disability insurance, childcare, family violence and related programs are cut.

Elder, Parent, Sibling and Adolescent Abuse

In searching for solutions to the various problems of family violence, a number of possible interventions have been suggested by professionals working in the field. Many of these involve dealing with the interactants of the abusive situation directly; for example, setting up shelters so that victims have somewhere to escape when violence occurs or passing legislation that enables police officers who attend at the scene of family violence to put an end to it and remove the perpetrator. Other types of interventions place more emphasis on the wider properties of family violence; in other words, on the social conditions that contribute to the creation of violent and abusive families. There are two such interventions. One consists of educational programs that are designed to teach people how to identify abusive behaviour when it happens to them or to someone else, either as perpetrator or victim. The other calls for community supports such as drop-in or care centres for teens or elderly people who need to get out of the family setting for a temporary period of time to reduce the amount of stress they and their family members experience. Both types of interventions are necessary if we are to successfully deal with the problem of violence and abuse in families.

In this section we review, in some detail, the different types of solutions and interventions that have been suggested in the literature and offer critical comments on their possible efficacy. (For a more comprehensive discussion of Canadian strategies for dealing with elder abuse, see MacLean 1995.)

The first point that must be made is that social policy must undergo a major overhaul in order to adequately address family violence. Any policy that focuses exclusively on cases of abuse, whether they are perpetrated against adults or children, and only deals with these cases as an individual phenomenon ignores the fact that poverty, or low income, is one of the most fundamental aspects of family conflict and troubles. The individualization of this problem cannot adequately correct these. Social policy must be reformulated to deal with the underlying *social* causes of violence within the family. Without an appropriate economic base, one which is not achieved at the cost of working extremely long hours outside the home under gruelling conditions, family relations cannot thrive. People's needs will not be met. When needs are not met, people tend to suffer from anxiety and depression, and hostility builds. Relations become damaged by these negative feelings and result in damage to the people who experience them and those upon whom they vent these feelings. Damaged individuals cannot form the basis for a healthy society. Damage, like shame, is contagious and may affect entire populations. Social relations in general suffer. Therefore, social policy must deal with issues of greater economic security for families that are vulnerable. The social safety net cannot be pulled from these families because the probable outcome will be more violence and abuse, not only contained within the families themselves, but spreading throughout the rest of society. Better income supplements, better wages and benefits, safer working conditions, lower-cost housing and accessible daycare facilities are essential to the optimal functioning of families and society as a whole. Deficit-cutting cannot be employed as an excuse for the greater impoverishment of families because the cost of such cuts to the social safety net will have to be borne by the entire society and will simply be too high.

Gelles and Cornell (1990: 139) offer five policy steps that they believe would help to bring violence in families to an end. The first is to eliminate social norms that glorify and perpetuate violence. Some examples they offer are an end to spanking of children, which has been argued by many to teach children nothing but the appropriateness of hitting a loved one when the perpetrator believes that the situation justifies it. Children learn that violence is a normal part of a loving relationship in this way. Blending love and violence in an intimate setting can have tremendous repercussions throughout our society. Therefore, social policy should be elaborated to put an end to child spanking. Furthermore, violence in the media should be curtailed. It is not necessary to show bloodied corpses strewn on streets in order to report the news. Nor is it necessary or desirable to fill prime time hours with various degrees of fighting, shooting and killing, all in the guise of "entertainment" or "real-life drama." Even situation comedies, the staple of television fare, are rife with instances of verbal abuse and denigration of characters. These types of programs normalize different kinds of abuse by offering them up as part of everyday scenes of life to which most people can relate at some level. We begin to believe that this is what happens to everyone and that it is part of "human nature" to behave and treat others in such a manner. Violent scenes pervade children's cartoons. Villains seeking to do harm to innocent people lurk around every corner while superheroes sometimes just barely manage to subdue them. The battle between "good and evil" is constantly being waged on children's programs but there is a great deal of similarity between the good characters and the bad in terms of their behaviour. Children may get warped messages about what it means to be good and how violence plays a role in being good.

The second policy proposal offered by Gelles and Cornell is that "violence-provoking" stress should be eliminated from society. This suggestion echoes what has already been stated pertaining to social policy. Poverty, social inequality, un- or underemployment, inadequate housing, education and nutrition are all factors that contribute to human misery and possibly to overwhelming stress. People who suffer from these types of deprivation are probably deeply angry over their life situation and are not, therefore, likely to be well equipped to handle daily stressors. They may lash out with violence when their profound anger is aroused by a family member over something relatively insignificant, doing much more damage than they might have intended.

Families must be integrated into a network of kin and community as a third step toward creating social policy that will enable us to prevent violence. It has been found that social isolation is a correlate of family violence. Whether the isolation precedes abuse or results from it is not clear but that it is closely associated with violence is evident. There are two ideas for communities to help families establish relationships outside the family and build a social bond. Perhaps neighbourhoods could be organized into committees that could set up visiting programs. Volunteers in these programs would reach out to families in the area in a non-threatening way. Or neighbourhood parties could be held where everyone is invited to meet and mingle with their neighbours. While these suggestions might have a "Rockwellesque" ring to them, something which seems outdated in our cynical society, they offer up possibilities in terms of providing connections for increasingly socially alienated individuals and families. If the social bond were strengthened, then there is a real chance that people might be able to overcome their tendencies to lash out at one another.

An important policy step in any program to decrease violence in families would be the removal of sexism from our social landscape. The power imbalance established by sexism leads to social inequality and low valuation of an entire social group. In addition, sexism provides a model for other types of -isms that reinforce power inequities and accomplish the same low valuations of, for instance, senior citizens, children and ethnic minorities.

Finally, the cycle of violence must be broken within particular families. Since violence is often transmitted from generation to generation, it is imperative to intervene and put an end to it. Parents must learn techniques to deal with children that do not lead to abuse and violence. Problem-solving and conflict resolution procedures could be taught to families. Neighbours could be encouraged to take children for a short period of time so that parents can reduce their stress levels. A community drop-in centre or even a hot line might help to decrease stress and provide another outlet for overburdened family members.

Ethical issues must be taken into consideration anytime intervention into an abusive family situation is contemplated. As Kryk (1995) notes, in our society we value self-determination but we also believe that society has an obligation to protect its citizens. We also cherish the notion that families themselves will safeguard their members. Competing societal values make the decision to intervene an extremely difficult one and require that it be approached with caution.

Individual rights must not be unduly trespassed upon, regardless of how well meaning professionals might be. Professionals must not arbitrarily decide to remove victims or perpetrators against the will of the parties involved. Alternatively, they must not attempt to keep victims or perpetrators from returning to their relationship if that is what they want. Despite frustration over repeated scenes of abuse between the same parties, professionals must at all times recall that people have the right to determine their own fates if they are legally and mentally competent to do so. Family relationships rarely involve *only* abuse and anger; there is usually love and loyalty as well. The intertwining of these emotions makes it hard for any individual, whether she or he is the victim or the perpetrator, to simply walk away from the relationship and never look back. Until she or he is ready to do so of her or his own volition, no professional, no matter how concerned or caring, should attempt to force her or him to leave the relationship. Such coercion could result in the possibility of greater damage to the victim.

Even when family relationships are marked by violence and abuse, intervention in the form of removal of either the victim or the perpetrator should not result in the destruction of these relationships if there is any possibility that they could be saved. Even temporary removal of abused children or elders could have a deleterious effect on their relations with other family members, in addition to the abuser. No professional should cause harm with whatever decision she or he makes. Therefore, before removal is even suggested, there should be no doubt that the family relationship is already damaged beyond repair and that there is nothing to salvage. Of course, if the victim's life is threatened, then removal may be the only recourse. However, removal of the perpetrator might be a more beneficial response than removal of the victim, depending on the circumstances.

In the case of sibling abuse, for example, removal may pose a serious dilemma for professionals since removal of siblings from the family may violate a number of rights. The rights of the parents may be violated if a professional steps in to remove a child abusing other siblings because it effectively destroys their parental role of disciplining their children and resolving their children's problems. It may be seen as a negative judgment of their parenting skills without strong enough justification. It may also stigmatize parents in the eyes of the community as well as in terms of their other children, possibly undermining their authority.

Another problem is that removal may destroy the integrity of the family unit. Removal of a sibling from brothers and sisters assumes that the only relationship that exists among them is the abusive one. This is too narrow a definition of sibling relationships. It may destroy the other sibling relationships if the other children take sides for or against the abusing sibling. The relationship between the abusing sibling and parents could be severely damaged if the child perceives that the parents did not fulfil their responsibilities in providing adequate guidance or discipline, or did not protect the abusing child from the authorities. The same may be true for the parent–child relationship with the remaining children. They may perceive the same failures in their parents.

The abusing child may suffer unduly in the sense of being socially stigmatized by being removed from the family unit and also because of being labelled an abuser. Removal fails to separate the behaviour from the person, reducing the child to a master status that denies the presence of other, positive qualities. It may isolate the child and exacerbate whatever factors may have contributed to the abusive behaviour in the first place. Furthermore, the child may be placed in a facility in which other children with similar problems may reside, once again isolating the child from more positive influences and relationships. Finally, being removed from the family does not allow the abusing child to learn how to develop more positive relationships with siblings.

It cannot be stated strongly enough that intervention must be careful not to alienate individuals from the other members of their family or from others in their lives. Once again, this prudence applies more to removal than to other less intrusive types of intervention. Removing siblings, adolescents, children or elders from their home and family environment may sever their other relationships if, for example, other members of the family or relatives cannot maintain contact with the removed party. Being removed might set up an us–them situation where those who are left behind in the family may feel that they are "guilty by association" in the sense that they remain within the family circle and possibly still have dealings with the victim or perpetrator, depending on which party was removed. These individuals might begin to feel shame that they did not stop the abuse or do something else to ameliorate the situation; the shame can have a corrosive effect on them and their relationship with the removed party. These family relationships might break down as a result of removal. The removed party will then have less family support because of this breakdown. Instead of removal, another type of intervention into an abusive family situation might consist of an outreach program that could provide the pertinent parties with an outlet for their anger and aggression or that might work in an advisory capacity to offer possible remedies for the abusive situation.

The punitive ethos of some types of intervention, such as those which fall under the rubric of legislation (for example, removal, mandatory reporting, prosecution), might exacerbate family violence rather than remedy it. It is the emotions of both the victim and abuser, along with those of other family members, that are exacerbated when a family member is removed or forced to leave due to abusive behaviour, or a professional is compelled to report abuse to the authorities and an official investigation is undertaken, or charges are laid. Some of the feelings likely to be heightened are stress, being overburdened with responsibilities, low self-esteem stemming from the family conflict itself or because of poverty, unemployment or problems with alcohol. These emotions could already be running high and could be pushed beyond control. Time spent in a detention centre could make an abuser that much more violent and more bent on seeking revenge. The same effect could result from a victim being placed in a shelter or foster home. Statistics demonstrate that a perpetrator's violence against a woman who leaves an abusive partner often escalates to the point of homicide. An elderly person forced to go into an institution due to violence in the family could become bitter, angry and depressed, creating problems for that person in the institutional setting. In short, intrusive solutions, such as those connected with legislation, could make the situation worse, inflicting more damage on the victim and family relationships in general. None of these hypothetical scenarios should completely rule out any sort of intervention or legal sanctions; they should simply serve to alert professionals and the general public to potential pitfalls inherent in such solutions.

Victims' self-determination must be a priority. Victims should not be made to feel as if they have *less* control over their situation when a professional or advocate attempts to intervene on her or his behalf. Podnieks (1988) points to the loss of privacy, when this takes place, as a factor that might contribute to loneliness and isolation of the victim. The professional must remain sensitive to the victim's desires at all times. This is especially true in light of Podnieks's (1992) finding that abused elderly women who felt in control of their lives and the decisions about their lives displayed the very positive quality of hardiness. Self-determination also applies to decisions to proceed with prosecution of abusive spouses despite the victims' recantings. In San Diego, California, and in Toronto, Ontario, such prosecutions have gone ahead. They raise important ethical questions. Should the legal system, in its representation of society, go against the wishes of the victim and prosecute the abuser? Who benefits from this prosecution? Is this truly an attempt to ameliorate conditions for victims or is it simply a way to present the public with a seemingly more efficient legal system and the image of a government pledged to protect its citizens and doing something to fulfil its promise? In the absence of cynicism, it is still possible that the good intentions of professionals and advocates working in the multifaceted and volatile field of family violence may lose sight of what their ultimate goal should be: helping families suffering from abuse. A lengthy feature in the *Toronto Star*, running in March of 1996, dealt with some of the complex issues surrounding prosecution of abusers in the case of wife abuse.

Kryk (1995) outlines some ethical issues that pertain specifically to elder abuse. The competence of the abused party must be taken into consideration. Is the victim in a position to make a reasonable decision concerning her or his own fate? Is she or he capable of caring for her or himself? What is best for the victim? This is a very delicate question. The professional contemplating intrusion into an abusive situation concerning a senior citizen should look at the responsibilities, rights and needs of caregivers. It is easy to charge caregivers with abuse and neglect but it may be more difficult to do so once the professional has seriously considered the many constraints and demands facing the caregivers. If the abuser turns out to be mentally incapacitated, should committal be recommended? What about the rights of the abuser? Also, when taking into account what is best for the victim, it may be found that what is best for her or his happiness is not necessarily best for her or his safety. In other words, the victim's happiness may be better ensured if she or he were to be left in the home with the abusive caregiver, although her or his safety would not be ensured in this case. Should safety take precedence over happiness? How is the quality of life to be measured (i.e., in terms of happiness or safety)? Along the same lines, if the victim's values commit her or him to the caregiver, even if said caregiver is violent and abusive, should the professional override these values and remove the victim or caregiver from the setting? Does that truly serve the needs of the victim? Should the victim's right to privacy be contravened to ensure safety? What if the victim is an abuser as well (as may often be the case when dealing with abuse involving adults, older or adolescent children)? All of these questions present a conundrum, yet all must be seriously considered before intrusive solutions are contemplated. Ethical concerns also apply to intrusive interventions.

Legislation

On the federal level, provisions under the Criminal Code of Canada address the various types of abuses experienced by siblings, adolescents, parents and elders. Sections 244 and 245.3 deal with physical assault. Sections 246.1 and 246.8 deal with sexual assault. Psychological or emotional abuse that consists of threats and intimidation is dealt with through sections 243.4 and 381. Neglect is covered by section 197 or section 247 if the neglect consists of forcible confinement (Gnaedinger 1989: 7). Material or financial abuse, which is virtually exclusive to elderly people, can be dealt with using section 304 (stopping mail with intent), section 324 (forgery), and sections 291 and 292 (theft by a person holding power of attorney). McDonald et al. (1991) provide more detailed references to the sections of the Criminal Code that deal with particular kinds of abuse. In addition, they provide an account of legislation that deals with elder abuse in institutional settings. Such legislation generally consists of government regulation of the institutions themselves and tort or civil contract law.

McDonald et al. (1991) also argue that existing provisions under the Criminal Code of Canada offer limited usefulness in dealing with mistreatment of the elderly. Their limitation is due to the fact that they can only deal with provable cases of abuse and, therefore, do nothing to facilitate prevention. In other words, legislation is *reactive* rather than *proactive*. As with criminal law, these laws that deal with governmental regulation of nursing homes and civil contracts place the onus of proof on the offended party, or victim, who must initiate the action and demonstrate to the court that she or he has been mistreated in some way. Such action requires knowledge of the system and the laws, in addition to financial means to pay for legal advice and to retain a lawyer to carry out the suit. Use of existing criminal, regulatory or civil legislation is always in reaction to an already perpetrated action.

Most provinces in Canada have enacted legislation to specifically deal with abuse of the elderly and other dependent adults. These laws are collectively known as "adult guardianship and adult protection legislation". Gordon (1995; see also McDonald et al. 1991; Gnaedinger 1989) provides an excellent overview of the evolution of this legislation, describing the evolution as occurring in three waves of reform.

According to Gordon, the first wave took place in the 1970s, beginning with Alberta in 1976. The Alberta legislation dealt primarily with the concerns of mentally disabled adults and their families. It removed terms such as "mentally incompetent" that stigmatized disabled adults and changed the purely medical basis for assessing decision-making capacity to one that encompassed an individual's functionality. In other words, an adult would, under the new provisions, be assessed as to how well she or he could make informed, competent decisions on the basis of how well she or he was able to function in her or his daily life. Provisions for guardianship were limited in terms of their duration and the scope of powers given to the guardian. Other jurisdictions in Canada (Saskatchewan, Northwest Territories), as well as Australia and some American states, followed this model. Unfortunately, as Gordon points out, the weakness of this legislation lay in its lack of specificity in terms of addressing cases of abuse and neglect.

The second wave of reforms was primarily concerned with intervention in cases of abuse and neglect. Newfoundland was the first

Canadian province to enact specific adult protection laws in 1973. Most of the significant reforms in the other provinces occurred in the 1980s, however. This type of legislation generally allows health and social service agencies to intervene wherever abuse or neglect is suspected. Self-neglect is included under this rubric. Services are offered to adults who may voluntarily accept them. Nevertheless, if it is deemed that the adult cannot, will not or is incapable due to mental impairment of making an informed decision, these agencies may forcibly intervene by obtaining court orders. Such orders are limited in duration and are open to review. The legislation nonetheless gives these professionals a good deal of power to enter premises, arbitrarily remove adults who are deemed to be suffering from abuse and neglect, report cases of abuse and neglect to the proper authorities, and obtain restraining orders against abusers.

The drawback of adult protection legislation in most provinces (with the exception of Prince Edward Island) is that it is very much like *child* protection legislation. As has already been noted, elderly people are *not* children; they are full-fledged adults and have civil and legal rights that differ from those of children. Therefore, legislation that treats them as *if* they were children is both problematic and insulting.

An attempt to balance intervention with autonomy and self-determination characterizes the third wave of reforms to adult guardianship and protection legislation in Canada. This incarnation of the legislation appears to place more control over their personal situation into the hands of the elderly, de-emphasizing the power of professionals. Mandatory reporting has been given less priority; voluntary reporting is preferred. Social or community advocacy is also a feature of this wave of legislation, allowing those senior citizens without caring friends and relatives to have someone who can offer support and assistance. Personal support networks are recognized and are preferred over court-ordered guardianship. British Columbia, Manitoba, Ontario and Quebec have implemented these reforms.

Gordon states that this third-wave legislation incorporates the best features of that of the preceding two waves. However, he cautions that there are potentially three problem areas in this new legislation. Combining guardianship and protection legislation is one problem area. Such a combination may lead to more intrusive and more restrictive methods of dealing with abuse and neglect, like court-ordered guardianship. One way to offset such a tendency is to have an advisory board oversee and periodically review guardianships and trusteeships. The cutbacks increasingly being made by provincial governments endanger advocacy services to elderly people.

This situation comprises another of the potential problems. Ontario may be especially vulnerable since social advocacy is an integral part of the new legal provisions for guardianship and protection of the elderly, provisions which rest on the assumption that, unless an elderly person objects, she or he can be ordered by the court to be placed under guardianship. If cutbacks result in the abolition or drastic reduction of advocacy services, seniors will not have anyone to object for them, so they may be placed under court-ordered guardianship against their will.

The third potential problem is an increase in abuse and neglect cases because the power of professionals to intervene whenever they deem fit has been greatly reduced. If elderly people have more control over their situation and they are able to rely more on personal support networks, there might be more opportunity for members of their support network to abuse them or to continue to abuse them and less opportunity for detection by professionals.

One of the very real problems with legislation that is aimed at prosecuting persons who are found to be abusers is that there is often scant attention paid to their own victimization. In other words, if someone is abusing a sibling, parent, adolescent or senior citizen, among others, but that person was the victim of abuse when she or he was younger or is perhaps still experiencing abusive treatment from a member of her or his family, being prosecuted by the court system as an abuser will do very little to remedy the dilemma posed by family violence. Although every individual is ultimately responsible for her or his behaviour, to punish someone who is already a victim for reproducing the behaviour which has made her or him into a victim is actually to punish her or him twice. Such double punishment can do very little to end abuse because it becomes another facet of the abuse the victim/abuser has already experienced. Victimization must be stopped at the source, or as close to the source as possible, in order to effectively deal with family violence.

This also applies to adolescents who come before the courts. When adolescents who have been violently mistreated by their parents come before the courts because they have ended up on the streets and committed criminal offences, officers of the court should be instructed to be more attuned to the needs of these abuse victims (for example, being able to spot them, serving their needs). The court should be lenient with them and intervene to get them and their family help rather than punish them. Cases should have specific workers to watch over adolescents to ensure that they are being dealt with fairly and having their needs met rather than just being processed. There should be less jail time and general institutionalization of teens since these methods are more damaging than rehabilitative (Garbarino and Gilliam 1980).

There is a great debate among professionals regarding mandatory versus voluntary reporting (Bond et al. 1995). The ability to intervene at an earlier stage, its effectiveness as a deterrent and the opportunity to give assistance to those who might be unable to give consent to such are among the arguments in favour of mandatory reporting. Those opposed contend that it is intrusive, creates problems with confidentiality and may increase the number of unsubstantiated cases.

Shelter

The provision of shelters for both victims and abusers could provide a resource for abusive families. Although there are shelters for battered women and hostels for men, it is generally found that elderly women and men do not fit into the shelter and hostel environments, nor do they feel comfortable with the often large age gap between themselves and the other residents. Furthermore, because younger abused women often bring their children with them, the atmosphere could be somewhat problematic for older victims due to noise and activity levels (see *Niagara Falls Review* 1997: A10; *Toronto Star*, August 23, 1994: C2). Older victims may also find that the other services available in the shelter, such as counselling, may not be suited to their needs, while there might not be services to meet the special needs of some elderly women, especially those with health problems. The same applies to men's hostels. Elderly men could have special needs that cannot be accommodated in these places. Shelters for abused men, if they exist at all, are few and far between. Because of these problems with shelter, so many abused elderly people are afraid to report. They fear that they will be placed into an institution for lack of alternatives. An article in the *Toronto Star* from 1994 stated that a shelter particularly designed for elderly victims of abuse was being planned for Toronto. It would be the second in Canada, the first having been opened in 1992 in Montreal. Shelters dedicated to victims of elder abuse would be more beneficial for these victims because they could be staffed with individuals trained to handle not only the effects of abuse but also the distinct needs of older people.

Shelters for children and adolescents fleeing from parental or sibling abuse could be of some benefit, especially if there were follow-up programs designed to assist victims in recovering from the effects of violence and to help other family members deal with the abuse that occurred within the family. Even those siblings who do not personally experience abuse need to come to terms with what happened in their family.

Potential or actual abusers could also be provided with shelters. An article in the *Niagara Falls Review* (March 10, 1997: A9) stated that a shelter for violent men was being opened in Winnipeg, Manitoba, to allow these men to leave the environment where the abuse was or might be taking place so that they could learn techniques for handling their anger. Such a place would serve men who fear that they may become abusers, as well as those who are already behaving in violent and abusive manners, because they would have the opportunity to deal with their problems in a way that would be empowering. Rather than being jailed and forced into some sort of counselling, they would have the choice of going to shelters; this could reduce the sense of being labelled and stigmatized and make them more positively disposed to change.

Group homes as a temporary or even permanent measure, or some other type of alternative living options (Podnieks 1992), could assist both abusers and victims. Such shelters could offer these individuals a separate space from the people and environments associated with the violence and abuse; distance could possibly help to defuse the situation and give all the interactants a chance to examine their relationships to see if there could be alternative methods for interacting. For children or adolescents, group or alternative homes would be able to give them a safe place to stay while they heal from the experience of abuse. The staff could also serve as a liaison between them and their families, offering ways to reintegrate family relationships in a more positive manner.

Affordable housing in senior citizens complexes could be another solution for elderly victims of abuse. Since older individuals usually balk at the notion of going into a nursing home, a complex designed with them in mind, including the state of their finances, where they could mingle with others their own age and receive needed services, might be an ideal situation. An apartment or suite could offer them the privacy they need, while being part of a complex would aid in combatting the social isolation elderly people often endure.

In a neo-conservative, cost-cutting environment, such recourse to shelters and alternative living arrangements may seem out of the question. However, governments should be made to recognize that the cost in human misery and the loss of human resources due to lives ravaged by violence and abuse are far higher than the cost of funding programs to create these services. Furthermore, private corporations might be induced to contribute to such facilities where job- or skills-training at some level might be offered to younger people staying there. Their profile in the community could only be heightened if these corporations and businesses were seen to demonstrate their desire to be part of the community and lend their assistance. Finally, perhaps shelters and group homes could be developed as small businesses by private individuals, subject to grants from governments to get started, possibly charging a small fee for room and board from those who can afford it and charging corporate sponsors for allowing them to place their products in these facilities. Government monitoring would, of course, be compulsory.

Education

Education is a preventative measure against all forms of family violence and has the potential to reap the greatest rewards if people can be taught new ways of seeing, thinking and interpreting. On the other hand, it is one of the most difficult measures because it requires ongoing and extensive work.

Friends or family members who are caregivers of the elderly need to learn about the special needs of their charges and how to handle them. Often, these caregivers assume they will simply know how to care for elders because they have affection for them or have raised children or given assistance in some other capacity. In addition, these caregivers need to learn how to handle stressful situations and ongoing stress and to learn effective conflict resolution methods that could help them deal with the problems they might encounter with the elderly.

The elderly should also be educated about what elder abuse is, what options are available to them if they find themselves in such a situation and how they themselves can help to prevent their own abuse (for example, having someone they can call, having cheques deposited directly into their bank accounts and bills paid automatically from them). This information could be transmitted via television shows elders are likely to watch, visiting homemakers, Meals-on-Wheels volunteers, or public health nurses (Gnaedinger

1989). Of course, the information should be available not only in Canada's two official languages but in other minority languages as well, since many of our seniors are immigrants who have been sponsored by their children (Beaulieu 1992).

The same methods could be employed in other types of abuse. Parents and children of all ages could benefit from educational sessions at the local school in the evenings or during the regular school day for the children. Methods of nonviolent conflict resolution and for handling anger appropriately would help children and parents cope with many of the frustrations endemic to family life so that violence does not become the only recourse. Parenting and family skills courses, as well as stress management courses, could be a part of every school curriculum in some form, and evening courses could be held for parents. Joint classes for parents and children/adolescents or siblings could also be held to deal with the family as a whole and assist members in handling problems. They could also be a source of empowerment, helping victims to take steps to stop their abuse and abusers to find an alternative way of coping with stress and tension (Goodwin and Roscoe 1990).

All schools that train professionals such as social workers, lawyers and nurses should have a required component dealing with gerontology or geriatrics. This type of instruction would promote greater sensitivity in these professionals so that they are better able to identify potential abuse. It might also facilitate an exchange of information about the factors and indicators of elder abuse among various professionals (Gnaedinger 1989).

In general, schools could help identify abuse victims, provide other assistance and help with prevention. For example, educators could inform policy makers about the many issues surrounding abuse so they can institute more protective policies. Parent-teacher associations could provide education in nonviolent conflict resolution and other aspects of family life to neighbourhood families or those with histories of abuse. And most importantly, schools should be more sensitive to students' learning needs and provide more encouragement when students are having a tough time (Garbarino and Gilliam 1980).

Finally, raising public consciousness about the problems many families face is essential. Educational programs should be launched to ensure that Canadians become aware that social conditions contribute to violence in families, not just individual pathologies. Everyone should be made aware of what constitutes an abusive situation, the many factors that can precipitate violence in any family, ways to deal with an abusive situation and what services are available to families and individuals who are experiencing violence or neglect. Canadians should be aware of the fact that the proportion of elderly people in the population is growing and that there are particular factors that make them more vulnerable to abuse, such as physical and cognitive disabilities and isolation (One Voice 1995). They should be made to understand that many families, not just those that live in low-income or impoverished homes, are suffering the effects of stress and economic insecurity and how these factors contribute to the impoverishment of family relations and members. In short, Canadians must be made to realize that family violence is an issue that touches the lives of all people who live in this country, not just those who experience it directly.

Community Support and Counselling Services

Without community support in various forms, education can do little to ameliorate family violence. If people have nowhere to turn for relief and advice when they find themselves caught up in an abusive or potentially abusive situation, education is a waste of time and energy. The entire community, including friends and neighbours, as well as professionals and agencies, such as legal and medical services, must get involved in stopping and preventing family violence.

There are few services available for abused adolescents. Often teens have little choice but to run away from home, preferring the harshness of living on the street to remaining at home with abusive parents. Those who attempt to avail themselves of services may encounter many problems and shortages. Group homes may be the best alternative for adolescents suffering maltreatment at the hands of their parents, but there are few of these. Foster homes are also scarce and are often underfunded and overcrowded, the caregivers poorly screened. Institutional settings like detention centres do not provide already-wounded adolescents with a nurturing environment, a fact which may exacerbate their problems. Furthermore, they often suffer more abuse within these institutions. Due to professional standards, extreme caseloads and bureaucratic procedures, social workers frequently do not devote sufficient attention to adolescent runaways. Believing that social workers do not care about them, teens may view them with a great deal of suspicion. Adolescents who run away to escape abuse typically have low self-esteem; as a consequence, they tend to put themselves in degrading positions (such as prostitution, panhandling and petty crime), which may lead to even lower self-esteem (Webber 1991; Garbarino and Gilliam 1980).

Support groups and both formal and informal counselling should be made available to individuals who need them. Drop-in centres for teens, parents and elders could offer people a non-threatening, non-stigmatizing place where they can go to get away from a volatile situation, seek camaraderie and talk about their problems in complete confidentiality. Telephone hot lines could also help in this regard. Sometimes just being able to talk to someone and share experiences with them, having these experiences validated, can assist individuals in coping with and working through their problems (Beaulieu 1992; Schlesinger 1988; National Clearinghouse 1986). It can also help identify an abusive situation. In addition, resources like this would ameliorate some of the social isolation many people experience.

Access to helping professionals, like social workers, medical /health care workers and legal workers, could be another resource offered in a community drop-in centre. These professionals should all be trained to be sensitive and non-judgmental in their dealings with individuals experiencing violence, whether they are victims, abusers, or potential abusers. For example, caregivers of elderly people could benefit from a combined educational and counselling atmosphere with peers and professionals sensitive to the stresses of their lives (Podnieks 1988). In terms of siblings who abuse or are likely to abuse, community-based strategies would be useful in providing alternatives for these children. In other words, if children had somewhere to go to escape an escalating situation, they might be able to defuse it effectively before abuse ensues. If there were neighbourhood drop-in centres where children could go, where trained and sympathetic adults could supervise them and give them an outlet to vent their frustrations or give them activities to pursue to redirect their energies, perhaps children would feel less inclined to turn on their siblings. A non-threatening environment where they could go to get away temporarily from irritants in their homes might be enough to assist them in dealing with siblings in a more positive fashion. This kind of solution would be consistent with research findings that demonstrate that, when children spend less time in the home with siblings, abuse decreases.

To resolve the problem of parent abuse, the best strategy might be training parents in parenting skills. Such skills would involve firmness, supportiveness, additional problem-solving techniques and more involvement in their adolescents' lives. Tackling the parents' own alcohol and drug abuse would help to strengthen the family system as a whole, which would, in turn, assist in improving inter-actions between parents and adolescents. An examination of the peer group may also assist in assessing how deeply embedded in violent behaviours the adolescent may be. A violent peer group would tend to reinforce abusive behaviour in the home (see Wilson 1996). Fam-ily therapy may be an optimal opportunity for dealing with all of the above-noted problems, as the therapist will have the opportunity to assess family interactions and structure and how they might contrib-ute to adolescent violence against parents. This more holistic ap-proach to therapy would probably be more beneficial than long-term individual therapy focusing on the abusing adolescent.

Professionals offering counselling services should concentrate on the history and quality of family relationships in an effort to pinpoint dysfunction and offer solutions, but they should also attempt to see patterns so that they can make prudent suggestions concerning pre-vention of abuse (Tindale et al. 1994).

To combat institutional abuse of the elderly, Pillemer and Moore (1992) propose that there should be more staff, better wages for staff members and better training in managing conflict situations that arise with difficult patients. In other words, define solutions that focus on those elderly patients who are difficult to deal with because of mental or physical impairment, solutions that teach staff how to use special skills to handle these situations. Learning to handle those situations that could potentially lead to the abuse of the elderly will, in the long run, prevent some of the abuses that arise in situations peculiar to institutions caring for them.

Research

DeKeseredy (1996) suggests that better research is a key to the amelioration of abuse and to future prevention. He states that re-searchers must focus on using more representative samples and must develop better instruments and more precise and universal definitions of abuse before real progress can be made. Until researchers are in a position to assert that they are all studying the same thing, that what they are studying is, in fact, the problem which needs to be better understood, and that they are measuring it in comparable fashion, we will continue to have a contradictory body of literature that obfus-cates more than illuminates the problem.

Research on family violence is a difficult endeavour. People are concerned about privacy. They are ashamed of talking about their experiences with violence and abuse. They fear that there will be negative repercussions for them if they reveal what is happening to them. Furthermore, people have a very real concern for their family members, even those who are abusing them. Family relationships are highly complex; emotions are often intertwined. There may be abuse, but there also may be love. For all these reasons, as Tindale et al. (1994) recommend, researchers might do better to redirect their focus from the people and the abuse itself to the family relationships and the factors that affect those relations in order to attempt to discern predictors and potential risk factors. They also propose that research be done on non-abusive families and how they manage themselves in order to see what the differences are in the way they relate to one another and to understand the factors that affect their relationships. In this way, researchers may be able to provide possible solutions to the social problem of family violence.

A brief overview of these solutions readily indicates that a great deal of both money and commitment are required from government and the citizenry of Canada. Neighbourhood or community task forces should be created to target specific problems and attend to their solutions (for example, care for teens, supervision, some place for teens to go for fun after school, hot meals, homemaking services). Services should be for all families, not just abusive ones. Implementing them seems to be a formidable and daunting task. Yet, both funding and community involvement must be present. Until people realize that family violence is not just something that happens to others, whether they are poor, unemployed, addicted or overstressed, that it happens to all of us, and until people realize that violence affects all our lives by contributing to crime, human misery and the impoverishment of generations of individuals, we will not be able to make a decisive move to end abuse.

Notes

1. Throughout the following discussion, the term "victim" will be used since it is consistent with everyday usage. It is important to note, however, that many activists object to this term on the grounds that it is stigmatizing and disempowering. They recommend the term "survivor."

2. Since the inception of the modern women's movement, feminist psychologists, social workers and counsellors have developed both a thorough-going critique of traditional psycho-dynamic

therapy and feminist alternatives. Feminist therapy seeks to encourage women to question, for example, the self-denial and self-sacrifice which are built into the traditional womanly caregiver role. The intent of therapy is to empower women and to provide them with the skills to question the role of the larger social order in their personal problems (Pressman 1989).

3. Dutton, however, counters that his approach to group counselling is effective. Based on a ten-year review of treated and untreated abusers, he concludes that for every 1,000 men, there were 350 fewer arrests and 10,500 fewer attacks than if the men were untreated. Not surprisingly, given this ongoing controversy about the benefits of treatment groups and treatment approaches, therapists and policy analysts are currently debating how to establish standards for batterer intervention (including treatment approaches, training of therapists, goals of programs and so on) (see Gondolf 1995; Geffner 1995).

4. According to the Health Canada survey, treatment programs last from eight weeks to one year (1994b).

5. A common-law peace bond is obtainable from a justice of the peace. The abusive husband has to sign the bond agreeing to the conditions (for example, to stay away from the woman's home or place or work). Failure to comply with the peace bond will result in a fine ($500) or six months in jail. If criminal charges are laid, the woman may obtain a second type of peace bond which carries more severe penalties (depending on circumstances). A restraining or non-molestation order under the *Ontario Family Law Act* is usually issued after a divorce or separation (*The Spectator* (Hamilton), April 2, 1988: A4).

6. There are other indications that family violence is not taken as seriously as other crimes by the courts. A recent study found that rapists who attacked a stranger average a sentence of 66.1 months, those who assaulted an acquaintance are sentenced to 52.8 months and those who raped a spouse, ex-spouse or relative are given 49.3 months. Despite the fact that under the Criminal Code, the crime is the same regardless of the relationship to the victim, it is clear that the courts tend to deal more leniently with family violence (Papp 1997b: A3).

7. This unintended consequence has been alleviated by instructing police officers not to automatically counter-charge, but rather, to record the details of the charge and present them to a Crown to decide whether further action is warranted (MacLeod 1995a: 22).

8. It should be noted that some analysts express concern about the application of the battered woman defence. They suggest that only "good," that is traditional, wives are seen to qualify. Women who are non-traditional (for example, women in lesbian couples) are often exempted from such a defence (Card 1995).

9. Another initiative to safeguard women has been the introduction of "panic buttons." These small electronic devices allow a woman to alert the police if her attacker assaults her while she is away from a phone. Clearly, such an individual-by-individual approach is expensive (US$300 per device) and may not eliminate the possibility of violence and injury (*Toronto Star* October 30, 1992: C10).

10. "Claiming space," which Virginia Woolf immortalized as "a room of one's own," is, according to Graham, basic to the struggle of oppressed people. Personally, it may entail having some private, separate space in the home. For organizations, it may mean having a space for women and their concerns — for example, shelters for women, women's centres and women's bookstores.

11. The names of child welfare agencies vary to some extent from province to province and region to region.

12. Trocme reports a growing emphasis on involving police in child abuse investigations (1994: 78).

13. Recently, a Calgary woman sued a B.C. man for sexual abuse that had taken place fifty years earlier (*The Standard* (St. Catharines) December 31, 1993: A8).

14. Trocme indicates that this is consistent with data from the U.S. (1994: iii).

15. The problem is not endemic to Canada. Of the 1,300 children who died as a result of child abuse in 1993 in the United States, 42 per cent had been previously reported to child protection

agencies. Clearly, children were returned to or allowed to live in dangerously abusive situations (Edmonds 1995: 2A).

16. Research indicates that on average, children under sixteen who become permanent wards of the state will be sent to eight different foster families and many will be placed in institutional settings (as cited in Dunsdon 1995: 453).

17. In Marshall's study of eighty cases identified to the police, twenty-two charges were laid, twelve individuals were convicted and six were incarcerated (1994: 271).

18. Ontario Children's Aid Societies recently expressed concern about the growing trend towards international adoption. Many parents are opting to adopt infants and young children from foreign countries because they believe that children are not available to adopt in Canada. The Societies point out that there are many children, often older and often with a history of upheaval, who are indeed available for adoption. They plan to launch an advertising campaign to encourage adoption within Canadian borders.

Some Concluding Thoughts

It may hint at arrogance to attempt to arrive at conclusions regarding family violence when we have demonstrated that it is a very complex and still not well-understood social phenomenon. At the same time, those very traits suggest some concluding remarks.

A review of the current literature available in Canada, the United States and the United Kingdom reveals that the fundamental issues remain unresolved. Despite the proliferation of research, journals devoted to and addressing the topic, institutes and special divisions of agencies, there is little agreement regarding definitions, measurement, causes or solutions. Progress has been made in the sense that twenty years ago the entire issue of family violence enjoyed scant legitimacy. Now it has gained acceptance as a public issue, secured a position on research and funding agendas, and generated its own industry in terms of professionals and advocates. The public has certainly become much more educated with regard to its various aspects. Yet, many of the original insights advanced by pioneers in the field, such as David Gil on child abuse, remain pertinent but have largely been ignored in the literature and research. For instance, it has been noted that social problems such as poverty, a violent cultural milieu, inequality and power imbalances, sexism and ageism, and a lack of community support, among others, all contribute to family violence in some form. However, many theories about the causes of abuse and suggestions for resolution still tend to psychologize and pathologize the phenomenon by implying or openly stating that personal traits of the victims and abusers, or their particular situations, are responsible for abusive behaviours. Sociological factors are often downplayed. Therefore, what we are left with is the impression that there are certain people who are waiting to abuse, certain others waiting to be abused, and certain situations that are abusive. Some suggest that if we could just treat these people, keep them separate, and disarm these situations, the problem of violence in families would simply disappear. Such, of course, is not the case. It is an attempt to apply an easy answer to a hard question.

Furthermore, as the edifice of research has grown, it seems to have lost touch with the lived experiences of the people themselves and the individuals who work at the grassroots level. These people would include those who are involved in the shelter movement, which has made some real inroads into the problem of family violence

On this note as well, despite the money, time and energy in the context of cutbacks at all levels that have been devoted to this matter, not only do we still not have universal definitions or measurements, but it would appear that the field of family violence research is becoming more fragmented. More and more viewpoints have crystallized into oppositional camps. While initially victims were believed when they came forward with reports of abuse, now there are those groups that argue that many of these reports have emerged from the therapeutic process itself. In other words, these incidents purportedly did not actually take place, but were "remembered," or created, when individuals went into treatment for personal problems and were unconsciously directed into conjuring up these "memories" as a way of explaining their troubles. While this may certainly be the case for some people, to dismiss accounts of victimization as a whole would seem to be a rash and hasty conclusion. Therefore, what at first appeared to be enormous progress has suffered a setback.

Similarly, the San Diego approach, adopted in Toronto to override the decision of women who recant their testimony of spousal abuse and pursue criminal prosecution against their abusers, may be another form of victimization. The court system takes control of the situation and the victim's life, forcing an issue she does not want, quite possibly inflicting more harm on the family. Treating elderly abuse victims like children who need guardianship and protection is another instance of victimization by the system. Instead of empowering these individuals and giving them back control over their lives, the system and its professionals, regardless of how well-meaning their intentions, actually oppress them even more.

In short, what we have is a kind of iatrogenesis, a condition wherein the remedy generates more problems. The issue fragments more as oppositions grow against solutions as well. Employing a feminist paradigm, one which deals with matters of control and power imbalances, we can argue that control is at the root of the problem, both the problem of violence itself, and the problem of the splintering of the field. Everyone seems to be vying for control.

Advocates want to take charge of victims. Other professionals, such as academics, lawyers, health and social services workers, want to control the definition, measurement and parameters of family violence. Abusers want to control their victims; victims want to regain control over their own lives. The courts want to take charge of abusers. Control is the problem, yet the solutions all seek some form of control. This search for control is causing more and more struggle within the field itself. How can we make progress on the issue when this type of climate prevails?

The approach to family violence to date has not been a holistic one, a fact which creates its own set of difficulties. Like the blind people positioned at various points on the elephant's body and trying to describe the whole thing, professionals in the field have tended to focus only on sections of the problem that coincide with their disciplines and approaches. Many policy analysts and advocates prefer to attempt solutions that attend to the problem on a case-by-case basis rather than a societal one. Not many are trying to see the "big picture" or working on how to deal with it. As daunting a task as this may be, without a more integrated approach to family violence, splintering is the best that may be achieved.

Furthermore, the punitive nature of the whole system, which again takes an atomistic approach rather than a societal one, does not address the root causes of family violence. It merely places Band-Aids on the symptoms. It also ensures that the problem will continue to be dealt with on an individualistic basis rather than a systemic one. In effect, it becomes another part of the problem, as it creates subsets of difficulties for the people involved (often those it attempts to assist), not part of the solution.

As conflict among professionals in the field escalates, as more and more terrain is claimed (for example, self-abuse and self-neglect by elderly people), factions emerge, but also the general public begins to lose its sympathetic stance. When family violence becomes conceptualized in such broad terms, the issue becomes meaningless. This consequence is ironic because of the broad scope of the root causes of family violence. It may be argued that expanding the terrain of the issue allows for overreporting of abuse and the possible growth of a kind of paranoiac attitude toward social relations, especially those within the family. Everyone becomes a "victim" or an "abuser." This burgeoning sense of victimization has been addressed by some members of the women's movement who oppose this type of negative labelling and propose that, instead, people see themselves as "survivors," not "victims," of abuse. What is left, however, is how to view "abusers." How do we separate the sin from the sinner and help that person to heal and reintegrate into society and the family?

Feminists themselves have been accused of contributing to growing paranoia and overreporting of abuse. They have been in the forefront of the family violence issue, having insisted that this matter, formerly considered part of the private domain, be put on the public agenda. Arguably, some feminists have not contributed greatly to the forging of a consensus on the matter among the various groups of professionals in the field. Their critical stance against patriarchal tendencies, often found in the approaches taken by other, non-feminist professionals tends to promote more infighting rather than consensus.

The overall lack of consensus makes it very difficult to gauge any progress. It makes it particularly difficult to see whether Canada has made any inroads into solving the problem, since the Canadian literature must depend so much on American information while the two countries differ fundamentally in many ways. Not only are the Canadian legal, cultural, health care and social systems so different, but cities in Canada do not suffer from the extent of urban decay found in most American cities. Urban decay contributes to the degeneration of the environment in which people are forced to live, making their lives more difficult and stressful, conditions which then influence their relationships with others. Therefore, family violence may not be quite as severe in this country. It is very hard to tell. Much more research, particularly in the area of prevalence studies, needs to be done.

The necessity for more research highlights yet another problematic area. In a neo-conservative sociohistorical context, when lowering government spending and the reduction of bureaucracy occupy such prominent positions on the public agenda, looking for more funding to undertake large studies and stepping up the amount of research will probably be very difficult to accomplish. Yet this very cost-cutting ethos is generating more human misery and contributing to family violence itself. Welfare spending is being reduced; jobs are being lost; wages are being cut and unions are fighting for their lives. People's lives are being impoverished, but, more importantly, the people themselves are being impoverished. Such a situation is highly likely to contribute to family violence and abuse.

Nevertheless, however tempting it may be to take a pessimistic stance on the future of the field of family violence, we must bear in mind that positive things are being done to tackle the problem. People are coming forward to reveal their personal experiences of abuse. Work is being done to demonstrate the scope of the problem and more people are being educated about it. There are many who are committed to ameliorating the situation and community-level work is being accomplished. When Canadians come to the realization that family violence concerns everybody, each individual may be empowered to take a stand and intervene whenever they are confronted by an abusive situation. Human agency is a powerful force and has the capacity to evoke great change.

Perhaps one of the most hopeful signs is that, amid protestations that feminism is dead, feminist activism is still taking place. Shelters remain open, sexual assault centres remain active and are on the cutting edge of educating people in schools and the community. Committed individuals are making a difference in the lives of those suffering abuse. By chipping away at the problem of family violence, we can make progress against it.

Bibliography

Aitken, Gail, and Andy Mitchell. 1995. "The Relationship Between Poverty and Child Health: Long-Range Implications." *Canadian Review of Social Policy*, 35 (Spring): 19-36.

Armstrong, Jane. 1996. "Ads target domestic violence." *Toronto Star* (May 10): A18.

Aronson, Jane, Cindy Thornewell, and Karen Williams. 1995. "Wife Assault in Old Age: Coming Out of Obscurity." *Canadian Journal on Aging* 14:2 (supplement): 72-88.

Badgley, Robin F. 1984. *Sexual Offences Against Children in Canada: Volumes 1, 2 and Summary*. Ottawa: Minister of Supply and Services.

Bagley, Christopher, and Kathleen King. 1990. *Child Sexual Abuse: The Search for Healing*. London: Tavistock/Routledge.

Baker, Maureen (ed.), 1996. *Families: Changing Trends in Canada*. 3rd ed. Toronto: McGraw-Hill Ryerson.

Baxter, Kate et al. 1995. "Ducking Bullets." Pp. 281-97 in Leslie Timmins (ed.) *Listening to the Thunder*. Vancouver: Women's Research Centre.

Beaulieu, Marie. 1992. *Intervention for Victimized Elderly People*. (September). Association quebecois Plaidoyer-Victimes.

Bindman, Stephen. 1995. "Battered women who killed win reviews." *Toronto Star* (July 14): A3.

Bindman, Stephen. 1997. "Free 5 women who have killed: Judge" *Toronto Star* (March 3): A2.

Bishop, Patricia. 1991. *Child Abuse: Emotional, Psychological and Sexual*. Toronto: Canadian Mental Health Association.

Bograd, Michele. 1988. "Feminist Perspectives on Wife Abuse: An Introduction." Pp. 11-26 in Kersti Yllo and Michele Bograd (eds.), *Feminist Perspectives on Wife Abuse*. Newbury Park: Sage.

Bond, Jr., John B., Roland L. Penner and Penny Yellen. 1995. "Perceived Effectiveness of Legislation Concerning Abuse of the Elderly: A Survey of Professionals in Canada and the United States." *Canadian Journal on Aging* 14:2 (supplement): 118-35.

Bowker, Lee H. 1993. "A Battered Woman's Problems Are Social, Not Psychological." Pp. 154-65 in Richard Gelles and Donileen Loseke (eds.), *Current Controversies on Family Violence*. Newbury Park: Sage.

Boyce, Sonja. 1995. "Wanted: Women of Colour Encouraged to Apply." Pp. 235-46 in Leslie Timmins (ed.), *Listening to the Thunder*. Vancouver: Women's Research Centre.

Bradbury, Bettina. 1996. "The Social and Economic Origins of Contemporary Families." Pp. 55-77 in Maureen Baker (ed.), *Families: Changing Trends in Canada*. 3rd. ed. Toronto: McGraw-Hill Ryerson Ltd.

Brinkerhoff, M., and E. Lupri. 1988. "Interspousal Violence." *Canadian Journal of Sociology* (13): 407-34.

Brown, Louise. 1994. "Group urges alternatives to spanking." *Toronto Star* (September 27): B1.

Callahan, Marilyn. 1993. "Feminist Approaches: Women Recreate Child Welfare." Pp. 172-209 in Brian Wharf (ed.), *Rethinking Child Welfare in Canada*. Toronto: McClelland and Stewart.

Cameron, Gary. 1989. "Community Development Principles and Helping Battered Women: A Summary Chapter." Pp. 157-65 in Barbara Pressman, Gary Cameron and Michael Rothery (eds.), *Intervening with Assaulted Women: Current Theory Research and Practice*. Hillsdale, New Jersey: Lawrence Erlbaum Associates.

Caplan, Paula. 1985. *The Myth of Women's Masochism*. New York: E.P. Dutton.

Card, Claudia. 1995. *Lesbian Choices*. New York: Columbia University Press.

Cardozo, Andrew. 1996. "Domestic violence doesn't know any ethnic boundaries." *Toronto Star* (April 16): A21.

Chalmers, Lee, and Pamela Smith. 1987. "Wife Battering: Psychological, Social and Physical Isolation and Counteracting Strategies." Pp. 15-38 in Kathleen Storrie (ed.), *Women: Isolation and Bonding*. Toronto: Methuen.

Cole, Susan G. 1988. "Child Battery." Pp. 517-37 in Bonnie Fox (ed.), *Family Bonds and Gender Divisions*. Toronto: Canadian Scholars' Press Inc.

Collins, Randall. 1975. *Conflict Sociology: Toward an Explanatory Science*. New York: Academic Press.

Connidis, Ingrid Arnet. 1989. *Family Ties and Aging*. Toronto: Butterworths.

Conway, John F. 1993. *The Canadian Family in Crisis*. Revised Edition. Toronto: James Lorimer and Company Ltd.

Coomaraswamy, Radhika. 1995. "Some Reflections on Violence Against Women." *Canadian Woman Studies* 15 (2,3) (Spring/Summer): 19-23.

Cordon, Sandra. 1997. "School strapping may end." *The Standard* (St. Catharines) (February 21): B6.

Coser, Lewis. 1956. *The Functions of Social Conflict*. New York: Free Press.

Cote, Andree. 1984. "The New Rape Legislation." *Status of Women News* (November): 8-17.

Cote, James E., and Anton L. Allahar. 1994. *Generation on Hold: Coming of Age in the Late Twentieth Century*. Toronto: Stoddart.

Crawford, Maria, and Rosemary Gartner. 1992. *Woman Killing: Intimate Femicide in Ontario: 1974-1990*. Women We Honour Action Committee.

Crook, Farrell. 1991. "Rage made abused wife mutilate mate, court told." *Toronto Star* (September 26): A25.

Crook, Farrell. 1992. "Wife is acquitted in man's mutilation." *Toronto Star* (October 2): A4.

Crowder, Adrienne. 1993. *Opening the Door: A Treatment Model for Therapy With Male Survivors of Sexual Abuse*. Waterloo: Family and Children's Services.

Dahrendorf, Ralf. 1958. "Toward a Theory of Social Conflict." *Journal of Conflict Resolution* 2:2 (June): 170-79.

Dahrendorf, Ralf. 1959. *Class and Class Conflict in Industrial Society*. Stanford, CA: Stanford University Press.

Daly, Rita, Caroline Mallan, and Jane Armstrong. 1996a. "Managing Anger." *Toronto Star* (March 11): A11.

Daly, Rita, and Tracey Tyler. 1996c. "Court to target spousal abuse." *Toronto Star*. A1, A18.

Daly, Rita, Caroline Mallan, and Jane Armstrong. 1996b. "Repeat Offender." *Toronto Star*. (March 13): A17.

Danica, Elly. 1988. *Don't: A Woman's Word*. Toronto: McClelland & Stewart Inc.

DeKeseredy, Walter S., and Ronald Hitch. 1991. *Woman Abuse: Sociological Perspectives*. Toronto: Thompson Educational Publishing.

DeKeseredy, Walter S. And Desmond Ellis. 1994. *Pretest Report on the Frequency, Severity and Patterning of Sibling Violence in Canadian Families*. Ottawa: Family Violence Prevention Division, Health Canada.

DeKeseredy, Walter S., Hyman Burshtyn and Charles Gordon. 1995. "Taking Wife Abuse Seriously: A Critical Response to the Solicitor General of Canada's Crime Prevention Advice." Pp. 67-69 in E.D. Nelson and Augie Fleras (eds.), *Social Problems in Canada Reader*. Scarborough: Prentice Hall Canada Inc.

Denham, Donna, and Joan Gillespie. 1996. "Ending violence against women and children requires new outlook." *Perception* 20 (2) (Fall): 3.

Dobash, Russell P., and R. Emerson Dobash, Margo Wilson, and Martin Daly. 1992. "The Myth of Sexual Symmetry in Marital Violence." *Social Problems* 39(1) (February): 71-91.

Donovan, Kevin, and Moira Welsh. 1996. "Child deaths : Task force to be set up." *Toronto Star* (September 19): A1, A34.

Donovan, Kevin and Moira Welsh. 1997. "Children's deaths ruled 'quite high.'" *Toronto Star* (March 25): A1, A24.

Doob, Anthony. 1995. "Understanding the Attacks on Statistics Canada's Violence Against Women Survey." Pp. 157-65 in Marianna Valverde, Linda MacLeod, and Kirsten Johnson (eds.), *Wife Assault and the Canadian Criminal Justice System*. Toronto: Centre of Criminology, University of Toronto.

Drake, Betty, and Shanta Pandey. 1996. "Understanding the Relationship Between Neighbourhood Poverty and Specific Types of Child Maltreatment." *Child Abuse and Neglect* 20 (11): 1003-18.

Dranoff, Linda Silver. 1977. *Women in Canadian Live: Law*. Toronto: Fitzhenry & Whiteside.

Duffy, Ann, and Norene Pupo. 1992. *Part-time Paradox: Connecting Gender, Work & Family*. Toronto: McClelland & Stewart Inc.

Dunsdon, Kelly. 1995. "Child Sexual Abuse: A Comparative Case Comment." *Canadian Journal of Family Law* 12 (2): 441-56.

Dutton, Donald, G. 1995a. *The Batterer: A Psychological Profile*. New York: Basic Books.

Dutton, Donald G. 1995b. *The Domestic Assault of Women*. Vancouver: UBC Press.

Duxbury, Linda, and Christopher Higgins. 1994. "Families in the Economy." Pp. 29-40 in Maureen Baker (ed.), *Canada's Changing Families: Challenges to Public Policy*. Ottawa: The Vanier Institute of the Family.

Edelson, Jeffrey L., Zvi Eisikovits, and Edna Guttman. 1985. "Men Who Batter Women." *Journal of Family Issues* 6 (2) (June): 229-47.

Edmonds, Patricia. 1994. "Poll: Abusive parents should lose children." *USA Today* (April 8): 1A, 8A.

Edmonds, Patricia. 1995. "Agencies ask: Is this parent fit, or not?" *USA Today* (March 2): 1A, 2A.

Federal-Provincial Working Group on Child and Family Services Information. 1994. *Child Welfare in Canada: The Role of Provincial and Territorial Authories in Cases of Child Abuse*. Ottawa: Minister of Supply and Services.

Finkelhor, David, and Kersti Yllo. 1985.*License to Rape: Sexual Abuse of Wives*. New York: Free Press.

Firestone, Shulamith. 1970. *The Dialectic of Sex*. New York: William Morrow and Company.

Ford, Catherine. 1996. "She's served her time but Alberta socialite still not off the hook." *Toronto Star* (October 19): E4.

Foucault, Michel. 1979. *Discipline and Punish: The Birth of the Prison*. New York: Vintage Books.

Fraser, Sylvia. 1987. *My Father's House*. Toronto: Collins.

Gadd, Jane. 1997. "More boys physically abused than girls." *Globe and Mail* (July 9): A1, A6.

Garbarino, James. "The Human Ecology of Child Maltreatment: A Conceptual Model for Research." *Journal of Marriage and the Family* 39 (November): 721-35.

Garbarino, James, and Gwen Gilliam. 1980. *Understanding Abusive Families*. New York: Lexington Books.

Geffner, Robert. 1995. "Editor addresses readers' concerns." *Family Violence and Sexual Assault Bulletin* 11 (3-4) (Fall/Winter): 29-32.

Gelles, Richard J. 1990. *Intimate Violence In Families*. 2nd ed. Newbury Park: Sage.

Gelles, Richard J. 1993. "Through a Sociological Lens: Social Structure and Family Violence." Pp. 31-46 in Richard J. Gelles and Donileen R. Loseke (eds.), *Current Controversies on Family Violence*. Newbury Park: Sage.

Gelles, Richard J., and Claire P. Cornell. 1990. *Intimate Violence in Families*. 2nd ed. Newbury Park: Sage.

Gelles, Richard J., and Murray A. Straus. 1988. *Intimate Violence*. New York: Simon and Schuster Inc.

Genuis, Mark, B. Thomlison, and C. Bagley. 1991. "Male Victims of Child Sexual Abuse: A Brief Overview of Pertinent Findings." *Journal of Child and Youth Care* (Fall):1-6.

Gil, David G. 1980. "Unraveling Child Abuse." Pp. 119-28 in J. Cook and R. Bowles (eds.), *Child Abuse: Commission and Omission*. Toronto: Butterworths.

Gnaedinger, Nancy. 1989. *Elder Abuse: A Discussion Paper*. Ottawa: National Clearinghouse on Family Violence.

Gold, Svea J. 1986. *When Children Invite Child Abuse*. Eugene, Oregon: Fern Ridge Press.

Goldner, Virginia, Peggy Penn, Marcia Sheinberg, and Gillian Walker. 1990. "Love and Violence: Gender Paradoxes in Volatile Attachments." *Family Process* 29 (4): 343-64.

Goldstein, Stanley E., and Arthur Blank. 1988. "The elderly: abuse or abusers." Pp. 86-90 in Benjamin Schlesinger and Rachel Schlesinger (eds.), *Abuse of the Elderly: Issues and Annotated Bibliography*. Toronto: University of Toronto Press.

Gombu, Phinjo. 1997. "Man guilty despite recanted claims." *Toronto Star* (March 27): A8.

Gondolf, Edward W. 1995. "Gains and Process in State Batterer Programs and Standards." *Family Violence and Sexual Assault Bulletin* 11 (3-4) (Fall/Winter): 27-28.

Goodman, Marilyn S. 1990. "Pattern Changing: An Approach to the Abused Woman's Problem." *Family Violence Bulletin* 6(4) (Winter 1990): 14-15.

Goodwin, Megan P. and Bruce Rosco. 1990. "Sibling Violence and Agonistic Interactions Among Middle Adolescents." *Adolescence* XXV: 98 (summer): 451-67.

Government of Canada. 1992. *Family Violence in Canada: A Call to Action*. Ottawa: Minister of Supply and Services.

Graham, Dee with Edna I. Rawlings and Roberta K. Rigsby. 1994. *Loving to Survive: Sexual Terror, Men's Violence and Women's Lives*. New York: New York University Press.

Granatstein, J.L. et al. 1983. *Twentieth Century Canada*. Toronto: McGraw-Hill Ryerson, Ltd.

Greven, Philip. 1990. *Spare the Child: The Religious Roots of Punishment and the Psychological Impact of Physical Abuse*. New York: Alfred A. Knopf.

Griffiths, C.T., and J.C. Yerbury. 1995. "Native Indian Victims in Canada: Issues in Policy and Program Delivery." Pp. 124-35 in E.D. Nelson and Augie Fleras (eds.), *Social Problems in Canada Reader*. Scarborough, ON: Prentice Hall Canada Inc.

Gurr, Jane, Louise Mailloux, Diane Kinnon, and Suzanne Doerge. 1996. *Breaking the Links Between Poverty and Violence Against Women*. Ottawa: Ministry of Supply and Services Canada.

Hanes, Tracy. 1994. "Women's shelter counts up its victories." *Toronto Star* (September 9): C1, C3.

Hannah-Moffat, K. 1995. "To Charge or Not to Charge: Front LineOfficers' Perceptions of Mandatory Charge Policies." Pp. 35-61 in Mariana Valverde, Linda MacLeod, and Kirsten Johnson (eds), *Wife Assault and the Canadian Criminal Justice System: Issues and Policies*. Toronto: Centre of Criminology, University of Toronto.

Hannen, Andrea. 1996/97. "Keeping Kids Safe." *Parent Quarterly Niagara*. (Winter): 27-33.

Harman, Lesley D. 1995. "Family Poverty and Economic Stuggles." Pp. 235-69 in Nancy Mandell and Ann Duffy (eds.), *Families: Diversity, Conflict and Change*. Toronto: Harcourt Brace & Company, Canada.

Harrison, Deborah, and Lucie Laliberte. 1994. *No Life Like It: Military Wives in Canada*. Toronto: James Lorimer and Company Ltd.

Harvey, Wendy. 1996. "Preparing Children for Testifying in Court." Pp. 251-63 in N. Bala, J. Hornick, and R. Vogl (eds.), *Canadian Child Welfare Law.* Toronto: Thompson Educational Publishing, Inc.

Health and Welfare Canada. 1993. *The Family Violence Audio-visual Source Guide.* Ottawa: Minister of Supply and Services.

Health and Welfare Canada. 1995. *Child Abuse: Awareness Information for People in the Workplace.* Ottawa: Minister of Supply and Services.

Health Canada. 1994a. *A Resource Guide on Family Violence Issues for Aboriginal Communities.* Ottawa: Ministry of Supply and Services Canada.

Health Canada. 1994b. *Canada's Treatment Programs for Men Who Abuse their Partners.* Ottawa: Ministry of Supply and Services Canada.

Health Canada. 1994c. *Child Sexual Abuse Initiative: Summaries of Funded Projects (1986-1991).* Ottawa: Minister of Supply and Services.

Health Canada. 1996. *Breaking the Links Between Poverty and Violence Against Women.* Ottawa: Ministry of Supply and Services Canada.

Hoff, Lee Ann. 1990. *Battered Women as Survivors.* London: Routledge.

Hotaling, G.T., and D.B. Sugarman. 1986. "An analysis of risk markers in husband-wife violence: The current state of knowledge." *Violence and Victims* 1: 101-24.

Hudson, J. Edward. 1988. "Elder Abuse: An Overview." Pp. 12-31 in Benjamin Schlesinger and Rachel Schlesinger (eds.), *Abuse of the Elderly: Issues and Annotated Bibliography.* Toronto: University of Toronto Press.

Jaffe, Peter G., David A. Wolfe, and Susan Kaye Wilson. 1990. *Children of Battered Women.* Newbury Park: Sage.

Janus, Mark-David, Francis X. Archambault, Scott W. Brown, and Lesley A. Welsh. 1995. "Physical Abuse in Canadian Runaway Adolescents." *Child Abuse & Neglect.* 19(4): 433-47.

Johnson, Allan G. 1997. *The Gender Knot: Unraveling Our Patriarchal Legacy.* Philadelphia: Temple University Press.

Johnson, Holly. 1995. "Response to Allegations About the Violence Against Women Survey." Pp. 148-156 in Mariana Valverde, Linda MacLeod, and Kirsten Johnson (eds.), *Wife Assault and the Canadian Criminal Justice System.* Toronto: Centre of Criminology, University of Toronto.

Johnson, Holly. 1996. *Dangerous Domains: Violence Against Women in Canada.* Toronto: Nelson.

Johnson, John M. 1989. "Horror Stories and the Construction of Child Abuse." Pp. 5-19 in Joel Best (ed.), *Images of Issues: Typifying Contemporary Social Problems.* New York: Aldine de Gruyter.

Johnson, Joyce. 1990. *What Lisa Knew.* New York: Kensington Publishing Corp.

Jones, Ann. 1996. "'Domestic Violence' Is Not Clearly Defined." Pp. 17-21 in A.E. Sadler (ed.), *Current Controversies: Family Violence.* San Diego, CA: Greenhaven Press.

Kalmuss, Debra S., and Murray A. Straus. "Wife's Marital Dependency and Wife Abuse." *Journal of Marriage and the Family* 44 (May 1982): 277-86.

Kaufman, Michael. 1987. "The Construction of Masculinity and the Triad of Men's Violence." Pp. 1-29 in Michael Kaufman (ed.), *Beyond Patriarchy:*

Essays by Men on Pleasure, Power, and Change. Toronto: Oxford University Press.

Kaplan, Tracey. 1996. "Slap more serious than it may sound." *Toronto Star* (January 20): H6.

Kempe, C. Henry et al. 1980. "The Battered Child Syndrome." Pp. 49-61 in J. V. Cook and R.T. Bowles. *Child Abuse: Commission and Omission.* Toronto: Butterworths.

Kendrick, M. 1988. *Anatomy of a Nighmare.* Toronto: Macmillan of Canada.

Kennedy, Leslie W., and Donald G. Dutton. 1989. "The Incidence of Wife Assault in Alberta." *Canadian Journal of Behavioural Science* 21(1): 40-54.

Killoran, M. Maureen. 1984. "The Management of Tension: A Case Study of Chatelaine Magazine 1939-1980." *Journal of Comparative Family Studies* XV: 3 (Autumn): 407-26.

Knudsen, Dean. 1992. *Child Maltreatment: Emerging Perspectives.* Dix Hills, New York: General Hall, Inc.

Krishnan, Vijaya, and Kenneth B. Morrison. 1995. "An Ecological Model of Child Maltreatment in a Canadian Province." *Child Abuse and Neglect.* 19 (1): 101-13.

Kryk, Vicki. 1995. "Three Case Studies of Elder Mistreatment: Identifying Ethical Issues." *Journal of Elder Abuse and Neglect* 7:2-3:19-30.

Kurz, Demie. 1993. "Physical Assaults by Husbands: A Major Social Problem." Pp. 88-103 in Richard J. Gelles and Donileen R. Loseke (eds.), *Current Controversies on Family Violence.* Newbury Park: Sage.

Kuypers, Joseph A. 1992. *Man's Will to Hurt.* Toronto: Fernwood.

La Novara, Pina. 1993. *A Portrait of Families in Canada.* Ottawa: Minister of Industry, Science and Technology.

Laframboise, Donna. 1995. "Battering is in eyes of beholder." *Toronto Star* (November 13): A17.

Landsberg, Michele. 1995. "Repeal law that lets parents spank kids." Toronto Star (May 20): G1.

Landsberg, Michele. 1996a. "Spare the rod: Spanking your children isn't normal." *Toronto Star* (October 6): A2.

Landsberg, Michele. 1996b. "Let's outlaw *any* hitting of children." *Toronto Star* (September 22): A1.

LaRocque, Emma D. 1994. *Violence in Aboriginal Communities.* Ottawa: Royal Commission on Aboriginal Peoples.

Larzelere, Robert E. 1994. "Should the Use of Corporal Punishment by Parents be Considered Child Abuse? No." Pp. 204-09 in M.A. Mason and E. Gambrill (eds.), *Debating Children's Lives.* Newbury Park: Sage.

Lasch, Christopher. 1977. *Haven in a Heartless World.* New York: Basic Books, Inc.

Lenton, Rhonda L. 1990. "Techniques of child discipline and abuse by parents." *Canadian Review of Sociology and Anthropology* 27 (2) (May): 157-85.

Lerner, Gerda. 1986. *The Creation of Patriarchy.* New York: Oxford University Press.

Leroux, Thomas G., and Michael Petrunik. 1990. "The Construction of Elder Abuse as a Social Problem: A Canadian Perspective." *International Journal of Health Services* 20:4: 651-63.

Lew, Mike. 1990. *Victims No Longer*. New York: Harper and Row.

Liddle, A. Mark. 1989. "Feminist Contributions to an Understanding of Violence against Women — Three Steps Forward, Two Steps Back." *Canadian Review of Sociology and Anthropology* 26:5 (November): 758-75.

Lindsay, Jocelyn, Francine Ouellet, and Marie-Christine Saint-Jacques. 1994. "Pour une intervention plus efficace auprès des conjoints violents." *Social Worker* (Fall): 104-08.

Lupri, Eugen, Elaine Grandin, and Merlin B. Brinkerhoff. 1994. "Socioeconomic Status and Male Violence in the Canadian Home: A Re-examination." *Canadian Journal of Sociology* 19(1): 47-73.

Lupri, E. 1990. "Male Violence in the Home." Pp. 173-76 in Craig McKie and Keith Thompson (eds.), *Canadian Social Trends*. Toronto: Thompson Educational Publishing.

Luxton, Meg. 1988. "Thinking About the Future." Pp. 237-60 in *Family Matters*. Scarborough: Nelson Canada.

Lynn, Marion, and Eimear O'Neill. 1995. "Families, Power, and Violence." Pp. 271-305 in Nancy Mandell and Ann Duffy (eds.), *Canadian Families: Diversity, Conflict and Change*. Toronto: Harcourt Brace & Company, Canada.

MacDonald, John A. 1995. "The Program of the Spallumcheen Indian Band in British Columbia as a Model of Indian Child Welfare." Pp. 380-91 in R.B. Blake and J. Keshen (eds.), *Social Welfare Policy in Canada: Historical Readings*. Toronto: Copp Clark Ltd.

Mackie, Marlene. 1991. *Gender Relations in Canada: Further Explorations*. Toronto: Butterworths.

MacLean, Michael J. (ed.), 1995. *Abuse and Neglect of Older Canadians: Strategies for Change*. Toronto: Thompson Educational Publishing, Inc.

MacLeod, Linda. 1994. *Understanding and Charting Our Progress Toward the Prevention of Woman Abuse*. Ottawa: Minister of Supply and Services.

MacLeod, Linda. 1995a. "Expanding the Dialogue: Report of a Workshop to Explore the Criminal Justice System Response to Violence Against Women." Pp. 10-32 in M. Valverde, L. MacLeod, and K. Johnson (eds.), *Wife Assault and the Canadian Criminal Justice System: Issues and Policies*. Toronto: Centre of Criminology, University of Toronto.

MacLeod, Linda. 1995b. "Policy Decisions and Prosecutorial Dilemmas: The Unanticipated Consequences of Good Intentions." Pp. 47-61 in M. Valverde, L. MacLeod, and K. Johnson (eds.), *Wife Assault and the Canadian Criminal Justice System: Issues and Policies*. Toronto: Centre of Criminology, University of Toronto.

MacLeod, Linda. 1995c. "Family Group Conferencing: A Community-Based Model for Stopping Family Violence." Pp. 198-204 in M. Valverde, L. MacLeod, and K. Johnson (eds.), *Wife Assault and the Canadian Criminal Justice System: Issues and Policies*. Toronto: Centre of Criminology, University of Toronto.

MacLeod, Linda. 1980. *Wife Battering in Canada: The Vicious Circle*. Ottawa: Canadian Advisory Council on the Status of Women.

MacLeod, Linda. 1987. *Battered But Not Beaten ... Preventing Wife Battering in Canada*. Ottawa: Canadian Advisory Council on the Status of Women.

MacLeod, Linda, and Cheryl Picard. 1989. "Towards a More Effective Criminal Justice Response to Wife Assault: Exploring the Limits and Potential of Effective Intervention." Working Paper. Ottawa: Department of Justice Canada.

Majonis, Joel. 1995. "Patterns of Social Interaction in Abusive and Non-Abusive Families." Pp. 334-53 in E.D. Nelson and Augie Fleras (eds.), *Social Problems in Canada Reader*. Scarborough: Prentice-Hall Canada Inc.

Mallan, Caroline. 1997a. "Child abuse probe called." *Toronto Star* (August 21): A1, A34.

Mallan, Caroline. 1997b. "Domestic courts set to expand." *Toronto Star* (July 3): A10.

Mallan, Caroline, Rita Daly, and Jane Armstrong. 1996. "The Accused." *Toronto Star* (March 10): E1, 4-7.

Mandell, Nancy (ed). 1995. *Feminist Issues*. Scarborough: Prentice Hall, Inc.

Manion, Ian G., and Susan Kay Wilson. 1995. *An Examination of the Association Between Histories of Maltreatment and Adolescent Risk Behaviours*. Ottawa: Minister of Supply and Services.

Margolin, Leslie. 1992. "Beyond Maternal Blame." *Journal of Family Issues* 13(3) (September): 410-23.

Marshall, Carolyn. 1994. *The Response of the Justice System to Family Violence in Nova Scotia*. Halifax: Nova Scotia Department of Justice.

Massecar, Bob. 1995. "Dad cleared in spanking not bitter." *Toronto Star* (April 27): A1.

Mawhinney, Janice. 1995. "The batterer." *Toronto Star* (November 13): E1, E3.

Maxim, Paul S., and Carl Keane. 1992. "Gender, age and the risk of violent death in Canada, 1950-1986." *Canadian Review of Sociology and Anthropology* 29:3 (August): 329-45.

McAteer, Michael. 1995. "Churches probe roots of domestic violence." *Toronto Star* (June 17): K16.

McDonald, Lynn, and Blossom Wigdor. 1995. "Editorial: Taking Stock: Elder Abuse Research in Canada." *Canadian Journal on Aging* 14:2 (supplement): 1-13.

McDonald, P. Lynn, Joseph P. Hornick, Gerald B. Robertson, and Jean E. Wallace. 1991. *Elder Abuse and Neglect in Canada*. Toronto: Butterworths.

McEvoy, Maureen, and Judith Daniluk. 1995. "Wounds of the Soul: The Experience of Aboriginal Women Survivors of Sexual Abuse." *Canadian Psychology* 36(3):221-35.

McGuire, Thom L., and Faye E. Grant. 1991. *Understanding Child Sexual Abuse*. Toronto: Butterworths.

McHutchion, John. 1997. "Canada tops U.S. in unaligned directors." *Toronto Star* (February 7): E3.

Messerschmidt, James W. 1993. *Masculinities and Crime: Critique and Reconceptualization of Theory*. Lanham, MD: Rowman & Littlefield Publishers, Inc.

Miller, Alice. 1983. *For Your Own Good: Hidden Cruelty in Child-Rearing and the Roots of Violence*. New York: Farrar, Straus, Giroux.

Miller, Leslie. 1990. "Violent Families and the Rhetoric of Harmony." *British Journal of Sociology*. 41:2 (June): 263-88.

Mones, Paul. 1991. *When a Child Kills: Abused Children Who Kill Their Parents*. New York: Pocket Books.

Moore, Timothy E., Debra Pepler, Reet Mae, and Michele Kates. 1989. "Effects of Family Violence on Children: New Directions for Research and Intervention." Pp. 75-91 in Barbara Pressman, Gary Cameron, and Michael Rothery (eds.), *Intervening with Assaulted Women: Current Theory, Research and Practice*. Hillsdale, New Jersey: Lawrence Erlbaum Associates.

Mulligan, Suzanne, and Donna Mitchell. 1992/93. "Family Violence Prevention and Curriculum Development." *Women's Education/Éducation des Femmes*. 10(1) (Winter): 34-37.

Muller, Robert T. 1995. "The Interaction of Parent and Child Gender in Physical Child Maltreatment." *Canadian Journal of Behavioural Science* 27 (4): 450-65.

Murray, Bonnie, and Cathy Welch. 1995. "Attending to Lavender Bruises." Pp. 109-126 in Leslie Timmins (ed.), *Listening to the Thunder*. Vancouver: Women's Research Center.

National Clearinghouse on Family Violence. 1986. *Abuse and Neglect of the Elderly*. Ottawa: Minister of Supply and Services.

National Clearinghouse on Family Violence. 1994. *Summaries of Projects Funded in Aboriginal Communities (1986-1991)*. Ottawa: Minister of Supply and Services.

National Council of Welfare. 1997. *Poverty Profile 1995*. Ottawa: Minister of Supply and Services.

Nett, Emily M. 1993. *Canadian Families: Past and Present*. 2nd ed. Toronto: Butterworths.

Noonan, Sheila. 1993. "Strategies of Survival: Moving Beyond the Battered Woman Syndrome." Pp. 247-70 in Ellen Adelberg and Claudia Currie (eds.), *In Conflict with the Law: Women and the Canadian Justice System*. Vancouver: Press Gang Publishers.

Northrup, David A. 1997. "The Problem of the Self-Report in Survey Research." *Institute for Social Research Newsletter* 12 (1) (Winter): 1-2.

O'Hagan, Kieran. 1993. *Emotional and Psychological Abuse of Children*. Toronto: University of Toronto Press.

O'Neill, John. 1994. *The Missing Child in Liberal Theory*. Toronto: University of Toronto Press.

One Voice, the Canadian Seniors Network. 1995. *National Action Plan to Reduce the Abuse of Older Adults in Canada*. Ottawa: One Voice, the Canadian Seniors Network.

Orenchuk-Tomiak, Natalie, Gemma Matthey, and Carole Christensen. 1989. "The Resolution Model: A Response to the Treatment of Child Sexual Abuse." *SIECCAN Journal* 4 (4) (September): 3-10.

Orwen, Patricia. 1997. "Women killed mostly by male partners." *Toronto Star* (April 30): A7.

Painter, Susan Lee, and Don Dutton. 1985. "Patterns of Emotional Bonding." *International Journal of Women's Studies*: 8(4): 363-75.

Palmer, Sally E., and Ralph A. Brown. 1989. "Effective Interventions with Assaultive Husbands." Pp. 57-73 in Barbara Pressman, Gary Cameron, and Michael Rothery (eds.), *Intervening with Assaulted Women: Current Theory,*

Research and Practice. Hillsdale, New Jersey: Lawrence Erlbaum Associates.

Papp, Leslie. 1997a. "Make spanking illegal, group urges." *Toronto Star* (August 15): A1, A32.

Papp, Leslie. 1997b. "Rapists get less jail time if victim a loved one, study finds." *Toronto Star* (June 20): A3.

Payne, Brian K., and Richard Cikovic. 1995. "An Empirical Examination of the Characteristics, Consequences, and Causes of Elder Abuse in Nursing Homes." *Journal of Elder Abuse and Neglect.* 7:4; 61-74.

Payne, Julien D., and Marilyn A. Payne. 1993. *Dealing with Family Law: A Canadian Guide.* Toronto: McGraw-Hill Ryerson Limited.

Pillemer, Karl. 1993. "The Abused Offspring Are Dependent: Abuse Is Caused by the Deviance and Dependence of Abusive Caregivers." Pp. 237-49 in Richard J. Gelles and Donileen R. Loseke (eds.), *Current Controversies on Family Violence.* Newbury Park, CA: Sage Publications.

Pillemer, Karl, and David Finkelhor. 1988. "The Prevalence of Elder Abuse: A Random Sample Survey." *Gerontologist.* 28:1: 51-7.

Pillemer, Karl, and David W. Moore. 1990. "Highlights from a Study of Abuse of Patients in Nursing Homes." *Journal of Elder Abuse and Neglect.* 2:1/2: 5-29.

Pittaway, Elizabeth Dow, Anne Westhues, and Tracy Peressini. 1995. "Risk Factors for Abuse and Neglect Among Older Adults." *Canadian Journal on Aging.* 14:2 (supplement): 20-44.

Pleck, Elizabeth. 1987. *Domestic Tyranny.* New York: Oxford University Press.

Pleck, Joseph H. 1995 [1974]. "Men's Power With Women, Other Men and Society: A Men's Movement in Analysis." Pp. 5-12 in Michael S. Kimmel and Michael A. Messner (eds.), *Men's Lives.* 3rd ed., Boston: Allyn and Bacon.

Podnieks, Elizabeth. 1988. "Elder abuse: it's time we did something about it." Pp. 32-44 in Benjamin Schlesinger and Rachel Schlesinger (eds.), *Abuse of the Elderly: Issues and Annotated Bibliography.* Toronto: University of Toronto Press.

Podnieks, Elizabeth. 1992. "The Lived Experience of Abused Older Women." *Canadian Woman Studies.* 12:2: 38-44.

Podnieks, Elizabeth, Karl Pillemer, J. Phillip Nicholson, Thomas Shillington, and Alan Frizzel. 1990. *National Survey on Abuse of the Elderly in Canada.* Toronto: Ryerson Polytechnical Institute.

Pressman, Barbara. 1989. "Treatment of Wife Abuse: The Case for Feminist Therapy." Pp. 21-45 in Barbara Pressman, Gary Cameron, and Michael Rothery (eds.), *Intervening with Assaulted Women: Current Theory, Research and Practice.* Hillsdale, New Jersey: Lawrence Erlbaum Associates.

Pressman, Barbara, and Michael Rothery. 1989. "Introduction: Implications of Assaults Against Women for Professional Helpers." Pp. 1-19 in Barbara Pressman, Gary Cameron, and Michael Rothery (eds.), *Intervening with Assaulted Women: Current Theory, Research and Practice.* Hillsdale, New Jersey: Lawrence Erlbaum Associates.

Priest, Lisa. 1996. "$4 billion toll of abuse." *Toronto Star* (August 9): A1.

Pron, Nick. 1997. "Custody is child abuse dilemma, Ecker says." *Toronto Star* (April 24): A2.

Pupo, Norene. 1997. "Always Working, Never Done: The Expansion of the Double Day." Pp. 144-165 in A. Duffy, D. Glenday and N. Pupo (eds.), *Good Jobs, Bad Jobs, No Jobs.* Toronto: Harcourt Brace.

Radbill, Samuel X. 1980. "Children in a World of Violence: A History of Child Abuse." Pp. 3-20 in C. Henry Kempe and Ray E. Helfer (eds.), *The Battered Child.* 3rd ed. Chicago: University of Chicago Press.

Raychaba, Brian. 1991. "Child Care Commentary: We Get a Life Sentence." *Journal of Child and Youth Care* (Fall): 129-37.

Renzetti, Claire M. 1992. *Violent Betrayal: Partner Abuse in Lesbian Relationships.* Newbury Park: Sage.

Rodgers, Karen, and Garry MacDonald. 1994. "Canada's Shelters for Abused Women." *Canadian Social Trends* (Autumn): 10-14.

Rose, Elizabeth S. 1993. "Surviving the Unbelievable." *Ms. Magazine,*3 (4) (January/February): 40-45.

Rossman, B.B. Robbie. 1994. "Children in Violent Families: Current Diagnostic and Treatment Considerations." *Family Violence and Sexual Assault Bulletin* 10 (3-4): 29-34.

Ruby, Clayton. 1996. "Spousal abuse: Establishment agenda just won't work." *Toronto Star* (November 16): D3.

Rush, Florence. 1980. *The Best Kept Secret: Sexual Abuse of Children.* Englewood Cliffs, New Jersey: Prentice-Hall, Inc.

Russell, Diana E.H. 1982. *Rape in Marriage.* New York: Macmillan Publishing Co.

Russell, Diana E.H. 1986. *The Secret Trauma: Incest in the Lives of Girls and Women.* New York: Basic Books.

Schlesinger, Rachel. 1988. "Grannybashing." Pp. 3-11 in Benjamin Schlesinger and Rachel Schlesinger (eds.), *Abuse of the Elderly: Issues and Annotated Bibliography.* Toronto: University of Toronto Press.

Schmidt, K. Louise. 1995. *Transforming Abuse: Nonviolent Resistance and Recovery.* Gabriola Island, British Columbia: New Society Publishers.

Scotton, Lindsay. 1994. "To spank or not to spank." *Toronto Star* (April 9): J1.

Segal, Uma. A. 1995. "Child Abuse by the Middle Class? A Study of Professionals in India." *Child Abuse and Neglect* 19 (2): 217-231.

Sinclair, Judge Murray, Donna Phillips, and Nicholas Bala. 1996. "Aboriginal Child Welfare in Canada." Pp. 171-194 in N. Bala, J. Hornick, and R. Vogl (eds.), *Canadian Child Welfare Law.* Toronto: Thomson Educational Publishing, Inc.

Smith, M.D. 1987. "The Incidence and Prevalence of Woman Abuse in Toronto." *Violence and Victims* 2(3): 173-87.

Smith, M.D. 1990a. "Patriarchal Ideology and Wife Beating: A Test of a Feminist Hypothesis." *Violence and Victims* 5(4): 257-73.

Smith, M.D. 1990b. "Sociodemographic Risk Factors in Wife Abuse: Results from a Survey of Toronto Women." *Canadian Journal of Sociology* 15(1): 39-58.

Smith, M.D. 1994. "Enhancing the Quality of Survey Data on Violence Against Women: A Feminist Approach." *Gender and Society* 8(1) (March): 109-27.

Snider, Laureen. 1995. "Feminism, Punishment, and the Potential for Empowerment." Pp. 236-59 in Marian Valverde, Linda MacLeod, and Kirsten Johnson (eds.), *Wife Assault and the Canadian Criminal Justice System.* Toronto: Centre of Criminology, University of Toronto.

Statistics Canada. 1993. "The Violence Against Women Survey." *The Daily.* November 18. Ottawa: Statistics Canada.

Statistics Canada. 1996. *Canadian Social Trends* 41. (Summer): 36.

Steed, Judy. 1994. *Our Little Secret.* Toronto: Random House of Canada.

Stefaniuk, Walter. 1996. "You Asked Us." *Toronto Star* (September 26): A7.

Steinmetz, Suzanne K. 1997. *The Cycle of Violence: Assertive, Aggresive, and Abusive Family Interaction.* New York: Praeger Publishers.

Steinmetz, Suzanne K. 1993. "The Abused Elderly Are Dependent: Abuse Is Caused by the Perception of Stress Associated With Providing Care." Pp. 223-36 in Richard J. Gelles and Donileen R. Loseke (eds.), *Current Controversies on Family Violence.* Newbury Park, CA: Sage Publications.

Stephens, William N. 1963. *The Family in Cross-Cultural Perspective.* New York: Holt, Rinehart and Winston.

Stevens, Cathy. 1995. "Stopping Violence Against Women with Disabilities." Pp. 223-34 in Leslie Timmins (ed.), *Listening to the Thunder.* Vancouver: Women's Research Centre.

Stone, Sharon. 1993. "Getting the Message Out: Feminists, the Press and Violence against Women." *Canadian Review of Sociology and Anthropology* 30:3 (August): 377-400.

Strange, Carolyn. 1995. "Historical Perspectives on Wife Assault." Pp. 293-304 in Mariana Valverde, Linda MacLeod, and Kirsten Johnson (eds.), *Wife Assault and the Canadian Criminal Justice System.* Toronto: Centre of Criminology.

Straus, Murray A. 1979. "Measuring Intrafamily Conflict and Violence: The Conflict Tactics (CT) Scales." *Journal of Marriage and the Family.* 41: 75-88.

Straus, Murray A. 1993. "Physical Assaults by Wives: A Major Social Problem." Pp. 67-87 in Richard J. Gelles and Donileen R. Loseke (eds.) *Current Controversies on Family Violence.* Newbury Park: Sage.

Straus, Murray. A. 1994. "Should the Use of Corporal Punishment by Parents be Considered Child Abuse? Yes." Pp. 195-203 in M.A. Mason and E. Gambrill (eds.), *Debating Children's Lives.* Newbury Park: Sage.

Straus, Murray A., and G. Hotaling. 1979. *The Social Causes of Husband-Wife Violence.* Minneapolis: University of Minnesota Press.

Straus, Murray A., Richard J. Gelles, and Suzanne K. Steinmetz. 1980. *Behind Closed Doors: Violence in the American Family.* Garden City, NY: Anchor Books.

Straus, Murray A., and Richard J. Gelles. 1986. "Societal Change and Change in Family Violence from 1975 to 1985 as Revealed by Two National Surveys." *Journal of Marriage and the Family* 48 (August): 465-79.

Straus, Murray A. and Richard J. Gelles. 1992. *Physical Violence in American Families.* New Brunswick, N.J.: Transaction Publishers.

Straus, Murray A., and Stephen Sweet. 1992. "Verbal/Symbolic Aggression in Couples: Incidence Rates and Relationships to Personal Characteristics." *Journal of Marriage and the Family* 54 (May 1992): 346-57.

Struthers, Marilyn. 1994. "At a Crossroads in the Work to End the Violence: A Rural Perspective." *Canadian Woman Studies* 14 (4) (Fall): 15-18.

Stubbs, Julie. 1995. "'Communitarian' Conferencing and Violence Against Women: A Cautionary Note." Pp. 260-289 in M. Valverde, L. MacLeod, and K. Johnson (eds.), *Wife Assault and the Canadian Criminal Justice System: Issues and Policies*. Toronto: Centre of Criminology, University of Toronto.

Sweet, Lois. 1986. "Child-abuse register is inadequate." *Toronto Star* (June 13): F1.

Swift, Karen J. 1995. *Manufacturing 'Bad Mothers': A Critical Perspective on Child Neglect*. Toronto: University of Toronto Press.

Synnott, Anthony. 1983. "Little angels, little devils: a sociology of children." *The Canadian Review of Sociology and Anthropology* 20 (1) (February): 79-95.

Teichroeb, Ruth. 1997. *Flowers on My Grave: How an Ojibwa Boy's Death Helped Break the Silence on Child Abuse*. Toronto: HarperCollins.

Tindale, J.A., J.E. Norris, R. Berman, and S. Kulack. 1994. *Intergenerational Conflict and the Prevention of Abuse Against Older Persons*. Ottawa: Family Violence Prevention Division, Health Canada.

Vadasz, Mish. 1988. "Family abuse of the elderly." Pp. 91-94 in Benjamin Schlesinger and Rachel Schlesinger (eds.), *Abuse of the Elderly: Issues and Annotated Bibliography*. Toronto: University of Toronto Press.

Voumuakis, Sophia E., and Richard V. Ericson. 1984. *New Accounts of Attacks on Women*. Toronto: University of Toronto Centre of Criminology.

Thomlison, Barbara, M. Stephens, J. Cunes, R. Grinnell, and J. Krysik. 1991. "Characteristics of Canadian Male and Female Child Sexual Abuse Victims." *Journal of Child and Youth Care* (Fall): 65-76.

Thompson-Cooper, Ingrid, Renee Fugere, and Bruno Cormier. 1993. "The Child Abuse Reporting Laws: An Ethical Dilemma for Professionals." *Canadian Journal of Psychiatry* 38 (8) (October): 557-62.

Thorne-Finch, Ron. 1992. *Ending the Silence: The Origins and Treatment of Male Violence Against Women*. Toronto: University of Toronto Press.

Tomes, Nancy. 1978. "A 'Torrent of Abuse': Crimes of Violence between Working-Class Men and Women in London, 1840-1875." *Journal of Social History* 2 (3) (Spring): 328-45.

Tower, Cynthia Crosson. 1996. *Understanding Child Abuse and Neglect*. 3rd ed. Boston: Allyn and Bacon.

Trocme, Nico et al. 1994. *Ontario Incidence Study of Reported Child Abuse and Neglect*. Toronto: Institute for the Prevention of Child Abuse.

Turner, Jan. 1995. "Saskatchewan Responds to Family Violence: The Victims of Domestic Violence Act, 1995." Pp. 183-197 in M. Valverde, L. MacLeod and K. Johnson (eds.), *Wife Assault and the Canadian Criminal Justice System: Issues and Policies*. Toronto: Centre of Criminology, University of Toronto.

Turner, Janice. 1994. "Out of the Shadows: Living in Fear." *Toronto Star* (August 2): C1, C2.

Ursel, E. Jane. 1995. "The Winnipeg Family Violence Court." Pp. 169-82 in M. Valverde, L. MacLeod, and K. Johnson (eds.), *Wife Assault and the Canadian Criminal Justice System: Issues and Policies*. Toronto: Centre of Criminology, University of Toronto.

Vadasz, Mish. 1988. "Family abuse of the elderly." Pp. 91-94 in Benjamin Schlesinger and Rachel Schlesinger (eds.), *Abuse of the Elderly: Issues and Annotated Bibliography*. Toronto: University of Toronto Press.

Valverde, Mariana, Linda MacLeod, and Kirsten Johnson. 1995. "Introduction." Pp. 3-9 in M. Valverde, L. MacLeod, and K. Johnson (eds.), *Wife Assault and the Canadian Criminal Justice System: Issues and Policies*. Toronto: Centre of Criminology, University of Toronto.

Van Rijn, Nicolaas. 1997. "Child abuse deaths spark major study by Ottawa." *Toronto Star* (August 15): A4.

Van Stolk, Mary. 1978. *The Battered Child in Canada*. Revised ed. Toronto: McClelland and Stewart.

Vienneau, David. 1992. "Court ruling helps woman overcome child incest horror." *Toronto Star* (October 30): A1, A36.

Vogl, Robin. 1996. "Initial Involvement." Pp. 33-54 in N. Bala, J. Hornick, and R. Vogl (eds.), *Canadian Child Welfare Law*. Toronto: Thomson Educational Publishing Inc.

Voumuakis, Sophia E., and Richard V. Ericson. 1984. *News Accounts of Attacks on Women*. Toronto: University of Toronto Centre of Criminology.

Walker, Gillian. 1990. *Family Violence and the Women's Movement*. Toronto: University of Toronto Press.

Walker, Lenore. 1979. *The Battered Woman*. New York: Harper Colophon Books.

Walker, Lenore. 1993. "The Battered Woman Syndrome." Pp. 133-53 in Richard Gelles and Donileen Loseke (eds.), *Current Controversies on Family Violence*. Newbury Park: Sage.

Wallace, Harvey. 1996. *Family Violence: Legal, Medical and Social Perspectives*. Boston: Allyn and Bacon.

Walters, Diane. 1995. "Mandatory Reporting of Child Abuse: Legal, Ethical, and Clinical Implications within a Canadian Context." *Canadian Psychology* 36 (3) (August): 163-82.

Washburne, Carolyn. 1983. "A Feminist Analysis of Child Abuse and Neglect." Pp. 289-92 in David Finkelhor, Richard J. Gelles, Gerald T. Hotaling and Murray A. Straus (eds.), *The Dark Side of Families: Current Family Violence Research*. Beverly Hills: Sage Publications.

Watchel, Andy. 1994. *Child Abuse and Neglect: A Discussion Paper and Overview of Topically Related Projects*. Ottawa: Minister of Supply and Services.

Webber, Marlene. 1991. *Street Kids: The Tragedy of Canada's Runaways*. Toronto: University of Toronto Press.

Welsh, Moira, and Kevin Donovan. 1997a. "How to save the children." *Toronto Star* (June 21): A1, A16, A17.

Welsh, Moira, and Kevin Donovan. 1997b. "Getting away with murder — of children." *Toronto Star* (May 18): A1, A6.

Welsh, Moira, and Kevin Donovan. 1997c "CAS seeks power to combat abuse." *Toronto Star* (April 22): A1, A26.

Welsh, Moira and Kevin Donovan. 1997d. "Panel cites rise in deaths under supervision." *Toronto Star* (March 26): A2.

Wharf, Brian. 1994. "Families in Crisis." Pp. 55-68 in Maureen Baker (ed.), *Canada's Changing Families: Challenges to Public Policy*. Ottawa: The Vanier Institute of the Family.

Wiehe, Vernon R. 1990. *Sibling Abuse: Hidden Physical, Emotional, and Sexual Trauma*. Lexington, MA: Lexington Books.

Wilson, Johanna. 1996. "Physical Abuse of Parents by Adolescent Children." Pp. 101-22 in Dean M. Busby (ed.), *The Impact of Violence on the Family: Treatment Approaches for Therapists and Other Professionals*. Boston: Allyn and Bacon.

Wilson, Margo, and Martin Daly. 1994. "Spousal Homicide." *Juristat Service Bulletin* 14(8): 1-15.

Woloschuk, Mike. 1996. "Silence of the Lions." *Elm Street* l(l) (October): 16ff.

Women's Research Centre. 1989. *Recollecting Our Lives: Women's Experience of Childhood Sexual Abuse*. Vancouver: Press Gang Publishers.

Wright, Lisa. 1996. "24-hour hotline to help domestic abuse victims." *Toronto Star* (November 22): A3.

Yllo, Kersti A. 1993. "Through a Feminist Lens: Gender, Power and Violence." Pp. 47-66 in Richard J. Gelles and Donileen R. Loseke (eds.), *Current Controversies on Family Violence*. Newbury Park: Sage.

Yorker, Beatrice Crofts. 1994. "Munchausen Syndrome by Proxy as a Form of Family Violence." *Family Violence and Sexual Assault Bulletin* 10 (3-4): 34-39.

Index

abuse
  compensation 173
  and gender 33-37
  abusers, and victimization 200
adolescent abuse
  community help 205-206
  and gender 88
  measurement 87-88
  psychology 152-153
  social context 1-2, 86-87, 89-91
adolescents
  and parent abuse 93-94
  and sibling abuse 82-84
adoption 183
adult protection legislation 198-201
affordable housing 202
ageism 212
aging
  and family 102-103
  and society 95-96
alcohol, and male abuse 39-40
arranged marriage 39

Badgley, Robin 58, 63
Battered Child in Canada 58
battered child syndrome 58
battered woman syndrome 34, 172
battered women *See* woman abuse
Blackstone, Sir William 24
Bobbitt case 27-28
Bradshaw, John 45, 49

Canada Evidence Act 183
Canadian Armed Forces 137
Canadian Association of Elizabeth Fry
  Societies 172
Canadian Children's Foundation 59
Canadian Council on Social
  Development 60
Canadian Foundation for Children,
  Youth and the Law 53
Canadian Nurses Association 108
Canadian Violence Against Women
  Survey 31-33, 37-40, 62, 132, 138,
  141, 169
capitalism 9, 127, 136
  feminist analysis 117
  and liberal democracy 120-123
  and poverty 114-116

caregiver dependency 158
caregivers
  and child abuse 149
  and elder abuse 110-112
  and elderly 105-107, 203
Centre for Research on Violence Against
  Women & Children (London, Ont)
  164
Centre for Research in Women's Health
  178
Charter of Rights 186
Chatelaine 10, 11-12
child abuse 1-2
  age range 46, 67
  characteristics 46-48
  criminal justice system 182-184
  definition 50-55
  feminist analysis 69, 148-150
  and gender 68-72
  government involvement 59-60, 189
  legislation 57-59, 183-184
  measurement 58-59, 61-66
  and neglect 69-70, 189
  and patriarchy 55-57
  psychology 4, 45, 68, 145
  and public education 188-189
  social context 46, 49, 52, 66-68,
  72-73, 145-147, 150-151
  and social welfare agencies 182-183,
  185
  therapy 180-182
*Child Abuse Prevention and Treatment
  Act* (U.S.) 58
child abuse registers 183, 186-187
child abuse *See also* Sexual abuse of
  children
Child Assault Prevention Program 189
Child at Risk 58, 64
child protection services 185-187
Child Victim-Witness Project (London,
  Ontario) 183
childrearing 49, 56, 61, 70, 144, 145, 150
Children's Aid Societies 57, 62, 65, 182,
  185-187
Clarke Institute of Psychiatry 64, 65
clinical samples 15
co-residency 109
common-law relationships 26, 28, 38

communitarian conferencing *See* family
   group conferencing
community advocacy 199
community support 99, 205-206, 212
competition
   and family 121
   and liberal democracy 121
conflict 151
   and society 7-10, 116
conflict resolution 204
Conflict Tactics Scale 30-31, 64
Connidis, Ingrid A. 98, 102
control
   and parent abuse 91
   personal 125
   relation to family violence 19, 125,
      136-137, 152-154, 166, 213-214
Cornell, Claire P. 191
corporal punishment 8, 126 *See also*
   spanking
Coser, Lewis 7
Criminal Code of Canada 53, 172, 183,
   197, 198
criminal harassment 172
criminal justice system 25
   and abused women 165, 167-176
   and adolescent abuse 200-201
   and child abuse 182-184, 187
   Manitoba 175
   Nova Scotia 184-185
   Ontario 173-175
   Saskatchewan 173
   sentencing 168-169, 174, 185
cycle of abuse 140-141
cycle of violence 132

Dakota Ojibwa Child and Family Services
   184
dangerous offenders 174
dark figure 11, 14
dependency 19, 98-99, 139, 144, 158
Design for a New Tomorrow program
   177
divorce 40
Domestic Abuse Intervention Project
   (Duluth, Minnesota) 137
domestic violence courts 174
domination 19, 28, 35, 123
Dunsdon, Kelly 187
Dutton, Donald G. 129, 166

ecofeminism 136
economic abuse 28
educational measures 59-60, 177-178,
   188-189, 203-205
elder abuse

   and caregivers 103-104, 110-112,
      156, 157-158
   definition 100-103
   and dependency 98-99
   ethical issues 196-197
   feminist analysis 158-159
   institutional 104-107, 207
   legislation 96-97
   measurement 97-98, 107-109
   psychology 155-159
   risk factors 99-100, 109-110, 200
   and shelters 201-202
   as social issue 95-97
emotional abuse 47-48
European Court of Human Rights 54

familicide 37
family
   and competition 121
   as myth 3, 11, 117-120
   social context 5, 6, 9
family group conferencing 179-180
family relations 3-4, 67, 133-34, 156,
   208
   and the elderly 103-104
   and power 9
   therapy 181, 207
family violence
   characteristics 3-4
   and control 125, 136-137, 152, 154,
      166, 213-214
   definition 11-14
   education 203-205
   feminist analysis 126, 131, 135-139,
      215
   and gender 5-6, 12, 27, 131
   as individual problem 117-118, 127,
      214
   intervention 193-196
   legislation 197-198
   and lower classes 25
   and male drunkeness 24-26
   and mass media 10-11, 126-128
   measurement 14-15
   and patriarchy 123-126
   psychology 117-118
   research 207-208, 212-216
   and social change 190-193
   social context 4-5, 114-116, 122-123,
      131-135
   and social isolation 4, 67, 192
Family Violence Initiative 60
fathers, and male abusers 129
Federal Initiative on Family Violence 60
feminism 10, 26
   and child abuse 150

and family violence 126, 131
and woman abuse 29, 141-144
feminist analysis, and societal change
176-180
feminist research 135-139
foster care 182, 186, 187
Fraser, Sylvia 146
freedom, and liberal democracy 120-121

Garbarino, James 146
Gelles, Richard 64, 131, 191
gender
and child abuse 68-72, 149
and elder abuse 158-159
and patriarchy 124-125
and sibling abuse 82-84, 152
gender inequalities, and social change
176
Gil, David 212
Goldner, Virginia 143
Goodman, Marilyn 140
Graham, Dee 137, 176
Grenier, Glenda 137
group homes 182, 202
guardianship 96, 198-200, 213

Hale, Sir Matthew 171
healing circles 179
healing lodges 179
Health and Welfare Canada. Family
Violence Division 97
homicide 36-37

incest 51, 142
individual
and liberal democracy 122
responsibility for family violence
117-118, 127, 214
and society 120-121
inequality 212
infanticide 55
Institute for the Prevention of Child
Abuse 59
International Order of Foresters 59
intervention 96, 200, 201
ethics 193-196
intimate abuse *See* woman abuse
intimate violence *See* family violence

Janus, Mark-David 89
Jones, Ann 12
Joudrie, Dorothy 38
Joudrie, Earl 38
Journal of Elder Abuse and Neglect 97
Judeo-Christian tradition 55
judicial mediation 176

Kempe, Dr. C.H. 57
Killoran, M. Maureen 10

LaMarsh Research Centre on Violence and
Conflict Resolution 60
learned helplessness 40, 140, 141, 156
Lenton, Rhonda 72
lesbian battering 34-35, 130, 142-143
liberal democracy 9
and capitalism 120-123
and individuals 122
liberal feminism 136
Liddle, Mark 131
life histories 5
Lincoln County (Ontario) Board of
Education 188

Maclean's Magazine 10, 11
MacLeod, Linda 26, 29, 38
McMaster University 64, 65
male abusers 18-21
and alcohol 24-26, 39-40
characteristics 37-39, 134-135
counselling 166-167
and fathers 129
feminist analysis 136-137
and patriarchy 148-149
psychology 18-21, 129-131
sentences 168-169, 174
socialization 130-132, 143
socioeconomic status 38, 132-133
therapy 129-130
male role 20
male sexual abuse 71
male violence 5-6, 8, 27, 36, 137, 143
and patriarchy 123-125, 132-133,
137
surveys 32
mandatory charging 168, 170, 171, 175,
176
mandatory reporting 96, 183, 185, 186,
199, 201
marriage 119, 171
See also family relations
Marshall, Carolyn 184, 187
masculinity 8, 72, 123-124, 143
masochism 139
mass media
and capitalism 127
and family violence 126-128
maternalism 141
medical records, confidentiality 186
Medicated Fraud Reports 105
Miller, Alice 49, 55, 145, 150
Mills, C. Wright 5, 146
Mones, Paul 52

multigenerational families 98
My Father's House 146

National Clearinghouse on Family Violence 59
National Longitudinal Survey of Children 63
Native people 8-9
    child abuse 73, 184, 187
    family violence 178-179
    woman abuse 38-39, 142
neglect of adults 198-199
    and child abuse 46-47, 51, 67, 69-70, 147-148
    and the elderly 100-101
neo-conservatism 115-116, 203, 215
Niagara Falls Review 112, 202
Niagara Region Sexual Assault Centre 189
no-drop policy 170, 171, 175
nonviolence, and feminism 178
nuclear family *See* family

Old Testament 55, 56
Ontario Centre for the Prevention of Child Abuse 59
Ontario Incidence Study of Reported Child Abuse and Neglect 62-63, 69
Ontario Native Women's Association 39

parent abuse 92-94, 153-155
parent-teen conflict 93-94
parent/child bond 155
parental violence 40-41, 156
parenting skills 206-207
partner abuse *See* woman abuse
patriarchy 9, 69, 71, 123, 136
    child abuse 55-56, 69-71, 148-149
    family violence 24-26, 123-126, 215
    feminist analysis 135
    and gender 124-125, 135
    male violence 123-125, 132-133, 137
patterned interaction 157
peace bonds 168, 172-173
peacekeeping 8
Penn, Peggy 143
Pennell, LeRoy 61
Pizzey, Erin 26
police, and domestic violence 15, 25, 167-171
population surveys 15
post-traumatic stress disorder 34
poverty 69, 73, 92, 114-116, 148, 189, 190, 212
power
    and parent abuse 91

relation to family violence 9, 123, 136-137, 152, 154, 158
pre-natal abuse 51
pregnancy 40
Prevention of Cruelty and Better Protection of Children Act (Ontario) 57
privacy of family 14, 120, 207
privacy of information 186
psychological abuse 28, 47, 147

racism 142
radical feminism 136
rape 171-172
remediation 174
Renzetti, Claire 34
restraining order *See* peace bond
ritualistic abuse 51
role strain 103-104
romance 18-19, 141
Rousseau, Jean-Jacques 57
Ruby, Clayton 174

Scheff, Thomas 7
Schmidt, K. Louise 178
science fiction 176
Scream Quietly or the Neighbours Will Hear 26
self-determination 196
self-esteem 19, 81, 93, 116, 139, 143, 205
sex roles 20, 36, 130, 133, 141, 144, 152, 158-159
sexism 8, 39, 192, 212
sexual abuse of children 48-49, 51, 62, 70-71
    and Christianity 56-57
    and gender 70-72
sexual assault 172
sexual harassment 137
Sexual Offenses Against Children 58, 63
shame 6-7, 124, 129, 142
Sheinberg, Marcia 143
shelter movement 27, 136, 213
shelters 29-30, 96, 165-166, 201-202
sibling abuse
    characteristics 81-84
    definition 85-86
    and gender 82-84
    intervention 194
    measurement 84
    psychology 151-152
    sexual 84-85
sibling rivalry 80, 121, 156
Smith, Michael 30
social advocacy 200

social bond 7, 13, 114, 116
social change, and feminism 149-150, 176-180
social isolation 4, 67
Social Sciences and Humanities Research Council of Canada 60
social welfare agencies, and individual rights 193
socialist feminism 136
Societies for the Prevention of Cruelty to Children 57
Society for the Protection of Women and Children 25
socioeconomic status 38, 72-73, 132-133
Spallumcheen Child Welfare program (B.C.) 184
spanking 52-55, 126, 147, 151, 191 *See also* corporal punishment
spousal abuse *See* woman abuse
stalking 172
Stockholm syndrome 137-139
Stone, Sharon 177
strapping *See* corporal punishment
Straus, Murray 30, 64, 131
street kids 1-2, 89-91
stress 111, 146, 157-158
substance abuse, and child abuse 66-67
Supreme Court of Canada 34, 172, 184

Talmud 56
telephone hot lines 165, 173-174, 206
temperance movement 24-25
Ten Commandments 55
The Spectator (Hamilton, Ontario) 168
The Standard (St. Catharines, Ontario) 176
tickling 86
Times of London 24
Tomes, Nancy 24
Toronto Star 64, 166-167, 169, 170, 173, 185, 196, 201
Toronto Women's Court 25
transition houses *See* shelters
traumatic bonding 140

underreporting 14-15, 65-66
Uniform Crime Reporting Survey 14
United Nations 8
United States Bureau of National Affairs 104
United States National Center for the Prevention of Child Abuse and Neglect 58
United States National Committee to Prevent Child Abuse 63

Van Stolk, Mary 58
Vanier Institute of the Family (Ottawa) 11
victim feminism 11
victim support programs 175
victim-witness testimony 183
victimization 8, 33, 66-68, 99-100, 135, 137, 181, 196, 200, 212-214
Victims of Domestic Violence Act (Saskatchewan) 173
violence
    feminist analysis 135-139
    and mass media 191-192
    social context 7-10, 36, 116
violence against women *See* woman abuse
Vis-a-Vis 60

Walker, Gillian 143
Walker, Leonore 34, 140
When Children Invite Child Abuse 67
Wife Battering in Canada 26
Winnipeg Family Violence Court 175, 183
woman abuse
    and alcohol 39-40
    community programs 178-179
    counselling 164-166
    definition 13-14, 26-27, 28-29
    economic costs 164
    and ethnic origin 39, 142, 176
    and feminism 29
    feminist analysis 26, 135-139, 141-144
    legislation 171-175
    male role 18-21
    measurement 30-32
    and Native people 38-39, 178-179
    police attitude 167-171
    psychology 18-23, 139-142
    public education 165, 177-178
    and rape 171-172
    risk factors 39-41
    socialization 143-144
women
    as caregivers 69, 104, 149
    and parenting 69-70
women and violence 23-27, 33-37, 130-131, 137-139
Women's Research Centre (Vancouver) 71, 72
women's status 23-26

Yllo, Kersti 143

Zero Tolerance (for Violence) Policy 171